HR Analytics and Digital HR Practices

Subhra R Mondal · Francesca Di Virgilio ·
Subhankar Das
Editors

HR Analytics and Digital HR Practices

Digitalization post COVID-19

palgrave
macmillan

Editors
Subhra R Mondal
Duy Tan University
Da Nang, Vietnam

Francesca Di Virgilio
Department of Economics
University of Molise
Campobasso, Italy

Subhankar Das
Duy Tan University
Da Nang, Vietnam

ISBN 978-981-16-7098-5 ISBN 978-981-16-7099-2 (eBook)
https://doi.org/10.1007/978-981-16-7099-2

This Palgrave Macmillan imprint is published by the registered company Springer Nature Singapore Pte Ltd.
The registered company address is: 152 Beach Road, #21-01/04 Gateway East, Singapore 189721, Singapore

Contents

1 **People Analytics and The Future of Competitiveness: Which Capabilities HR Departments Need to Succeed in the "Next Normal"** 1
Teresina Torre, Daria Sarti, and Gilda Antonelli
Introduction 1
Background: Big Data and the Current Challenge for the HR Departments 4
HR Proactive Orientation and Big Data Analytical Capabilities 6
Discussion on HR Department Role and Capabilities 11
HRD New Capabilities 12
HR Department Should Assume the Role of BD Architect by Designing Structures and Systems 12
Effective HR Department Should Assume a Guidance Role for the Organization in the Shift Toward BD, Thus Promoting the Newness While Protecting the Social and Human Dimension 13
HR Department Should Assume the Role of Guardian and Promotor of Ethics in the Management of Data 14
Conclusion and Future Research Directions 15
Conclusions 15
Future Research 18
References 18

2	**The Influence of Social Media Usage on Firm Performance During the COVID-19 Era: An Empirical Study**	25
	Francesca Di Virgilio, Mohammad Soliman, and Muhammad Anwar ul Haq	
	Introduction	25
	Background: Main Focus of the Chapter	27
	Bed and Breakfast in the Hospitality Industry	27
	Social Media Platform at Work and the Central Role of Human Resources	29
	The Entrepreneurial and Management Supporting Social Policy Implementation	31
	Social Media Usage and the Relationship with Firm Performance	32
	Research Model and Hypotheses	33
	Methodology	34
	Findings	35
	B&B Characteristics and Demographic Profile of Respondents	35
	Assessing the Measurement Model	35
	The Structural Model and Hypotheses Testing	37
	Solutions and Recommendations	38
	Future Research Directions	40
	Conclusion	41
	Appendix 1	42
	References	43
3	**Effects of Covid-19 on Public Administration: Smart Working as an Organizational Revolution**	51
	Lucio Todisco, Gianluigi Mangia, Paolo Canonico, and Andrea Tomo	
	Introduction	51
	The Role of Technology in Organizational Flexibility	53
	Smart Working: Constitutive Features	55
	Methods	58
	Results and Discussion	59
	Smart Working Pilot Project Before Covid-19 Health Emergency	59
	Smart Working During Covid-19 Health Emergency	61

Conclusion, Limitations, and Future Research Directions 64
References 66

4 **Digitalize Work in Pandemic Time: Practices for Remote Working and Job Redesign in Public Organization** 73
Rocco Reina, Marzia Ventura, Concetta L. Cristofaro, and Walter Vesperi
Introduction 73
Review of Literature 76
Digitalization and ICT for Public Organizations 76
The New Forms of Work: Remote vs Smart 77
Objective of Chapter 81
Method 81
Context 82
Case Study: The Interview 84
Solutions and Recommendations 88
Future Research Directions 89
Conclusion 89
References 90

5 **Effective Management of a Remote Workforce for Covid-19: A Proposed Research Model Toward Smart Working Adoption Within Organizations** 101
Concetta Metallo, Rocco Agrifoglio, and Ferrara Maria
Introduction 101
Smart Working Within Organizations 104
Advantages and Disadvantages of Remote Working 106
Designing Smart Working & HRM Within Organizations 109
The Mobility and Development HRM System 110
The Evaluation HRM System 114
The Rewards HRM System 117
References 120

6 **Remote Work at the Time of COVID-19 Pandemic and Beyond: A Scoping Review** 127
Aizhan Tursunbayeva, Stefano Di Lauro, and Gilda Antonelli
Introduction 127
Background 129

Remote Work Definition 129
Generic Research on Remote Work 129
COVID-19 and Remote Work 131
Methodology 131
Literature Review Approach 131
Data Collection 132
Results 133
Academic Literature: Publication Characteristics 133
Gray Literature: Publication Characteristics 134
Analysis and Discussion 134
Benefits for Employees 135
Benefits for Companies 137
Benefits for Employees and Companies 137
Challenges for Employees 139
Challenges for Employees and Companies 141
Solutions and Recommendations 141
Conclusion and Future Research Directions 145
Appendix 1: Included Academic Literature 149
Appendix 2: Included Gray Literature 157
References 160

7 **Dynamic Role of Technology in Managing Workforce in Service Delivery During COVID-19 Pandemic** 171
Dora Almeida, Maria José Sousa, and Antonio Miguel Pesqueira
Introduction 171
Technology 172
Digital Information 173
Virtual Working 175
Smart Working 176
Methodology 177
Data Analysis and Discussions 177
Discussion 190
Limitations and Future Scope of Research 191
Conclusion 192
References 193

8 **Technological Dynamism of Workforce Management for Effective Education Service Delivery During and After Covid-19** 199
Mansi Tiwari and Subhra R. Mondal
Introduction 199
Background 202
Objective of the Chapter 204
Issues, Controversies, Problems 204
Strength 207
Weakness 207
Opportunities 208
Challenges 208
Suggestions 209
Conclusion 211
References 212

9 **Human Governance Analytics for Public Organizations** 217
Maria José Sousa, David Ferraz, António Sacavém, and João Salis Gomes
Introduction 217
Background 219
Human Governance Conceptualization 219
Human Governance Analytics 220
Empirical Research 223
Bibliometric Analysis 223
Case Studies in Public Administration 225
Case Study 1— Metrics for Senior Civil Servants Recruitment in the Public Administration Context 228
Introduction 228
Procedure 229
Metrics 230
Final Considerations 232
Case Study 2—Metrics for Human Governance Regarding Talent Development and Talent Performance Evaluation in the Context of Public Administration 232
Introduction 232
Procedure 232
Metrics 233

Case Study Final Considerations 234
Discussion and Conclusions 234
Future Research Directions 236
References 237

10 Analysing Users' Engagement with eSports Team: Does Covid-19 Matter? 243
Francesca Di Virgilio, Mohammad Soliman, Muhammad Anwar ul Haq, and Sara Fantini
Introduction 243
Background: Main Focus of the Chapter 245
ESports Overview 245
Users' Engagement with eSports 247
Users' Sentiment Expressions 248
Methodology 250
The Case 250
Data Collection and Analysis Procedures 251
Phase 1: Data Collection of Trends (RQ1) 251
Phase 2: Analyzing Sentiments Express Through Comments (RQ2) 251
Findings 253
Initial Analysis of Trends 253
Content Analysis 255
Word Frequency 255
Identification of Moods 256
Analyzing the Trend of Engagement 257
Sentiment Analysis 260
Conclusions 261
Discussion 261
Theoretical Contributions 262
Contribution to Practice 264
Limitation and Future Research 265
References 266

Index 273

Notes on Contributors

Rocco Agrifoglio, Ph.D. is an Assistant Professor of Management Information Systems at "Parthenope" University (Naples, Italy). He has earned his Ph.D. in Management and Business Administration from the same University and he has also been a visiting scholar at the University of Westminster (London, UK) and University of Castilla-La Mancha (Ciudad Real, ES). His primary research interests are communities of practice, technology acceptance and usage, IS continuance, and e-court. He has participated as a speaker in several international conferences and has published numerous papers in journals, including *Journal of Computer Information Systems* (JCIS), *Information Systems Management* (ISM), *Behaviour & Information Technology* (BIT), *Production Planning & Control*, and *Technological Forecasting and Social Change* (TFSC).

Dora Almeida Degree in Psychology, by the *Lusíada University of Lisbon* (specialization in organizations and work), she has always had her professional activity linked to human resources, especially in team coordination and training in various areas, such as *motivation*, *human resources management*, and *leadership*. With experience in various branches of the private sector, she identifies human resources as drivers of the company's success and increase of its human capital. She has a master's degree in Entrepreneurship and Innovation Management by the *European University of Lisbon* and has been focused on its specializations in education and positive psychology in the last years.

Gilda Antonelli (B.Sc., Ph.D.) is a full professor of Organizational Design and Human Resources Management at the Law, Economics, Management and Quantitative Methods Department of the University of Sannio, Italy. Her research focuses on innovation and change management at different organizational levels (individual, team, organization, and network), and on organizational identity. She is now focused on studying organizational change driven by Human Research Analytics methods. She is responsible for several research funds and she is a member of the Italian Academy of Organizational Studies.

Paolo Canonico is a Full Professor of Organization Studies at the University of Napoli Federico II, Italy. He holds a Doctorate in Business Administration from the University of Naples Federico II and a Master of Science in Analysis, Design, and Management of Information Systems from The London School of Economics and Political Science (UK).

Concetta L. Cristofaro is a post-doc Research Fellow at the Magna Graecia University (Catanzaro) in Italy, where, she received her Ph.D. in Health Economics and Management. Currently, she is an adjunct Professor of Organization theory, Conflict Management and Human Resource Management, Public and Private Organization at the Magna Graecia University. Her research is focused on the fields of intellectual capital, small and medium business, ITC, digitalization, family business, performance, gender diversity, and knowledge management. Her publications appeared in academic journals and presented her research at several international conferences. She is a member of Research Center "Economics and Management of Services" of the "Magna Graecia" University.

Dr. Subhankar Das is currently working as Professor and Researcher in the Honors Program, Duy Tan University, Da Nang, Vietnam. He is a Ph.D. in Social Media Advertisement & Media Planning with professional certification from Google, Manipal in digital marketing, IIM Lucknow, IIM Bangalore for Media planning & University of British Columbia for Advertisement along with other 15+ Globally Recognized Professional Certifications.

Stefano Di Lauro (Ph.D., Doctor Europaeus) recently completed his doctoral studies in Management at the University of Naples Federico II. His Ph.D. focused on Organizational Identity, Corporate Identity, and Social Media. During the doctoral studies, he was a visiting researcher at the Business School of the University of Edinburgh. He has international work and teaching experience and for the last three years in Organization science-related topics at the University of Molise. Currently he is working in the University of Sannio, Italy.

Dr. Francesca Di Virgilio is a Tenured Associate Professor of Organization Design and Human Resource Management at the University of Molise in the Department of Economics, Italy. She received her Ph.D. degree in "Organization, Technology and Development of Human Resources" from the University of Molise, in joint with the University of Naples Federico II and LUISS University (Italy).

Sara Fantini is a doctor in Management, Entrepreneurship and Innovation, (with a thesis titled: Social media and new organizational performances) University of Molise (Italy). She is an assistant teaching for the courses Organization Design and Human Resources Management at the Department of Economics-University of Molise (Italy).

Her current research focuses on social media at work and eSport.

Maria Ferrara is a Full Professor of Organization at the "Parthenope" University of Naples, Italy. Author of several books, essays, and articles on Business Organization and Information Systems, she has been Conference Chair at itAIS2010 and itAIS2019, the Italian Chapter of the Association for Information Systems (AIS), and at WOA2011, the Italian Workshop of Professors and Researchers of Organization. Scientific Coordinator of a major Research Project on Innovation Systems, funded by the European Union, her research topics are the Information Systems and the impact of innovations on individuals and organizations.

David Ferraz holds a Ph.D. in Public Policy (2018), a Master in Administration and Public Policy (2008), and a degree in Management and Public Administration (ISCSP-UL 2004). He is also graduated with a course in Advanced Studies in Public Management (CEAGP—2006), with a specialization in Organizational Development, Leadership and People Management, and has the INA's "Public Management Training Course for managerial functions" (FORGEP—2012). He is currently a Professor at ISCTE and ISCSP-UL, General-Secretary of the Portuguese Economic and Social Council, and a researcher of the Center for Administration and Public Policy. Since 2004, he has been teaching in various courses at INA, ISCTE-IUL, and ISCSP-UL. Between 1999 and 2004, he held positions in several private sector companies. He served in the Research and Consulting Unit of the National Institute of Administration, I.P. (2006–2010) and was the head of the Training Unit in Management and Public Administration (2010–2012). He also was the head of INA's Recruitment and Selection Division, providing this support to CRESAP (Senior Civil Servants Recruitment Commission—2012–2017). He is the author and co-author of various national and international publications in the areas of Management, Administration, Public Policy, and Human Resource Management.

João Salis Gomes Graduate in Law and Post Graduate in Juridical/Political Sciences (Faculty of Law, University of Lisbon). Ph.D. in Public Policies (ISCTE—University Institute of Lisbon). He has been teaching since 1977, first at the Faculty of Law, University of Lisbon. Since 1995, he teaches at ISCTE-IUL, Constitutional Law, Administrative Law, Economic Law, Education Law, Administrative Sciences, and Public Management in several BA and Masters. He is also the Director of the Master in Public Administration and of the training program for Top Management in Public Administration (CADAP, FORGEP and CAGEP) as well as the Scientific coordinator of the postgraduation course on Public Finance for the Audit Court of Angola and senior staff of the Ministries of Finance of PALOP (Portuguese Speaking African Countries) and East- Timor (EU-UNDP). He was also the Sub-director of the Department of Political Science and Public Policies and is a member of the Board of the Institute for Public and Social Policies (IPPS-IUL). He was elected in 2019 to the Board of Management of the International Association of Schools and Institutes of Administration (IASIA).

Muhammad Anwar ul Haq is a Ph.D. in Management from Wuhan University of Technology, Peoples' Republic of China. He is currently an Assistant Professor of Management at the University of Gujrat, Pakistan. His research interests are leadership, innovation, and positive organizational scholarship. Currently he is engaged in researching the impact of COVID-19 on business at various levels. He is a regular contributor to various international journals as author/reviewer. He has more than five years of teaching experience at the undergraduate and graduate level. He is also the program coordinator for M.Phil. and Ph.D. Management at the Department of Management Sciences, University of Gujrat, Pakistan. He is also a founding member of the Pakistan Chapter of Product Development and Management Association.

Gianluigi Mangia is a Full Professor of Organization Studies at the University of Napoli Federico II, Italy, where he currently teaches Organization theory and information systems, and human resources topics. He holds a Ph.D. in Organization and Business Administration from the University of Molise. He was a visiting scholar at Cardiff Business School, a visiting researcher at the London School of Economics, and visiting doctoral student at Warwick Business School.

Concetta Metallo, Ph.D. is an Associate Professor of Organization and Information Systems at "Parthenope" University (Naples, Italy). Her research interests are: technology adoption and usage behaviors, social media usage, e-participation. She has participated as a speaker in several international conferences and she has published papers in journals such as *Government Information Quarterly*, *Technological Forecasting and Social Change*, *Production Planning & Control*, *Behaviour & Information Technology*, *Information Systems Management*, *International Journal of Technology Management*, *Journal of Computer Information Systems*, *International Journal of Public Administration.*

Dr. Subhra R Mondal is a researcher in the Honors Program at Duy Tan University. She received her Ph.D. in Management in Retail studies. Her research interests are concerned with brand management, brand equity with innovative tools, smart tourism, destination marketing, social media marketing, AI & Web 5.0, & digital recruitment.

Antonio Miguel Pesqueira has been focused on leading the international commercial operations team in driving new competencies, capabilities, and processes. His core focus has been to launch new technologies and processes in the commercial and medical affairs space; maximize the advanced analytical lifecycles, and enhance operational systems like CRM, Business Intelligence, and Content Management across all international regions. He has his marketing degree from the European University of Lisbon and his master's degree in Innovation Management. He also earned his IBM Data Science Professional certification and has served as Scrum Master in several different professional & personal projects after earning his Scrum Master certification from SCRUM ALLIANCE®.

Rocco Reina is a Full Professor of Organizational Studies. He is a Professor in Organization Theory and Human Resource Management at the Magna Graecia University. His research is focused on the fields of HRM, ITC, HTA, Family business, and knowledge management. His publications appeared in academic journals and presented her research at several international conferences. He is a member of Research Center "Economics and Management of Services" of the "Magna Graecia" University and Scientific Coordinator of Master and Degree.

António Sacavém is an assistant professor at Universidade Europeia and IPAM and an invited professor at CATÓLICA LISBON School of Business and Economics. He holds a Ph.D. in management (Universidade Europeia) with a dissertation in leadership and communication, a master's degree in organizational behavior (ISPA), an executive M.B.A. (ISCTE Business School), and he also attended several executive programs (e.g.: leadership & organisational transformation at London Business School; executive education—IHRSA-U at IESE Business School). He is been teaching at FORGEP, which is a training program in management for public administration leaders at IPPS-ISCTE. António facilitates training in leadership, negotiation and communication skills in several National and International companies (ex: Toyota, Fujitsu, Farfetch, Natixis, Delta, José de Mello Group, Impresa Group, Instituto de Informática, etc.). He provides support through mentoring and coaching to change management processes, organizational development, strategic reflection, team motivation, and profiling. António is the former business director at SONAE TURISMO. He is an executive coach (PCC by ICF), international presenter, and author. António Sacavém is also a Partner at Leadership and Communication Academy® and he is the founder of Microexpressões Faciais® and Linguagem Corporal® brands. He is the author and co-author of various national and international publications in the areas of leadership and management. His work has been shared on several television channels including SIC, RTP1, TVI, and TVI24.

Daria Sarti is an associate professor of Organization and Human Resource Management at the University of Florence (Italy) where she received her Ph.D. in 2005. Currently she teaches in classes on Organization design and People management. Her primary research interests are: knowledge management and innovation of SMEs and human resource management for employees' engagement. Her present research also includes an investigation of the relationship between organizational design and employees' wellbeing when new information systems and technologies are implemented by organizations.

Mohammad Soliman is currently an Assistant Professor at the University of Technology and Applied Sciences, Salalah CAS, Oman. He has published multiple papers in reputed journals indexed in WoS and Scopus (e.g., *Journal of Destination Management & Marketing*; *Geoheritage*; *Journal of Medical Systems*; *Journal of Consumer Behaviour*; *International Journal of Hospitality & Tourism Administration*; *European Journal of Tourism Research*; *Anatolia*). Additionally, he sits on the editorial board of some academic journals (e.g., *Journal of Tourism & Hospitality*; *Tourism & Management Studies*; *Journal of Responsible Tourism Management*; *Journal of Global Hospitality and Tourism*), and serves as a reviewer of some top-tier journals (e.g. *International Journal of Hospitality Management*; *International Journal of Contemporary Hospitality Management*; *Journal of Hospitality and Tourism Technology*). He has successfully supervised and examined a number of Master and Ph.D. theses. His research interests include tourism management and marketing, tourism behavior, PLS-SEM, and bibliometric studies.

Maria José Sousa (Ph.D. in Industrial Management) is a University Professor at ISCTE, a research fellow at the Business Research Unit, and a collaborator of IPPS-ISCTE. She has developed major research in the innovation policies with articles published in high-level journals (as the *Journal of Business Research*, *European Planning Studies*, *Information Systems Frontiers*, *Systems Research*, and *Behavioral Science*, *Computational* and *Mathematical Organization Theory*, and others). She is also the guest-editor of more than 5 Special Issues from Springer and Elsevier. She is also an External Expert of the COST Association, and President of the ISO/TC 260—HRM, representing Portugal in ISO.

Dr. Mansi Tiwari has 12 years of experience in teaching & currently working as an Associate Professor at Unitedworld School of Business, Karnavati University, Gandhinagar, Gujarat. Her area of expertise is Human Resource Management & Marketing Management. Her research expertise lies in particular for understanding the impact of glass ceiling & glass cliff on working female's attitudinal outcomes. She has many Scopus indexed publications to her credit.

Lucio Todisco is a Post-doctoral researcher at the Department of Economics, Management, Institutions, University of Naples Federico II, Italy. He holds a Ph.D. in Management from the University of Naples Federico II. He has a master's degree in human resource management.

Since 2017 he is a licensed Labor Consultant and has carried out activities of payroll specialist. He has carried out tutoring activities for workshops and masters and assists the Chairs of Organization Studies, Organizational Behavior, and Negotiation.

Andrea Tomo is an Assistant Professor of Organization Studies at the Department of Economics, Management, Institutions, University of Naples Federico II, Italy. In 2018 he gained the national qualification as Associate Professor. He holds a Ph.D. in Management from the University of Naples Federico II and has been visiting researcher at Cass Business School, Copenhagen Business School, Stockholm Business School, and Leuphana University of Luneburg.

Teresina Torre is a full professor of Organization and Human Resources Management, University of Genoa. She is a coordinator of the Master Course of Management (Genoa) and president of the M.B.A.—Internacional en Gestion Estrategica. Finanzas e Internacionalizacion de las Empresas (with the Catholic University "Sedes Sapientiae" of Lima-Perù). She is a vice-president of the Italian Academy of Organization. Her main research interests are human resources and digitalization and soft skills. She is a co-editor of *Impresa Progetto Electronic Journal of Management* and a member of the scientific board of journals, author of books and papers on qualified national and international journals.

Aizhan Tursunbayeva (Ph.D., Doctor Europaeus, GRP) is an Assistant Professor at Parthenope University of Naples, Italy. Her previous professional roles include Management Consultant at KPMG Advisory and HR Manager at HSBC Bank. Her research lies at the intersection of HRMHR management (HRM), information systems, and healthcare. She has published in a range of journals including Information Technology and People, Journal of the American Medical Informatics Association, Management Learning, and International Journal of Information Management.

Marzia Ventura is a Research of Organizational Studies at the Magna Graecia University (Catanzaro) in Italy, where she received her Ph.D. in Health Economics and Management. Currently, she is an adjunct Professor of Organization theory and Human Resource Management at the Magna Graecia University. Her research is focused on the fields of HRM, ITC, HTA, Family business, and knowledge management. Her publications appeared in academic journals and presented her research at several international conferences. She is a member of Research Center "Economics and Management of Services" of the "Magna Graecia" University.

Walter Vesperi is Ph.D. in Management and Economics in the University of Messina. His research is focused on the fields of HRM, knowledge management, and startup & spin-off. His publications appeared in academic journals and presented his research at several international conferences.

List of Figures

Fig. 1.1	BDAC, BD sources, and exploration–exploitation processes (*Source* Authors' elaboration)	10
Fig. 2.1	The research model	34
Fig. 4.1	Organizational chart of Commerce of Catanzaro (CCIAA) (*Source* Website Chamber of Commerce of Catanzaro [CCIAA])	83
Fig. 5.1	A proposed research model for effective management of a remote workforce	103
Fig. 6.1	Benefits and challenges for organizations and employees	135
Fig. 7.1	Descriptive analysis of the age groups from the questionnaire respondents (*Source* Authors' own data analysis)	179
Fig. 7.2	Descriptive analysis of the gender from the questionnaire respondents (*Source* Authors' own data analysis)	179
Fig. 7.3	Descriptive analysis of the main professional area from the questionnaire respondents (*Source* Authors' own data analysis)	180
Fig. 7.4	Selected block of questions from the questionnaire to perform comparative analysis (*Source* Authors' own data analysis)	181
Fig. 7.5	First selected question (*Source* Authors' own data analysis)	182
Fig. 7.6	Second selected question (*Source* Authors' own data analysis)	182
Fig. 7.7	Third selected question (*Source* Authors' own data analysis)	183

Fig. 7.8 Fourth selected question (*Source* Authors' own data analysis) 184
Fig. 7.9 Question 6 from the before COVID and question 5 from the during phase (*Source* Authors' own data analysis) 184
Fig. 7.10 Question 7 from the before COVID and question 6 from the during phase (*Source* Authors' own data analysis) 185
Fig. 7.11 Question 9 from the before COVID and question 8 from the during phase (*Source* Authors' own data analysis) 185
Fig. 7.12 Question 9 from the before COVID and question 8 from the during phase (*Source* Authors' own data analysis) 186
Fig. 8.1 Depiction of transformation of education system 201
Fig. 9.1 Flowchart outlining the literature review (*Source* Authors' own conception) 224
Fig. 10.1 Followers' growth on Instagram (*Source* Authors' own analysis by NVivo 11) 253
Fig. 10.2 Number of comments (*Source* Authors' own analysis by NVivo 11) 254
Fig. 10.3 The trend of Instagram likes by followers (*Source* Authors' own analysis by NVivo 11) 254
Fig. 10.4 Dominantly used expressions (*Source* Authors' own analysis by NVivo 11) 256
Fig. 10.5 Thematic trend analysis (*Source* Authors' own analysis by NVivo 11) 259
Fig. 10.6 Sentiment analysis-overall (*Source* Authors' own analysis by NVivo 11) 260
Fig. 10.7 Sentiment analysis-positive (*Source* Authors' own analysis by NVivo 11) 261

List of Tables

Table 2.1	Characteristics of the B&Bs	36
Table 2.2	Profile of respondents	36
Table 2.3	Constructs reliability assessment	37
Table 2.4	Constructs validity assessment	37
Table 2.5	Structural model and hypotheses testing	38
Table 3.1	Summary table of the relevant aspects highlighted in the Italian local public employees on Smart Working in public administration before and during COVID-19 health emergency	65
Table 4.1	Remote and smart working elements	80
Table 4.2	Personnel distribution of the Chamber of Commerce of Catanzaro	83
Table 6.1	Recommendations that emerged from the literature	142
Table 7.1	Data sheet	178
Table 7.2	Descriptive key indicators for statistics and quantile statistics key indicators selection	181
Table 7.3	Collected open text from questionnaire questions analysis	187
Table 8.1	Glimpse of adoption for e-learning before COVID-19 in different countries	203
Table 9.1	Number of articles ($N = 28$)	224
Table 9.2	Human governance analytics in public administration studies	225
Table 9.3	Human governance analytics description	226

Table 9.4 Factors which influence the selection of top public servants component matrix (Top public servants) 231
Table 9.5 Human governance training analytics 233
Table 9.6 Human governance talent performance appraisal analytics 233
Table 10.1 Top 20 expressions 255
Table 10.2 Examples related to themes 258

CHAPTER 1

People Analytics and The Future of Competitiveness: Which Capabilities HR Departments Need to Succeed in the "Next Normal"

Teresina Torre, Daria Sarti, and Gilda Antonelli

Introduction

The COVID-19 pandemic brought with it a necessary rethinking and a related redesign of processes, ways of working, communication management and talent management methods, the evaluation of performance and

T. Torre
University of Genova, Genova, Italy
e-mail: teresina.torre@economia.unige.it

D. Sarti
University of Florence, Florence, Italy
e-mail: daria.sarti@unifi.it

G. Antonelli (✉)
University of Sannio, Benevento, Italy
e-mail: gilda.antonelli@unisannio.it

S. R. Mondal et al. (eds.), *HR Analytics and Digital HR Practices*,
https://doi.org/10.1007/978-981-16-7099-2_1

motivation of people in their work, as well as a rethinking of the general and specific culture of companies. And as a non-secondary effect, the importance of the human resources function emerges with even greater emphasis. Human Resources Department (HRD) has played a central role in supporting companies to manage the pandemic crisis, focusing first on people and their needs, but also on their ability to manage change, and only soon after, on the economic side of the business.

In a recent article by The Economist (March 24, 2020) the role of the Chief People Officer in the pandemic is compared with the central role played by the Chief Financial Officer in the global financial crisis: the HRD is considered crucial to respond to the crisis. A renowned article published in the Harvard Business Review points at the importance of Human Resource Management (HRM) in the new challenge that each company needs to face with the "advent" of Big Data (BD) (Cappelli, 2017; Manyika et al., 2011). Indeed, if before the pandemic the role of Chief People Officer was considered of less importance than that of other functional roles, the pandemic has brought him back among the most essential executives for the success of the company. Human resources departments, in fact, had little time to change their way of working, to put aside the value they reserved for empiricism and the execution of decisions made by others and move on to a more objective decision-making process based on data and learn to manage people with more innovative methodologies. These challenges were considered so strategic that several authors voice their concern on the possible failure of the HR Departments in facing them (Angrave et al., 2016; Rasmussen & Ulrich, 2015) and they confirmed their relevance especially nowadays, since the pandemic is forcing companies to redefine the way they work.

Much of the management writings show worry about the chances of HRDs meeting with this challenge (SHRM Foundation, 2016; Tracey et al., 2019). On the contrary, practitioners are devoting great importance to the use of BDs to handle people management processes and to show how the introduction of key analysis index can contribute to individual activities (e.g. recruitment, performance evaluation, careers,..), starting from the assumption that '*most HR professionals are oriented generalists who have experience in employee benefits, wages and employment relationships*' (Charan, 2014: 33). Other researchers verify that HRD' capabilities of analyzing data in order to manage HR functions were really poor (Collins & Bennet, 2015). Furthermore, most of the recent reports on HRDs show a lack of clarity in the definition of the meaning of BD and the lack of a systematization of the existing studies, while progressively more researches focus on the risks associated with the use of data (Diebold, 2018).

In the academic field, the interest on BD topic is quickly growing, however, the number of works is still limited and largely delimited to the domains of computer science and business. Indeed, the lack of a psychological and organizational perspective is claimed in relation to the impact of BD on HR (Zhang et al., 2018). As suggested by Caputo et al. (2019), the present research approaches are mainly oriented to firms' processes and infrastructures rather than to human resources. Lengnick-Hall et al. (2018) emphasizing the relevant role that HRD plays in the development of new individual and organizational knowledge incorporating the perspective offered by BD. The researchers also underline how BDs can represent a great competitive advantage if applied to human resources as they would guarantee greater efficiency in managing people (see for example: Campion et al., 2018; Cheng et al., 2018; Martin-Rios et al., 2017) in both large and small firms (Larsen et al., 2015).

Roger Cude, senior vice president at Humana Inc., in a recent interview with Nicole Lewis (21 September 2020) stresses the attention on the increased importance of acquiring the capability to use and analyze the data and the need of depth and scope of these necessary skills. He therefore believes that companies need a very advanced and reliable technological infrastructure but, above all, more skills in scrutinizing data and greater ability to use the simulations obtained. In a recent article Butler and Rivera (2020) underline as actions leaders need to take with respect to coronavirus crisis, various activities within the competence of human resources such as review workforce locations and travel, find potential weaknesses, produce the most effective communication, and use scenario analysis. Companies that invested in people analytics in the previous years have a competitive advantage in managing the present situation (Das, 2021a; Mondal, 2021).

At the same time, some drawbacks are put in evidence such as the rising concern on data risk management for HR data (Calvard & Jeske, 2018). The present paper focus on the key role of the HR Managers—and of the HR Departments in general—in dealing with BD to manage the companies. It is suggested that all the organizational units "*feel compelled to outline how they are going to use it [BD] to improve their operations*" (Cappelli, 2017: 1) and it is stressed, in particular, that the

Human Resource Department (HRD) cannot be excluded in the change inevitably produced accepting this challenge.

In this vein, interpreting the recent debate on Big Data through the lens of the resource-based theory, the researchers will use the concept of Big Data Analytics Capability (BDAC) (Gandomi & Haider, 2015; Wamba et al., 2017) and focus on the key role of the HR Departments in dealing with BD and the capabilities they need to have to be effective. In this perspective, the present paper presents a theoretical model that mixes the skills required of HRDs to use analytics appropriately and maximize their predictive potential, connecting different information and information flows to each other, with exploration and exploitation business strategies, aiming to be able to respond to future scenarios (Dua et al., 2021; Duy et al., 2020; Van et al., 2020). The Big Data Analytics Capabilities will be discussed considering the dual strategy that companies can play to succeed (Siri et al., 2020; Singh et al., 2020b; Singh, Mondal, and Das, 2020a).

Background: Big Data and the Current Challenge for the HR Departments

Many authors, including McAfee and his colleagues (2012), argue that using BDs to support decision-making can produce enormous changes by replacing traditional sequential logic and process rules as well as the scientific method undergoing it, and having it evolving from a static approach to a dynamic one. Indeed, BD "has the potential to support firms in identifying opportunities related to decision-making processes and in defining more efficient organizational processes through the data acquisition, filtering and coding" (Caputo et al., 2019: 4). At the same time, it becomes of fundamental importance that specific skills are developed, in order to enrich and make more effective decision-making activities that have an effect on both employees and organizations and, consequently, would have an impact on the organizational culture (De Mauro et al., 2015).

In this context, HR Departments need to face two big and different questions (Das, 2020; Mondal, 2020; Sharma & Das, 2020). On one hand, there is a general call for them to make new efforts in order to improve organizations' human capital through training so to develop new "hybrid" professions—that means with a double focus, on their specific professional profile and on the basis of new technologies (Oding, 2015)—able to deal with and manage BD (Angrave et al., 2016). Coherently, it becomes necessary that organizations invest in training programs for providing companies' workers and experts with "interdisciplinary business intelligence" and "analytics education", so that they use and finalize data properly and incorporate them in "new" decision processes understanding how and why (De Mauro et al., 2016). Conversely, there are other researches which enlighten that HR managers and professionals lack of the "must-have capabilities" (Angrave et al., 2016), thus stressing the usefulness of developing of new skills linked to the use and employment of Big Data Analytics (BDA) for HR purposes, but also suggesting the growth of new competences for HR Departments to help organizations in managing BD (Mondal & Sahoo, 2020; Nadanyiova & Das, 2020).

These challenges are considered so strategic that numerous authors declare their concern over the possible failure of HRDs to address them (Angrave et al., 2016; Rasmussen & Ulrich, 2015). Among other things, the difficulties for HR departments to provide uniquely quantifiable results of their activities (Lengnick-Hall et al., 2018) are considered to have a serious impact on the significance of HR Departments compared to other corporate functions. Indeed, it is argued that "*HR analytics is taken over by other functions that are more mature in their analytics path (particularly finance, IT and marketing*" (Rasmussen & Ulrich, 2015: 236). Some scholars indicate as one of the reasons for this subordination of HR Departments in the fact that decisions about people are often based on beliefs and impressions and less on the collection and punctual analysis of data (Angrave et al., 2016). In fact, HR Departments are less likely to have collected data on the activities of their employees both for a characteristic cultural approach that has always been linked to this function and the low propensity to quantitative analysis, and for the increasingly burning issues related to privacy on the use of some data. On this point, however, Rasmussen and Ulrich (2015) observe that the HR Departments actually lack skills and therefore are unable to create key indicators on which to query the data available to them, thus underlining how difficult it is for them to align themselves with competitive contexts in which data ownership and analysis is now considered vital. Furthermore, a prevalent lack of analytical thinking in HRDs is highlighted along with the old paradigm—expressed in these terms "HRM cannot be a data-driven function" (Lengnick-Hall et al., 2018) represent conditions characterizing the

HR Departments (and not the other Departments, which are readier in moving toward the approach implicated in BD). In the pandemic crisis companies that already used a people analytic approach to manage the emergence much better since they have at disposal many important data to control the productivity of workers from home, manage their interactions, and lead and motivate them (Behera et al., 2019; Gupta et al., 2019; Mohanty et al., 2019).

In the end, the shortage of competences of HR Departments and their limited awareness about BD potentialities may deteriorate their "power" in the organization so prejudicing the chance to take on the role of the key player in this relevant organizational challenge which, on the contrary, asks for the vision that considers more the people and ethical aspect connected to them, more than the technical mastery.

HR Proactive Orientation and Big Data Analytical Capabilities

The inclusion of a BD system in any organization inevitably introduces a deep change—as authors remarks (Shah et al., 2017; Wamba et al., 2015a, Wamba et al., 2015b; McKinsey & Company, 2016; Sivarajah et al., 2017) it is about a disruptive one—toward which a proactive orientation is necessary, just for anticipating the unpredictable evolution organizations are experimenting (Scholz, 2017).

Indeed, this process requires first the comprehension of what BD really are and then the awareness of their usefulness so to learn to manage them. And it is exactly the detailed aspects which decline the ability in managing to represent the challenge: this necessarily leads to a knowledge of the nature of BD, to the awareness of their usefulness in managing people, to the necessary ability to use them profitably by elaborating significant indices (Kim et al., 2014).

Moreover, to be able to use the BD in a conscious and effective way it is necessary a sociotechnical dimension and the separation of the HR management processes into sub-steps that can be controlled. This entails a substantial change in the traditional and consolidated method used and the need for new multifaceted capabilities and, consequently, has an impact on the technology and culture of the organization (Lagoze, 2014).

So, first and foremost, it is natural to suggest that the HR Department, besides its consolidated functions, has to play the key role of change agent (Brown et al., 2017; Ulrich, 1997) which implies its continuous effort in promoting processes of transformation within the organizations leading to improve "*the organization's capacity for change*" (Ulrich, 1998, p. 125). Indeed, it is suggested that the HR Department has to operate as a "ferryman" in this process focused on BD system rethinking and implementation, especially because it is necessary to train the specific skills of employees and, at the same time, to redesign different organizational processes. Coherently, it can be seen as a destroyer of certainties rather than promoter of the status quo. In some sense, it can play the role of the guardian acting in preventing the "core rigidities" (Leonard-Barton, 1992), which might arise against such an organizational change and rather promote core competencies enabling the organizational learning, so necessary to foster adaptation to the new conditions. Therefore, it would be necessary for HRD to become a sort of "devil's advocate" of the choices made, so that its contribution to the organizational change process becomes effective and proactive.

Thus, interpreting the recent discussion on BD through the fundamental principles of resource-based theory, the concept of Big Data Analytics Capability (BDAC) is proposed (Gandomi & Haider, 2015; Wamba et al., 2017). According to authors, Big Data Analytic (BDA) is "*a holistic approach to managing, processing and analysing the 5 Vs data-related dimensions*" (Wamba et al., 2017: 356)—as know they are variety, velocity, volume, value, and veracity (Demchenko et al., 2013)—which enable organizations "*to analyze and manage strategy through a data lens*" (Wamba et al., 2017: 357). Coherently, BDAC is the appropriate organizational capability, which enables the adoption of BDA.

In order to facilitate the implementation of a company's BDAC, consideration should be given to specific resources (Gupta & George, 2016) and organizational factors (Davenport & Patil, 2012; Wamba et al., 2017). It becomes important for organizations to focus on the "resources, in addition to technology, that are needed to build" enterprise-specific BDA capabilities which are difficult to replicate (Gupta & George, 2016: 3).

BDACs are divided into three specific areas: people, technology, and management. Skills on people is labeled as "*knowledge of people and data*" and serves to be able to understand, develop and apply analysis models. It is also mentioned to as "*people*" (Davenport & Patil, 2012), "*data science skills*" (Barton & Court, 2012), "*employee analytical skills*" (Kiron et al., 2014) or "*management of staff*" (McAfee et al., 2012), so as to highlight as a new capability (McAfee et al., 2012), to put in evidence how a new way of managing people arises with data at disposal. A simple and clear example are wearables tools, which produce information on organizational behaviors—personal feature, commitment, emotion, satisfaction, and so on—and can be used together with data that are coming from other part of the company (Waber, 2013)—productivity, sales, customer service, quality system—to have useful information to better design appropriate HR policies. Specifically, HR Analytics is an area of HRM practice, research, and innovation concerned with the use of information technologies, descriptive and predictive data analytics, and visualization tools for generating easy to interpret information on workforce transformations, individual and group performance, compensation dynamics, and other processes that can be used strategically to improve both organization effectiveness and efficiency and employees' experience (Tursunbayeva et al., 2018). In order to acquire this capability, one need to know the specific people management methods and have the familiarity with numbers and the elaboration of indicators.

The second critical element, that is "technology"—also referred as "technology capability" (Baron & Court, 2012)—is necessary to explore and manage data (Barton & Court, 2012). Having in mind the infrastructural support needed for this dimension authors named it also as: "analytics platform" (Kiron et al., 2014) and "technology infrastructure" (McAfee et al., 2012). Since the data can provide an analysis of the status quo, but also be interpolated to ensure a more complex interpretation or, even, thanks to the use of statistical methods and simulation models, design the diverse possible scenarios resulting from the different managerial actions, it becomes essential to have at least the quantitative basis competence for the construction of the main indices.

The third dimension is "management" (Davenport & Patil, 2012) and has to do with the use of forecasting and predictive decision-making models. Several authors refer to this competence with a broader vision, for example considering it as: 'management skills' (Barton & Court, 2012), 'corporate decision making' (McAfee et al., 2012), and 'organizational culture'. In this last case, in particular, it is once again underlined how it is necessary for managers to be familiar with the use of systems based on the simulation of probabilistic scenarios in their organizational context (Kiron et al., 2014).

Therefore, BDAC becomes "the" new organizational competence which, analyzing in an effective way that considers the organizational dimensions and resources, guarantees a 'systemic vision', and, therefore, contributes to have a strategic vision of the whole company, coordinating the various departments and the many company functions. In this case, the management aspect can be compared to that of the translator who unifies the different languages used by the organizational units so that they can understand and consider their different perspectives. Further, as Galbraith (2014) states, the development of specific Bid Data Analytic Competence entails the employment of a dual strategy. The first one is related to building *"a digital capability"* for the improvement of existing products and to make the decision process faster and increasingly effective; the second strategy is connected to the use of data and analytics for the generation of customized insights and reports *"that can be sold to customer and became a new profit center"* (p. 12).

In other words, if we consider the exploration–exploitation approach to organizational learning (March, 1991), the former strategy can be associated to an exploitation strategy and the latter to an explorative one. In relationship with this approach, we could imagine different organizational configurations for BD in the continuum between exploration and exploitation strategy. One more effect will be a continuum between a configuration in which BD are pervasive toward the whole organizations, coordination mechanisms are chosen according to a decentralized logic and competencies on BD are diffused and varied among employees and HR members. The other extreme, more internal process focused, in which BD are situated in a single organizational unit so that the centralized and top down logic of data governance prevails, and competencies are hold by individuals or single organizational units.

Organizations are requested to combine the two strategies into a dual system and seek complementarity (Tushman & O'Reilly, 1996) which allows the support of the whole structure (see Fig. 1.1) and shape, when possible, a dual-face organizational configuration—the ambidextrous organization—that is defined as an established organization able to develop radical innovations and protect, as well, its traditional businesses (O'Reilly & Tushman, 2004).

The model shown in Fig. 1.1 depicts BD analytics capabilities which a company should possess to enhance an effective BD strategy. In this vein it is crucial the role assumed by HR Department and its capability of proactively participate in governing BD analytics within the company.

This role asked to HR Department can be achieved by its re-orientation which leads it to assume also "meta-roles", meaning not only the HR roles identified by the original Ulrich and Grochowski

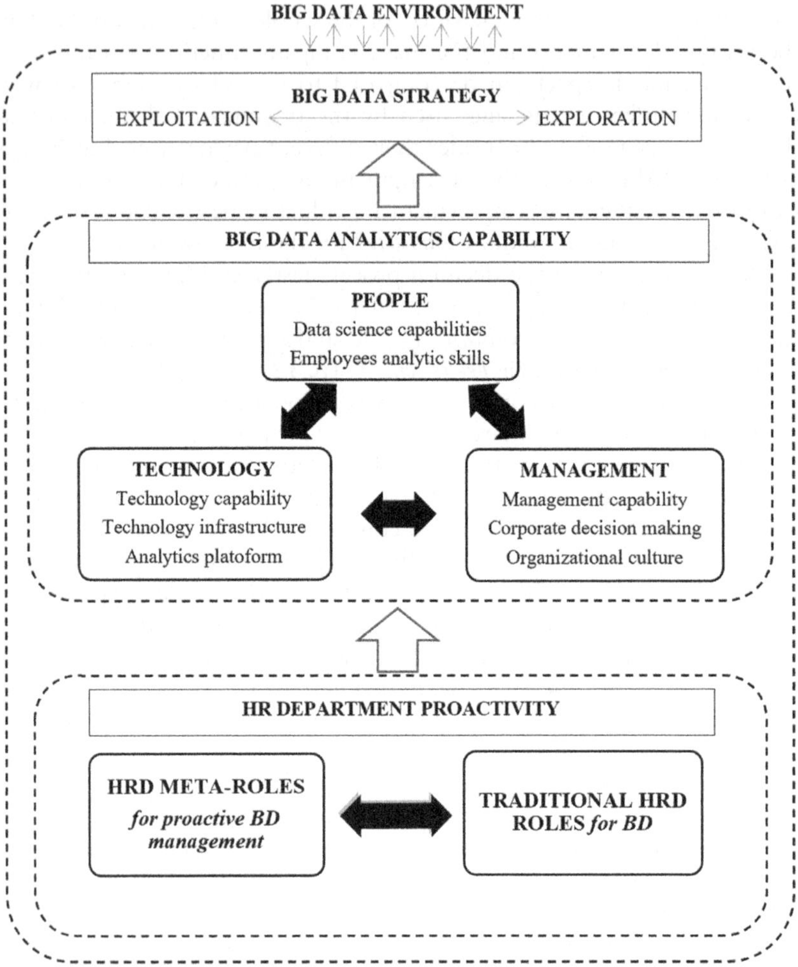

Fig. 1.1 BDAC, BD sources, and exploration–exploitation processes (*Source* Authors' elaboration)

(2012) categorization and readapted by the same authors for BD specific purposes, but rather roles that may directly facilitate the HR proactive action further enabling it in assuming a cross-sectional perspective. These roles—named by Scholz as 'BD watchdog", "BD centaur" and "HR

Daemon"—and referred by us as 'meta-roles', should be played by the HR Department to (1) facilitate employee usage of BD by informing them on potential risks arising from BD faultiness, favoring employees' BD literacy and favor managers empowerment toward decisions; (2) protect data authorship, privacy and conservation; (3) "make big data available and usable for everybody within the organization and, by that, to transform big data into a resource of pro-activity [...] rather than the organization just reacting on big data." (Scholz, 2017: 86).

The adoption of a different HR roles seems to be essential in terms of: employees' promotor of knowledge awareness, guidance for change, strategic counselor for the top management, protector of the human side of the organization, stimulus for knowledge acquisition, facilitator for data sharing, protector of data and privacy. Indeed, all these activities meet the natural vocation of every HR Department. By assuming these roles, and combining them appropriately and in a proactive manner, the success in this epochal change not only will be fostered, but it will also be possible to establish definitively the centrality of HR Department in the management of crisis and change in turning to a "new" normality.

Discussion on HR Department Role and Capabilities

BD's is one of the most impactful challenges of the last few years and will become even more so in the near future as it involves every aspect of the life of companies and their employees. Different kinds of company because of their business, strategy and history have to deal with BD employment in different way and must be able to foster and model distinct solutions. Human Capital Trends Survey (Deloitte Insights, 2018) reported People Analytics as being important or very important, making it the second highest-ranked HR trend. Recently, machine learning and artificial intelligence (AI) have begun to feature in these innovations to analyze complex performance data, screen potential employees, develop personalized training recommendations, enable smart scheduling, predict future performance, infer employee satisfaction, or gear payments to employee "value" (e.g. Nunn, 2018). Moreover, the COVID-19 pandemic asks for a big change in people processes and management that is totally transforming the organizations leading to a "next normal" era. The COVID-19 pandemic has required emergency changes that are likely not to be fully adopted into the new normal due to the systems chosen or the ways in which they were implemented in an emergency phase. However, they still lead us to reflect on the new way of working in the near future and on what we have learned from this experience, freeing ourselves from "lessons" that we will not need and treasuring those we will need.

The ability to analyze people's data, technology, and management skills are strategic and essential in dealing with "next normal" management. The HR Departments are considered to be the most conservative in the use of the methodologies used to carry out their functions as they are the ones that historically, having to do with people, find more difficulties in using new technologies (Camuffo, 2016). On the other hand, the adoption of new technologies in organizational processes makes a huge impact on people. Furthermore, the use of data analysis from an organizational point of view pushes companies to redesign structures, coordination mechanisms, and decision-making processes as well as the methodologies they use to manage employees.

All this requires a deep change to the managers of human resources both in the content of the numerous roles they have to cover and in terms of their professional profile. In fact, they must develop the ability to integrate information and different information flows using analytics. This will make them able to exploit the predictive potential of the analyzes and to design and interpret future scenarios to adapt their actions, strengthened by traditional skills on basic HR processes.

HRD New Capabilities

HR Department Should Assume the Role of BD Architect by Designing Structures and Systems

Data science, technology, and management capabilities appear strategic and essential in facing the "next normal" management. As a consequence, the role of HR Department is essential and should be improved through different capabilities related to the three areas People, Technology and Management. Adopting a system based on data analysis requires a change both from the side of redesigning the structure and processes, both of developing new mechanisms for coordinating them, both of re-planning the human resource management system. Starting from the HR department structure redesigning, it is important to stress teamwork. Using BD analysis and interpretation, teams can be vital for the successful implementation of this new methodology. It will also be necessary to review the coordination systems between the different units and between individuals who, due to the pandemic, have faced new ways of working (e.g. remote working). In this case the BD analysis (such as the control of emails, face to face but also web meetings and phone calls) become crucial to verify and, feasibly, redesign individual and team coordination mechanisms. Furthermore, the same tools for controlling the performance or the effectiveness of some work behaviors through the preparation of ad hoc key performance indexes, will allow to identify any structural trouble or wrong procedures, as well as to report any misalignments between units. For this reason, the HRD should be able to have among its members an organizational analyst, who studies and maps the entire organization through the BD. This capability can be condensed not only in a single person but also in different team members, coherently with the new managerial trend, which shows the need of creating teams with varied skills that act as a real center for data analysis and interpretation.

Larger companies have already integrated several specific roles such as, for example, data analysts or data scientists, together with the classic ones—training manager, the talent manager, the head of the legal area, and so on in the HRD.

Effective HR Department Should Assume a Guidance Role for the Organization in the Shift Toward BD, Thus Promoting the Newness While Protecting the Social and Human Dimension

In this sense a key capability would be the dialog promotion, that allows the balance between dualities (people and technology or soft and hard dimensions) which is described by different strategic aims and structural logics. This is coherent with the aim of the HR Department to be the caretaker of the human side. HR Department should assume the role of promoter of BD knowledge and culture among employees. The strategic use of BD needs a clear and systematize methodological approach to interpret different situations and decisions must lay on measurable observations. All business challenges can be translated into analytical expressions and analyzed throughout key performance indicators that refer to organizational processes, people behaviors and tasks. Furthermore, having the capabilities to interpret the results of the analyzes performed, relates to the ability to have a broader strategic vision.

Furthermore, HRD is responsible to create the culture of an appropriate comprehension of data and technologies and technological systems devoted to gather, store and analyze them, so developing appropriate training strategies. The critical capacity with respect to the tools adopted for the analysis of the BD, for example, the method of collection, storage and use of IT tools (entirely the prerogative of IT systems) can "hide" from a less attentive analyst information that could be key. The culture, essentially, seems to be affecting the way the companies face the BD challenge. The widespread culture within organizations of the use of data on which to base decision-making processes favors, over time, greater familiarity of all people with statistical and simulation tools but also with the use of IT tools and, therefore, it increases the possibility of reading the different symbols in a broader strategic framework that includes the different parts of the company.

HR Department Should Assume the Role of Guardian and Promotor of Ethics in the Management of Data

The HR teams need a new special expertise that supports the propensity to use data throughout the structure but also the protection of the same one. In fact, the perception of individuals but also the organizational context, are fundamental in guiding the way in which companies face the challenge with BD. Considering to incorporate this new competence into the team will certainly have a double advantage: on the one hand, being one of the HRD team's skills, it will be mediated by the other's capabilities and there will be no risk of following a mere logic guided by IT and, on the contrary, technology will be used with awareness. On the other, the climate and the internal organizational identity will be favored as individuals will not feel threatened by the unethical use of data.

Indeed, it is necessary to become aware of another important aspect of data management: the problem of ethics. In this sense, precisely if we consider the reorganization phase linked to the "next normality", the HR Department must pay particular attention to how the data are processed and the information that is generated is used, since it is necessary to have in mind that behind cold numbers there are people and their related situations. As a matter of fact, according to 84% of respondents in Global Viceversa 2018, organizations may not be truly aware of how the PA could give rise to unethical practices, for example giving rise, as has happened in recent years, to more or less volunteers discrimination based on gender, health conditions or disproportionate control over performance that does not contemplate the variability of people's general conditions from one day to the next (e.g. Holeman et al., 2016). Balancing these ethical requirements is challenging (Delios, 2010) and magnifies existing ethical dilemmas for HRM professionals faced with the need to produce efficiency gains without demoralizing the workforce (e.g. Ekuma & Akobo, 2015).

Conclusion and Future Research Directions

Conclusions

The COVID-19 pandemic has accelerated the change toward a different way of doing and organizing business; particularly, it has favored the adoption of so many ICT tools as they were available, which generate a large amount of data in any direction, and it has maximized the need for a more reliable picture of the different processes developed into every organization. And tools adoption implies nowadays the access of a different technological context, the depth of which we are understanding while it is invading the organizational context.

This, in our view, is the real reason behind the interest in the subject here examined. Especially small and medium-sized enterprises seem not to consider central a widespread approach to data analysis, probably due to their chronic lack of resources which may impede an integrated investment in ICT systems, except for applications related to the external market (consumers, sales, purchases), which are evidently and inevitably necessary; rather, the analysis related to data involving human resources risks to be considered of little significance, both for their features, which are assumed to be well known, and for the small number of skilled employees.

In this myopic evaluation, it is not considered that rather than effective BD, it is often the "smart" data which provides important information, specifically from an analytical and predictive perspective. The traditional functions of HR—such as the attraction of talents, the evaluation processes, the motivation of employees, and their retention—are even more important in a time of psychological loss of workers (destabilized also by the fear of getting sick, them and their loved ones) and of reorganization of work processes both in terms of localization (work from home) and time (asynchronous working), and in terms of coordination (new management and leadership methods to be improved) and they produce data, which offer many opportunities, if well managed and understood.

In a historical period of uncertainty and change, the HR Department has acquired a central role in managing the pandemic crisis and reorganizing work procedures, structures, and coordination mechanisms, and it has done so by reassuring people, managing their stress, sustaining their motivation and, at the same time, maintaining their productivity.

At the same time, it has become evident that the increasingly accelerated BD 'revolution', which has overwhelmed and will overwhelm all companies wishing to maintain their competitiveness on the market, cannot be the result of emerging and unrelated strategies or partial adoptions within organizations as it risks, doing so, of being downright loser. In this perspective, the HR Department in its role as facilitator and keeper includes all the skills to manage this change based on data analysis and it has to assume a leadership role in guiding organizations toward the "next normal", while paying great attention to people, in respects of their needs, potential and critical issues.

Since the real source of competitive advantage is to put people at the center of organizations, so that their job satisfaction and their motivation represent the lever for supporting the entire business and guarantee the success of the strategies implemented, traditional HR processes take on a renewed centrality consistently with the strong need to preserve purpose and focus, but revisited in light of the changed scenario. This change involves specific attention to the acquisition of talents, which becomes the first critical process in order to ensure that the organization is equipped with skills aligned with the context, and their rapid evolution through a continuous and strategic investment in internal training, so to support the people already employed in companies, in acquiring the skills they need to keep abreast with changes. But HR Departments become critical as their post-pandemic role transforms from creating value to delivering value. Indeed, HR "customers" are not just employees, leaders, or business strategies within the organization, but also stakeholders such as customers, investors (debt or equity), and communities outside the company (Ulrich, 2020a). Therefore, they create value not simply by managing the activities of employees with scorecards, dashboards, and insights, but also by ensuring the impact of human resources activities on the main stakeholders, through the creation and maintenance of a "just" corporate culture that creates, provides and captures value for customers and investors. "*The right culture can be defined as the identity of the company in the minds of its best customers which then shapes employee behaviours and HR practices*" (Ulrich, 2020b).

In the model presented in this chapter, the environmental dimension is also included. It relates to the exogenous pressures which may have a huge influence on the decision related to the way in which organizations adopt BD systems, enabling management to undertake an exploitation or exploration perspective in approaching to them (Benders et al., 2006). This has to be considered with specific attention. Indeed, the general attitude toward the emulation following competitors in the use of methodologies for BD presents a relevant risk, because the adoption of imitative strategies that do not consider a careful assessment of the actual peculiarities of the company (Scholz, 2017). On the contrary, an explicit decision is requested so to follow it evaluating together internal elements and external ones. Similarly, BD's sociotechnical vision emphasizes the importance to carefully and a priori evaluate the factors of the context in order to adapt the analyzes to the specificities of the organization and not to replicate senseless models used by different communities or for different purposes (Lagoze, 2014).

Furthermore, many researchers have stressed the importance of not letting oneself been guided in the implementation of such systems by an IT logic, but rather to thoroughly analyze the specificities of the organization and to search for responses starting from them and interpreted through IT resources (Dery et al., 2006).

Finally, it has to be remarked that the theoretical model here presented wish to contribute both to academic literature, where the number of works in PA is still limited and delimited to the domains of computer science and business, and to the practitioner field, since companies are preparing to face these new challenges and they need to create HR teams ready at the "next normal" management, that means that these teams have to move with agility and awareness in the just present future (Das, 2021b). A future in which the increasing use of data about any aspect of work, any attitude, and sentiment becomes the effective challenge to be understood first and to which standards have to be modified coherently with higher results, which are now possible to reach.

Future Research

As it has been underlined, we are quickly entering a different world. So, future research asks for in-depth analysis in any direction, just because the effects of the change we are living with go in any direction. In this scenario, we think that a specific attention has to be paid toward how HRDs are preparing to be protagonist, assuming all the different roles they are asked to interpret, and interiorizing a different mindset which incorporates data, being it BD or simply more data than before, and help in seeing people through them so having a global view, developing traditional processes and traditional goals in a different and more efficient way helpful for improving quality. Also, in a more focused perspective, leaders' role is changing dealing with the need of interpreting data in a strategic way and in supporting his/her employees, whose work is constantly becoming more effective if made in team when team works—so to create conditions for an appropriate climate in team. Preserving a focus on psychological dimension is a fundamental issue for HRDs, starting from the awareness of big stress-test that was caused by COVID-19 pandemic to which they had to offer responses both on working hand and on human hand. Indeed, it brought out many unexpected dimensions, such as entering private dimensions of most co-workers and superiors: this might have been a benefit in reshaping the social dimension as well as it has broken boundaries between social and private life, but it has to be managed with care and respect toward individuals perceptions and availability to share their intimacy. This aspect is strictly connected to the ethnic dimension of organizations, which with BD assumes a more critical profile asking for awareness and conscious decision.

References

Angrave, D., Charlwood, A., Kirkpatrick, I., Lawrence, M., & Stuart, M. (2016). HR and analytics: Why HR are set to fail the big data challenge. *Human Resource Management Journal, 26*(1), 1–11.

Barton, D., & Court, D. (2012). Making advanced analytics work for you. *Harvard Business Review, 90*, 79–83.

Behera, M., Dash, M., Ayasa Kanta Mohanty, A. K., & Das, S. (2019). Entrepreneurial ecosystem: A geographical upliftment. *Revista Espacios, 40*, 26–36. http://www.revistaespacios.com/a19v40n01/19400126.html

Benders, J., Hoeken, P., Batenburg, R., & Schouteten, R. (2006). First organize, then automate: A modern socio-technical view on ERP systems and teamworking. *New Technology, Work and Employment, 21*(3), 242–251.

Brown, M., Kulik, C. T., Cregan, C., & Metz, I. (2017). Understanding the change-cynicism cycle: The role of HR. *Human Resource Management, 56*(1), 5–24.

Butler, M., & Rivera, K. (2020). Seven key actions business can take to mitigate the effects of the COVID-19 Virus. *Strategy+Business.* Retrieved March 6, 2020, from https://www.strategy-business.com/blog/Seven-key-actions-business-can-take-to-mitigate-the-effects-of-COVID-19

Calvard, T. S., & Jeske, D. (2018). Developing human resource data risk management in the age of big data. *International Journal of Information Management, 43*, 159–164.

Campion, M. C., Campion, M. A., & Campion, E. D. (2018). Big data techniques and talent management: Recommendations for organizations and a research agenda for IO psychologists. *Industrial and Organizational Psychology, 11*(2), 250–257.

Camuffo, A. (2016). Le nuove sfide dell'HR: Big data, rilevanza e sostenibilità. *Economia & Management, 5*, 117–125.

Cappelli, P. (2017). There is no such thing as big data in HR. *Harvard Business Review, 2.*

Caputo, F., Cillo, V., Candelo, E., & Liu, Y. (2019). Innovating through digital revolution: The role of soft skills and Big data in increasing firm performance. *Management Decision,* 57, 2032–2051. Retrieved September 12, 2019, from https://doi.org/10.1108/MD-07-2018-0833

Centre for International Governance Innovation & Ipsos. (2018). *CIGI-Ipsos global survey on internet security and trust.* https://www.cigionline.org/internet-survey-2018

Charan, R. (2014). It is time to split HR. *Harvard Business Review, 92*(7), 33–34.

Cheng, Z., Xu, Y., & Cui, J. (2018). The formation of employee retention basing on computer communication networks. *Wireless Personal Communications*, 1–15.

Collins, L., & Bennet, C. (2015). *HR and people analytics.* Deloitte Insights. Retrieved November 10, 2017, from https://www2.deloitte.com/insights/us/en/focus/human-capital-trends/2015/people-and-hr-analytics-human-capital-trends-2015.html

Das, S. (2020). Innovations in digital banking service brand equity and millennial consumerism. In *Digital transformation and innovative services for business and learning* (pp. 62–79). IGI Global. https://doi.org/10.4018/978-1-7998-5175-2.ch004

Das, S. (2021a). A systematic study of integrated marketing communication and content management system for millennial consumers. In *Innovations in digital branding and content marketing* (pp. 91–112). IGI Global. https://doi.org/10.4018/978-1-7998-4420-4.ch005

Das, S. (2021b). *Search engine optimization and marketing: A recipe for success in digital marketing* (1st ed.). CRC Press. https://doi.org/10.1201/9780429298509

Davenport, T. H., & Patil, D. J. (2012). Data scientist. *Harvard Business Review, 90*(5), 70–76.

De Mauro, A., Greco, M., & Grimaldi, M. (2015). *What is big data? A consensual definition and a review of key research topics.* Paper presented at Proceedings of the 4th International Conference on Integrated Information, Madrid, Spain, 1644 (1), 97–104.

De Mauro, A., Greco, M., & Grimaldi, M. (2016). A formal definition of Big data based on its essential features. *Library Review, 65*(3), 122–135.

Delios, A. (2010). How can organizations be competitive but dare to care? *Academy of Management Perspectives, 24*(3), 25–36.

Deloitte Insights. (2018, May 8). *The rise of the social enterprise, Deloitte Global Human Capital Trends.*

Demchenko, Y., Membrey, P., Grosso, P., & De Laat, C. (2013, May 20–24). *Addressing Big data issues in scientific data infrastructure.* Paper presented at first International Symposium on Big Data, California Conference.

Dery, K., Hall, R., & Wailes, N. (2006). ERPs as 'technologies-in-practice': Social construction, materiality and the role of organizational factors. *New Technology, Work and Employment, 21*(3), 229–241.

Diebold, F. (2018). *A personal perspective on the origin (s) and development of 'Big data': The phenomenon, the term, and the discipline, second version.* Retrieved May 25, 2018, from https://www.sas.upenn.edu/~fdiebold/papers/paper112/Diebold_Big_Data.pdf

Dua, S., Singh, I., & Das, S. (2021). Banking innovative service with digital brand equity for new age consumers: Internet banking and millennial consumerism. In *Innovations in digital branding and content marketing* (pp. 134–159). IGI Global. https://doi.org/10.4018/978-1-7998-4420-4.ch007

Duy, N. T., Mondal, S. R., Van, N. T. T., Dzung, P. T., Minh, D. X. H., & Das, S. (2020). A study on the role of web 4.0 and 5.0 in the sustainable tourism ecosystem of Ho Chi Minh City, Vietnam. *Sustainability, 12*(17), 7140. https://doi.org/10.3390/su12177140

Ekuma, K., & Akobo, L. (2015). Human resource management ethics and professionals' dilemma: A review and research agenda. *Human Resource Management Research, 5*(3), 47–57.

Galbraith, J. R. (2014). Organizational design challenges resulting from big data. *Journal of Organization Design, 3*(1), 2–13.

Gandomi, A., & Haider, M. (2015). Beyond the hype: Big data concepts, methods, and analytics. *International Journal of Information Management, 35*(2), 137–144.

Gupta, D. K., Jena, D., Samantaray, A. K., & Das, S. (2019). HRD climate in selected public sector banks in India. *Revista ESPACIOS, 40*(11).

Gupta, M., & George, J. F. (2016). Toward the development of a big data analytics capability. *Information & Management, 53*(8), 1049–1064.

Holeman, I., Cookson, T. P., & Pagliari, C. (2016). Digital technology for health sector governance in low and middle income countries: A scoping review. *Journal of Global Health, 6* (2).

Kim, G. H., Trimi, S., & Chung, J. H. (2014). Big-data applications in the government sector. *Communications of the ACM, 57*(3), 78–85.

Kiron, D., Prentice K., Ferguson P., & Boucher R. (2012). Innovating with analytics. *MIT Sloan Management Review, 54*, Fasc. 1, 47–51.

Kiron, D., Prentice, P. K., & Ferguson, R. B. (2014). The analytics mandate. *MIT Sloan Management Review, 55*, 1–25.

Lagoze, C. (2014). Big data, data integrity, and the fracturing of the control zone. *Big Data & Society, 1*(2), 1–11.

Larsen, C., Rand, S., Schmid, A., Mezzanzanica, M., & Dusi, S. (Eds.). (2015). *Big data and the complexity of labor market policies: New approaches in regional and local labor market mentoring for reducing skills mismatches*. Rainer Hampp Verlag.

Lengnick-Hall, M. L., Neely, A. R., & Stone, C. B. (2018). Human resource management in the digital age: Big data, HR analytics and artificial intelligence. In Pedro, N. M. & Carolina, M. (Eds.), *Management and technological challenges in the digital age* (pp. 13-42). CRC Press.

Leonard-Barton, D. (1992). Core capabilities and core rigidities: A paradox in managing new product development. *Strategic Management Journal, 13*(S1), 111–125.

Lewis, N., (2020). *HR data analytics in the time of the COVID-19 pandemic*. Retrieved September 21, 2020, from https://www.shrm.org/resourcesandtools/hr-topics/technology/pages/hr-data-analytics-time-covid19-pandemic.aspx

Manyika, J., Chui, M., Brown, B., Bughin, J., Dobbs, R., Roxburgh, C., & Byers, A. H. (2011). *Big data: The next frontier for innovation, competition, and productivity*. Retrieved June 2, 2017, from https://www.mckinsey.com/business-functions/digital-mckinsey/our-insights/big-data-the-next frontier for innovation

March, J. G. (1991). Exploration and exploitation in organizational learning. *Organization Science, 2*(1), 71–87.

Martin-Rios, C., Pougnet, S., & Nogareda, A. M. (2017). Teaching HRM in contemporary hospitality management: A case study drawing on HR analytics and big data analysis. *Journal of Teaching in Travel & Tourism, 17*(1), 34–54.

McAfee, A., Brynjolfsson, E., Davenport, T. H., Patil, D. J., & Barton, D. (2012). Big data: The management revolution. *Harvard Business Review, 90*(10), 60–68.

McKinsey & Company. (2016). *The age of analytics: Competing in a data-driven world*. Global McKinsey Institute.

Mohanty, P. C., Dash, M., Dash, M., & Das, S. (2019). A study on factors influencing training effectiveness. *Revista Espacios, 40,* 7–15. http://www.revistaespacios.com/a19v40n02/19400207.html

Mondal, S. (2021). A systematic study of new age consumer engagement and exploration for digital entertainment for over-the-top platforms in various digital media. In *Innovations in digital branding and content marketing* (pp. 113–133). IGI Global. https://doi.org/10.4018/978-1-7998-4420-4.ch006

Mondal, S., & Sahoo, K. K. (2020). A study of green building prospects on sustainable management decision making. In *Green building management and smart automation* (pp. 220–234). IGI Global. https://doi.org/10.4018/978-1-5225-9754-4.ch011

Mondal, S. R. (2020). A systematic study for digital innovation in management education: An integrated approach towards problem-based learning in Vietnam. In *Digital innovations for customer engagement, management, and organizational improvement* (pp. 104–120). IGI Global. https://doi.org/10.4018/978-1-7998-5171-4.ch006

Nadanyiova, M., & Das, S. (2020). Millennials as a target segment of socially responsible communication within the business strategy. *Littera Scripta, 13*(1), 119–134. https://doi.org/10.36708/Littera_Scripta2020/1/8

Nunn, J. (2018, May 9). How AI is transforming HR departments. *Forbes*.

O'Reilly, C. A., III., & Tushman, M. L. (2004). The ambidextrous organization. *Harvard Business Review, 82*(4), 74.

Oding, N. (2015). The use of Big data: Challenges and perspectives in Russia. In C. Larsen, C., S. Rand, A. Schmid, M. Mezzanzanica, & S. Dusi, S. (Eds.), *Big data and the complexity of labor market policies: New approaches in regional and local labor market mentoring for reducing skills mismatches* (pp. 153–164). Rainer Hampp Verlag.

Rasmussen, T., & Ulrich, D. (2015). Learning from practice: How HR analytics avoids being a management fad. *Organizational Dynamics, 44*(3), 236–242.

Scholz, T. M. (2017). *Big data in organizations and the role of human resource management*. Peter Lang LTD International Academic Publishers.

Shah, N., Irani, Z., & Sharif, A. M. (2017). Big data in an HR context: Exploring organizational change readiness, employee attitudes and behaviors. *Journal of Business Research, 70*, 366–378.

Sharma, E., & Das, S. (2020). Measuring impact of Indian ports on environment and effectiveness of remedial measures towards environmental pollution. *International Journal of Environment and Waste Management, 25*(3), 356–380. https://doi.org/10.1504/IJEWM.2019.10021787

SHRM Foundation. (2016, May). *Use of workforce analytics for competitive advantage, preparing for future HR trends report*. Retrieved June 15, 2016, from https://www.shrm.org/foundation/ourwork/initiatives/preparing-for-future-hr-trends/Documents/Workforce%20Analytics%20Report.pdf

Singh, L. B., Mondal, S. R., & Das, S. (2020a). Human resource practices & their observed significance for Indian SMEs. *Revista ESPACIOS, 41*(7). http://www.revistaespacios.com/a20v41n07/20410715.html

Singh, S., Mondal, S., Singh, L. B., Sahoo, K. K., & Das, S. (2020b). An empirical evidence study of consumer perception and socioeconomic profiles for digital stores in Vietnam. *Sustainability, 12*(5), 1716. https://doi.org/10.3390/su12051716

Siri, R., Mondal S. R., & Das, S. (2020). Hydropower: A renewable energy resource for sustainability in terms of climate change and environmental protection. In *The handbook of environmental Chemistry*. https://doi.org/10.1007/698_2020_635

Sivarajah, U., Kamal, M. M., Irani, Z., & Weerakkody, V. (2017). Critical analysis of Big data challenges and analytical methods. *Journal of Business Research, 70*, 263–286.

The Economist. (2020). *The coronavirus crisis thrusts corporate HR chiefs into the spotlight*. Retrieved March 24, 2020, from https://www.economist.com/business/2020/03/24/the-coronavirus-crisis-thrusts-corporate-hr-chiefs-into-the-spotlight

Tracey, M., Shekar, N. V., & Wen, W. (2019). *Big data is a big deal for the HR function*. Tower Watson. Retrieved May 10, 2019, from https://www.willistowerswatson.com/en-HK/Insights/2019/03/big-data-is-a-big-deal-for-the-hr-function

Tursunbayeva, A., Di Lauro, S., & Pagliari, C. (2018). People analytics, A scoping review of conceptual boundaries and value propositions. *International Journal of Information Management, 43*, 224–247. https://doi.org/10.1016/j.ijinfomgt.2018.08.002

Tushman, M. L., & O'Reilly, C. A., III. (1996). Ambidextrous organizations: Managing evolutionary and revolutionary change. *California Management Review, 38*(4), 8–29.

Ulrich, D. (1997). *Human resources champion*. Harvard Business School Press.

Ulrich, D. (1998). A new mandate for human resources. *Harvard Business Review., 76*, 124–135.

Ulrich, D. (2020a, November 10). What are the results of your HR initiatives? *HRD Connect*. https://www.hrdconnect.com/2020/11/10/what-are-the-results-of-your-hr-initiatives/

Ulrich, D. (2020b, December). *HR's ever-evolving contribution*. https://www.linkedin.com/pulse/hrs-ever-evolving-contribution-dave-ulrich/

Ulrich, D., & Grochowski, J. (2012). From shared services to professional services. *Strategic HR Review, 11*(3), 136–142.

Van, N. T. T., Vrana, V., Duy, N. T., Minh, D. X. H., Dzung, P. T., Mondal, S. R., & Das, S. (2020). The role of human–machine interactive devices for post-COVID-19 innovative sustainable tourism in Ho Chi Minh City, Vietnam. *Sustainability, 12*(22), 9523. https://doi.org/10.3390/su12229523

Waber, B. (2013). *People analytics: How social sensing technology will transform business and what it tells us about the future of work*. Pearson Education Inc.

Wamba, S. F., Akter, S., Edwards, A., Chopin, G., & Gnanzou, D. (2015a). How 'big data'can make big impact: Findings from a systematic review and a longitudinal case study. *International Journal of Production Economics, 165*, 234–246.

Wamba, S. F., Edwards, A., & Rajeev S. (2015b, December 15). 'Big data' as a strategic enabler of superior emergency service management: Lessons from the New South Wales State Emergency Service. *ICIS 2012 MIS Quarterly Executive Workshop*. Available at SSRN: https://ssrn.com/abstract=2191155

Wamba, S. F., Gunasekaran, A., Akter, S., Ren, S. J. F., Dubey, R., & Childe, S. J. (2017). Big data analytics and firm performance: Effects of dynamic capabilities. *Journal of Business Research, 70*, 356–365.

Zhang, Y. E., Liu, S., Xu, S., Yang, M. M., & Zhang, J. (2018). Integrating the split/analyze/meta-analyze (SAM) approach and a multilevel framework to advance big data research in psychology: Guidelines and an empirical illustration via the human resource management investment–firm performance relationship. *Zeitschrift Für Psychologie, 226*(4), 274.

CHAPTER 2

The Influence of Social Media Usage on Firm Performance During the COVID-19 Era: An Empirical Study

Francesca Di Virgilio, Mohammad Soliman, and Muhammad Anwar ul Haq

Introduction

The usage of social media within the workplace is growing rapidly in the private and public sector, enhancing increasingly the strategic value into business processes (McDonald & Thompson, 2016). Technological change rapidly is making the social media even more pervasive and powerful to help achieve business goals within the company, and distinct

F. Di Virgilio (✉)
University of Molise, Campobasso, Italy
e-mail: fradivi@unimol.it

M. Soliman
University of Technology and Applied Sciences, Salalah, Oman
e-mail: msoliman.sal@cas.edu.om

Tourism & Hotels, Fayoum University, Faiyum, Egypt

S. R. Mondal et al. (eds.), *HR Analytics and Digital HR Practices*,
https://doi.org/10.1007/978-981-16-7099-2_2

departments took advantage of their potential (Gensler et al., 2013; Nisar & Whitehead, 2016). The human resources are one of the main corporate area (entrepreneurial, managers, employees) that benefits from using social media because, through their implementation, it has become more productive and competitive (Zyl, 2009). Companies with a social media profile can communicate the lack of staff in a more effective strategy posting a message on it and, at the same time, has the opportunity to analyse professional and personal skills of future employees by online recruitment (Gibbs et al., 2015). On the other side, people interested to work in a firm, through the research and examination on social media, can identify fundamental values at the base of the company, understand if they are compatible with them and then they will contact them. In fact, the organization becomes attractive through social media, matching potential employee's needs, values, and personality, with the organisation's image (Ladkin & Buhalis, 2016). Social media can offer potential benefits in all business sectors (Kaplan & Haenlein, 2010), in the hospitality industry has created extremely convenient and unlimited online customers' service experiences (Gibbs et al., 2015; Lew et al., 2020).

In recent years, social media is an increasingly important area in applied business strategies in the hospitality industry, because there has been an increasing interest to maximize its values and benefits in terms of usage and implementation (Gibbs et al., 2015). It is now well established from a variety of studies in tourism and hospitality sector to make the usage of social media tools to interact with customers, monitor the market and competition, improving customer service, reducing marketing costs, and improving the company's external perception (Leung et al., 2011). Furthermore, there are no studies focused on social media use and the relationship with performance and the role of entrepreneurs and managers, to promote policy implementation in the B&Bs segment, to increase dynamic range and power of their networks.

The segment of B&Bs is rapidly growing in the hospitality industry (Jeon et al., 2017; Shih-Tse & Jua, 2016) supported by integrating social media applications into their websites to enhance online purchase opportunities for customers (Jeon et al., 2017). Although these findings are

M. Anwar ul Haq
University of Gujrat, Gujrat, Punjab, Pakistan
e-mail: anwar.haq@uog.edu.pk

a starting point in our study in the hospitality industry, due to lack of sufficient data in the literature related to understanding the effect of social media use (SMU) on B&Bs performance, and the role of top management and entrepreneurial orientation (Tajudeen et al., 2018) to implement and to improve the usage, in particular during lockdown due to global pandemic coronavirus. Coronavirus (COVID-19) is a global pandemic, begun since the beginning of 2020, there was been a dramatic interruption of the activities during the lockdown, with effects on the global economy and in a business shutting down in all sectors in the worldwide (Ratten, 2020) and with consequent effects on hospitality industry (Gursoy & Chi, 2020).

In this vein, the aim of this exploratory research is to deeply understand the influence of SMU on B&Bs' performance in terms of profitability and how SMU influences the orientation of owner-managers to apply a social media policy and its subsequent impact on PP (Das, 2021b; Dua et al., 2021; Mondal, 2021). It also evaluates the intervening role of top management orientation between SMU and performance (Duy et al., 2020; Van et al., 2020; Siri et al., 2020).

The chapter is organized as follow. In the next part, we discuss the emerging role of B&Bs in the hospitality industry, past studies related to the usage of social media in organizations, and the potential influence on firm performance, and the role of ownership to support social policies into their business. Then, we develop a research model with hypotheses and present methods. In the following section, empirical results were provided. The last part presents discussions, in terms of solutions and recommendations, future research directions, and conclusion.

Background: Main Focus of the Chapter

Bed and Breakfast in the Hospitality Industry

The spreading of the B&B significantly developed in the last years, with its success in terms of business and number of structures, the main reasons relate to a number of contributing factors, such as the breakfast, the location, the design of the structure, pricing, and relevant role the development of social media strategies adopted by an increasing number of entrepreneurs in the hospitality industry in the global businesses (Chiu, 2018; Jeon et al., 2017). Therefore, B&Bs are seen by scholars and governments, as an innovative product in the hospitality industry and a tool for sustainable economic tourism development in traditional rural areas governed by agriculture (Chiu, 2018). The B&B concept is well established in the worldwide and in the last years, it is a development phenomenon in Italy and key in terms of sustainable growth in the hospitality industry (WTTC Travel & Tourism Economic Impact, 2019). It is now well established from a variety of studies that B&B operations are the new innovative sustainable tourism areas (Lituchy & Rail, 2000).

Research to date has not yet determined a single classification of the different forms of B&B into hospitality industry in Italy (Regional Law n. 18/1997; www.federalberghi.it; www.bed-and-breakfast.it), however, in this research we can be classified B&Bs by considering three aspects:

1. The quality of the structure (one-star to three stars), according to Núñez-Serrano et al. (2014) that explain as the official stars might be considered the most common classification to indicate the level of quality of a standard hotel;
2. The prevailing position (in the countryside, in the big city or immediate vicinity and set near the sea) (www.bed-and-breakfast.it);
3. Number of rooms and services: all receptive structures made up of no more than 6 rooms, other services are offered, but without food, beverage, or centralized services (www.bed-and-breakfast.it).

B&B sector positions compose an increasingly high proportion of the hospitality industry in Italy, for many facets the regions of Southern Italy represent a stage that can be termed "emerging" (www.federalberghi.it; www.bed-and-breakfast.it). The growing of the challenging to demand tourism, for constant tourist destination differentiation in terms location, context, and opportunities to be exploited heritage and resources by tourism services encountering customer needs (Trunfio et al., 2006). In the south of Italy there is a great availability of B&Bs located in the big city or immediate vicinity and often in the countryside, driving forces in the agribusiness and rural tourism, to make significant progress increase economic sustainability in this crucial area (Del Chiappa, & Presenza, 2013). The social media provides sharing information and consumers' experience, to combine services from the hospitality industry and the tourism industry together responding promptly to the tourists' need in the choice of a tourist destination (Di Pietro et al., 2012). In other words, policies implementation to use social media on B&Bs sector can contribute to increasing a sustainability-based destination in each country or region such as Southern Italy.

Social Media Platform at Work and the Central Role of Human Resources

Social media is a dynamic environment based on Web 2.0 applications where the content is powered by users through web services or aggregating the content from other sites where everything is mutable and based on interaction (Kaplan & Haenlein, 2010). A considerable literature has grown up around the theme of social media's effect on organizations for different sectors and respective managerial vantage points (Di Virgilio, 2018a; López-Bolás et al., 2019). The increasing usage of social media is a pervasive way in all business and it is mainly due to the online learning and sharing information about services and products to encourage the impulse purchase, and to influence the consumers on decision-making intention to buy (Di Virgilio & Antonelli, 2018; Tajudeen et al., 2018). The usage is growing rapidly by organizations in order to increase their business in range and richness since with quick turnarounds at a competitive cost. Subsequently, existing research recognizes the critical role played by social media for business (Kim et al., 2015; Tajvidi & Karami, 2017), adding value into the organizations to reduce advertisements and communications costs, increasing customer service, strengthening sales contacts (Schaupp & Bélanger, 2014) and improving corporate identity (Devereux et al., 2017). Managers may gather valuable information through firms' contents and innovative ideas that could be suggested directly by their customers. This is the main reason why more and more organizations are thinking the ways of integrating social media into their business strategies (Gaál et al., 2015).

Social media represents the fundamental key to validate companies to receive information and gain technological knowledge competencies (Garcia-Morales et al., 2018) due to the upgrade of the internal communication between employees and managers that allows them to learn faster and better to develop new items or to produce processes to respond the market demand. Furthermore, social media strengthens external interaction too, it is a competitive advantage that will certainly develop online networking among firms, customers, and suppliers (Aichner & Jacob,

2015) and enables them to make enjoyable and influential communications beyond geographical and cultural boundaries. Networking activities by social media usage creates great connectivity combining innovative solutions and creating added value for companies and customers (Siamagka et al., 2015). The combination of network and organizational skills represents a competitive advantage because it reveals as an impressive and superior performance that will lead to high future incomes (Naudé et al., 2014).

A strategic usage provides the opportunity to increase efficiencies in the organizations monitoring the market and competitors, and to lead the communication with stakeholders (O'Leary, 2011). The measurements of SMU are of crucial importance into its corporate setting and may concern both externally and internally contest (Demek et al., 2018). Internal usage involves activities related knowledge sharing tools to increase productivity (Di Virgilio, 2018b), to discuss a new project or new product or service (Palacios-Marques et al., 2015; Roberts & Candi, 2014), and to receive employees' feedback about the management (Demek et al., 2018). However, external usage covers communication with customers (Zhang et al., 2017), the recruitment process (Ouirdi et al., 2016), brand awareness activities (Nisar & Whitehead, 2016). Extremely helpful in terms of competitiveness is to analyse the impact of social media as a resource on value creation for firms (Palacios-Marques et al., 2015), through the Resource-Based View perspective (Barney, 2001) which supports the role of firm resources and capabilities as the true engine of competitive advantages (Colbert, 2004) and place a strong emphasis on the central drivers of the resources in a firm (Gannon et al., 2015).

To meet the above, the last two decades have seen a growing trend towards studies on SMU and its applications in the tourism and hospitality sector (e.g., Noone et al., 2011; Xiang & Gretzel, 2010; Xiang et al., 2017).

The web services and social media, in tourism and hospitality sector, are varied and articulated, and a question of great interest in a wide range of fields such as the emerging role of the online review platforms and online travel agencies in relationship with the diverse sociocultural model and different business systems (Scott & Orlikowski, 2012). From the business viewpoint, social media by persuasive communication has the common goal to support consumer and potential consumer during the decision-making for the choice of a tourism destination through its website (Yoo et al., 2016). Social media incorporate a range of user data and tools, photos and videos, building credibility, trust to influence user's behavior (Zhang et al., 2016). Mkono and Tribe (2016), in their research, analyse how during travelling, the users play different roles on social media sites such as online activist, information seeker and in addition to being the most important product evaluators. A considerable literature has grown up around the themes of motivation and sentiments related to hospitality products (Xiang et al., 2015), opinions about the nature and utilities of online reviews as data and online reservation by online travel agents (Jeon et al., 2017; Zhang et al., 2016) and the relationship between online reviews and hotel business performance (Xie et al., 2014). And in spite of the key aspect of the analysis SMU as a formative construct in the literature, surprisingly, the effects of SMU on the performance of the B&Bs have not been closely examined. B&Bs operate their own websites and the most common functions used is to manage online availability for the booking services to customers, underestimating the relationship between performance indicators and the usage of social media.

The Entrepreneurial and Management Supporting Social Policy Implementation

SMU by employees in the B&Bs sector provides many advantages that need improvement with implementing policies (Jeon et al., 2017). Social media policy implementation refers the set of actions that managers or owners have designed to manage social media through specific policies implementing across all areas, with main objective to clarify how organizations shall be responsible for using social media for business with activities carried out by employees in the workplace (Singh et al., 2020; Singh, Mondal, and Das, 2020; Sharma & Das, 2020). Several studies on the impacts of social media use in the organizational context point out the centrality issue of the border line to employees, between to spend more time into social media than meaningful relationships in the real world, often it becomes unclear to analyse for an organization or business (Turkle, 2012).

For the above reason, social media usage in an organization requires an effective management policy for the profitable usage by continuous and planned monitoring and competent staff to update the data of the internal and external social activities (Das, 2020; Mondal, 2020; Mondal & Sahoo, 2020; Nadanyiova & Das, 2020). Considering all these issues, in the B&B social media management, entrepreneurial orientation to designing a social media policy can be a strategic corporate asset, to include in the organizational strategies (Behera et al., 2019; Gupta et al., 2019; Mohanty et al., 2019). According to Tajudeen et al. (2018) entrepreneurial orientation is the combination of decision-making styles managers, technological and managerial practices, that require methods and entrepreneurial actions to be able to effectively guide organizations, to adapt the challenges and to update competencies. Therefore, the entrepreneurial orientation or top management supporting the social media usage, constitute the necessary beginning associated with real values for firms to compete in a web environment. Nevertheless, several researchers in tourism and hospitality industry have remarked the weaknesses of the entrepreneurial orientation for the small and family business ownership (Shih-Tse & Jua, 2016). Jaafar et al. (2011) analyse in the hospitality industry, the issues and problems between the small and medium hotel owners and managers in relation to their survivability in the industry. Peters and Kallmuenzer (2018) show in their study the embeddedness in the destinations of family firms and their weaknesses of behaviour against growth-oriented entrepreneurship.

Social Media Usage and the Relationship with Firm Performance

In the hospitality industry, we can highlight different resources such as human resources (employees, staff, and manager), organizational resources (technology, knowledge sharing, processes, and strategies), and physical resources (building, location, finances, and facilities) (Tajvidi & Karami, 2021). According to Sigala and Chalkiti (2012), social media is an internet-based resource capability, which builds that provides mutually reinforcing with organizational and human resources. In this context, a strategic role is playing into organizational resources of the social media, to improve networking activities (Trainor et al., 2014), to knowledge sharing among firms and consumers (Sigala & Chalkiti, 2012). The usage becomes a connecting tool between customers' decision-making and the choice of accommodation in a tourism destination (Barreda et al., 2015) and achieves increased organizational performance (Harrington & Ottenbacher, 2011).

Today the presence and activities with high-level engagement on social networks can have various positive and different effects, including the influencing potential tourist behaviour for purchasing and decision-making (Hajli, 2015), in addition, by the use of like, share, comment among users increase brand awareness and rate new product or services on different social media platforms (Gensler et al., 2013). The customers' comments with their evaluation provide information to hotel managers about their performance in products and services provided and in their management fields (Jeong & Mindy Jeon, 2008). Hospitality marketing is in continuous evolution, in the era of information and communication technology by social media and website, to book an accommodation or other travel services may be directly from social media or directly online from a link to hotel websites, influencing positively profitability reducing costs and optimizing performance (Harrigan et al., 2017). The opportunities through social media policy implementation may provide effects on the sales growth of the hotel industry reaching a great number of customers and consequently higher profitability (Harrigan et al., 2017). With advanced "handy services" provided by social media will continue to create novel and applied tools that lead the hospitality industry to all potential tourists in the world. B&Bs like small hotels with typically budget limitation, a positive entrepreneurial and managerial orientation to implement a social media policy for marketing campaigns, would enhance their growth and profitability (O'Connor, 2008).

In particular, in our study, the concept of performance is associated to profitability (Yen & Tag, 2015; Watson, 2012), with a central role of the ROI (Return on Investment), since up to now, far too little attention in the literature, has been paid to in the measurement into performance's B&B. The ROI index measures profitability and economic efficiency of an investment. Since ROI is measured as a percentage, it can be easily compared with returns from diverse types of investments, against one to another (David et al., 2012). Nowadays, in the B&B sector, performance management can support the evaluation of market research to be englobed in the firm, and ROI can be considered as one of the principal indexes to provide scientific reasons to clarify the motivation for which a strategy is so relevant that will be undoubtedly involved and integrated into numerous multiple analysis into the evaluation of profitability (Yen & Tag, 2015; Watson, 2012).

Research Model and Hypotheses

Figure 2.1 shows the research model. We proposed that usage of social media (SMU) has a significant association with firm performance in terms

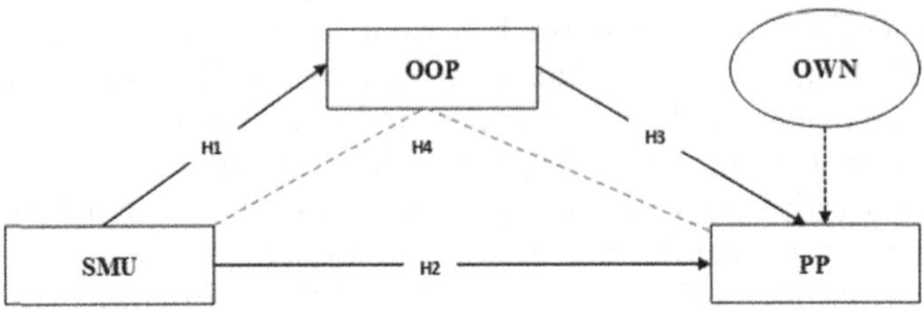

Fig. 2.1 The research model

of profitability (PP) and ownership/managers orientation to apply social media (OOP). We also postulated that OOP has a significant association with PP. In addition, we hypothesized that OOP mediates the association between SMU and PP. Finally, ownership pattern was tested, as a control variable.

Based on the research model, we tested the following hypotheses:
H1: SMU has a significant association with OOP.
H2: SMU has a significant association with PP.
H3: OOP has a significant association with PP.
H4: OOP significantly mediates the association between SMU and PP.

Methodology

The current research employed a quantitative approach to better understand the effect of SMU on the performance of B&Bs sector in Italy by investigating some variables which are not previously investigated in past studies and to generate initial insights needed for future research in the tourism and hospitality industry. In doing so, an online survey was used to gather data from a convenience sample of 278 owner-managers of B&Bs in Southern Italy. The data were collected within a period of three months, between January and March 2020, during the first lockdown in Italy due to the outbreak of Covid-19. Participants were randomly selected from "www.bed-and-breakfast.it," and they are representative of the larger population of B&B operators in Southern Italy.

The online survey is divided into three sections. The first section was used to gather data relating to the B&Bs characteristics: quality stars rating, number of employees, location, and number of operating years in the hospitality industry. The second section was to collect data about the demographic profile of participants such as gender, age, education, and ownership. The third section includes 14 items of the studied constructs: SMU (7 items), OOP (4 items) and PP (3 items) that were all adapted from prior studies (Appendix 1). A five-point Likert scale was used: 1 = strongly disagree and 5 = strongly agree.

With regard to data analysis process, SPSS software was used to analyse the descriptive data, including B&Bs' characteristics and demographic profile of respondents. Next, we employed PLS-SEM to assess the measurement model, the structural model and to test the research hypotheses by utilizing WarpPls 7.0 (Kock, 2020). In this vein, PLS-SEM has been widely employed in several studies within the tourism context (e.g. Soliman, 2019; Soliman & Wahba, 2019). PLS-SEM is a fitting technique used to perform mediation analysis (Kock, 2020).

Findings

B&B Characteristics and Demographic Profile of Respondents

The results (Table 2.1) revealed that 27.7% of B&Bs have one-star rating, 42.8% of them have two stars, while 29.5% of them have three stars, 43.17% of them are located in big cities or immediate vicinity, 34.53% are in the countryside, and 22.3% located near the sea. Regarding the number of employees, 77.7% of the B&Bs have less than 10 employees and 22.23% have more than 10 employees. The majority (95.32%) of B&Bs operated for more than 3 years.

Table 2.2 presented the demographic profile of the B&B owners/managers. Most of the respondents were men (79.14%), while 20.86% were women, around half of them were between 30–40 years old and 28.42% aged between 41–50 years. Concerning the education level, 67.98% of participants had a bachelor's degree and 26.26% had a postgraduate degree. Regarding the ownership pattern, 70.14% of the studied B&Bs are family-owned, while 29.86% of them are corporate-managed.

Assessing the Measurement Model

Table 2.3 shows the assessment of construct reliability. First, the outer loadings should have a cut-off point of at least 0.60 (e.g., Amaro & Duarte, 2015). Therefore, we removed only 2 items that had loadings less than 0.60 (Appendix 1). Therefore, we performed the analysis again and indicator reliability was accordingly confirmed since all loadings were

Table 2.1 Characteristics of the B&Bs

Characteristics	*Category*	*Frequenecies*	*Percentage (%)*
Stars	1 star	77	27.70
	2 stars	119	42.80
	3 stars	82	29.50
Location	Countryside	96	34.53
	Big city	120	43.17
	Near the sea	62	22.30
Employees	10 employees or less	216	77.70
	More than 10 employees	62	22.23
Time in operation	1–3 years	13	4.68
	More than 3 years	265	95.32

Table 2.2 Profile of respondents

Characteristics	*Category*	*Frequencies*	*Percentage (%)*
Gender	Male	220	79.14
	Female	58	20.86
Age	Less than 30 years	35	12.59
	30–40	140	50.36
	41–50	79	28.42
	More than 50 years	24	8.63
Education	High school graduate	16	5.76
	Bachelor's degree	189	67.98
	Post-graduate degree	73	26.26
Ownership	Corporate-owned	83	29.86
	Family-owned	195	70.14

above the value of 0.6. Next, construct reliability was established, as all composite reliability (CR) values are higher than the recommended value of 0.70 (Hair et al., 2020). In addition, it is clear that all VIF values are less than 3.0, indicating that multicollinearity is not a problem in this study (Hair et al., 2020).

Next, convergent and discriminant validity were measured. As shown in Table 2.4, all AVEs' values were higher than 0.50, proving conver-

Table 2.3 Constructs reliability assessment

Construct/items	*Loadings*	*Composite reliability*	*VIF*
SMU		0.845	1.679
SMU1	(0.774)		
SMU2	(0.811)		
SMU3	(0.754)		
SMU4	(0.640)		
SMU5	(0.618)		
OOP		0.829	2.019
OOP1	(0.750)		
OOP2	(0.770)		
OOP3	(0.746)		
OOP4	(0.697)		
PP		0.833	1.824
PP1	(0.770)		
PP2	(0.813)		
PP3	(0.787)		

Note SMU = Social media usage; OOP = Ownership orientation to apply social media policy; PP = performance in terms of profitability

Table 2.4 Constructs validity assessment

Constructs	*AVE*	*1*	*2*	*3*
SMU	0.523	**(0.724)**		
OOP	0.549	0.594	**(0.741)**	
PP	0.624	0.537	0.643	**(0.790)**

gent validity (Hair et al., 2020). In addition, discriminant validity was confirmed, since the square root of the AVE of each construct exceeded its corresponding correlation among other constructs, establishing discriminant validity (Fornell & Larcker, 1981).

The Structural Model and Hypotheses Testing

Based on the findings in Table 2.5, it is revealed that SMU positively and significantly impacted both OOP ($\beta = 0.594$; $p < 0.001$) and PP ($\beta = 0.240$; $p < 0.001$). As a result, H1 and H2 were supported. In addition, there is a significant and positive association between OOP and PP ($\beta =$

Table 2.5 Structural model and hypotheses testing

Hypotheses	*Path coefficient*	*P value*	*Effect size*	*Outcome*
Direct effect				
H1: SMU → OOP	0.594	< 0.001	0.353	Supported
H2: SMU → PP	0.240	< 0.001	0.129	Supported
H3: OOP → PP	0.500	< 0.001	0.322	Supported
Indirect effect				
H4: SMU→OOP → PP	0.297	< 0.001	0.159	Supported
OWN (control variable)	-0.012	0.418	–	–
R^2: OOP = 0.353; PP = 0.451				

0.500; $p < 0.001$), confirming H3. Moreover, the results indicated that the indirect association between SMU and PP was positive and significant (β = 0. 0.297; $p < 0.001$). This means that OOP partially mediates the link between SMU and PP and supports H4.

Moreover, as shown in Table 2.5, SMU explained 35% of the total variation in OOP (R2 = 0.353).Both SMU and OOP explained 45% of the variance in PP (R2 = 0.451), indicating that the structural model has a proper explanatory power (Cohen, 1988). With regard to the effect size, the results in Table 2.5 showed the relations between the independent and dependent variables had large (more than 0.35) and medium (more than 0.15) effects (Cohen, 1988). As we controlled for the impact of ownership concerning PP, it is evident that the aforementioned results outlined hold regardless of the variation in this variable.

Solutions and Recommendations

Our hypotheses that SMU has positive impact on PP (firm performance in terms of profit) and OOP (ownership/managers orientation to apply social media) were accepted. Similarly, OOP had also positive impact on PP. This is novel evidence, the research on tourism and hospitality have primarily been concentrated on hotel and restaurants industry. B&B industry is an emerging phenomenon with a strong potential to attract the low budget commuters, and therefore calls for attention from researchers (Chiu, 2018). Hence this is timely evidence.

The results have important guidelines for the organizations to implement a social media usage policy. An effective presence of the organization on social mediate platforms such as Facebook, Twitter, Instagram, and YouTube help organizations to outreach a larger audience base in an easy, efficient, effective, and faster manner. Furthermore, organizations can easily scan the customers' habits and tastes to launch the new offerings. However, certain guidelines are given for an effective social media usage policy particularly with reference to B&B industry.

The consumers, the tourists, of B&B industry usually have strong social media presence. They are onlookers for the new destinations and services. One of the important factors in their decisions to choose the destination is the availability of B&B facilities. The results help B&B management make prudent decisions for the development of marketing strategies while allocating their limited marketing budgets.

One of the important aspects of social media usage is that B&B organizations can share information about their offerings in an instant manner for which customers had to use E-mail or phone. Social media platforms can also provide an easy and frequent interactive platform between the organization and the customers. The B&B industry should therefore be wary of feedback received to them through social mediate platforms. They should also engage with the customers by frequently responding to queries which customers post on social media pages. Furthermore, they should also subscribe to the pages of competitors to get information about the offerings, activities, and tactics and branding (Ainin et al., 2015). Therefore, brand profiles should be managed on social media platforms to enhance the interest of customers (Muntinga et al., 2011). The marketing strategists should adopt social communication channels in their brand communication plans (Laroche et al., 2012). The B&B marketing managers should keep in mind the assertion made by Amchai-Hamburger (2008) who reminds that social media offers opportunity to not only engage with customer but to also affect their day-to-day conversation, since, people discuss with each other about the information they receive from internet. Furthermore, the use of social media can bring openness, disclosure, transparency, and access to information (O'Neil, 2014; Das, 2021a).

Though this study proves the significance of social media for firm performance, an important aspect to be considered is that a mere access to social media is not enough, rather an understanding of the better utilization of social media platforms is more important. Since B&B are smaller entities and do not have bigger budgets for advertising on multiple platforms, they should develop capabilities on how to do online branding and innovative digital marketing (Tajvidi, & Karami, 2017). This is reiterated based on the observations made by Ahmad et al. (2018) also. Some firms have adopted social media just because everyone else is doing likewise and they just joined a bandwagon (Xie et al., 2016). An earlier study reported that an inefficient usage of social media does not affect business performance. The B&B organizations should develop a clear strategy on how to position themselves on social media while moving online (McCann & Barlow, 2015). Such planning is becoming even more important with the increasing complexity in the virtual world (Noone et al., 2011). It is now more pertinent to understand the type of the segment that is targeted, for instance, for some organizations Facebook might be a more relevant space, for others Twitter and for some other organizations Instagram might fit better into the context (Ahmad et al., 2018). Therefore, an informed social media usage policy based on the evaluation of the internal strengths and of the opportunities in the market place is recommended.

Future Research Directions

The present research has some limitations to be outlined and addressed for further research directions. Firstly, this paper examined the impact of using social media on the profitability of the B&Bs sector. Thus, future research is recommended to test this link among other sectors within the tourism and hospitality field (e.g., hotels, motels, resorts, travel agents, etc.). Secondly, this research employed an online survey, as a data collection tool, to gather the primary data from concerned surveyors. Therefore, other data collection instruments (e.g., a self-administrative questionnaire, a semi-structured interview, a face to face interview, etc.) can be used to achieve this purpose. Thirdly, the context of the current paper was B&Bs enterprises in Southern Italy. Thus, future studies can examine the research model within another region within the same country (e.g., Northern Italy, Western Italy, etc.). A comparative study is also suggested in this regard to provide clear and solid findings and implications. Moreover, the research model can be investigated in another country with a similar culture and conditions (e.g., a Western Europe country) and/or a nation with different culture and conditions (e.g., a country from the Middle East and North Africa, Asia, South America, etc.). This can help in providing rigorous results and outlines concerning the links between the studied constructs. Lastly, the current study focuses on the perspective of owners or managers of the B&Bs in Southern Italy. As a result, future research can concentrate on the perspectives of other stakeholders such as employees, locals, and/or customers using different variables and items.

Conclusion

Due to the outbreak of COVID-19, a number of precautionary measures (e.g., travel restrictions, lockdown) were taken to restrain this pandemic. These measures have negative consequences on the performance of tourism and hospitality businesses (Hassan & Soliman, 2021) including bed and breakfasts. Thus, many tourism and hospitality enterprises used digital platforms (i.e., social media), as an effective tool to communicate with customers. According to Mathew and Soliman (2020), digital content marketing tools (e.g., social media platforms) substantially influenced consumers' attitudes and behaviors toward tourism products and services, which in turn have positive outcomes in tourism organizations. To this end, the current study sought to evaluate the relationships between SMU, top management's orientation to use social media (OOP) and the performance of B&Bs. Moreover, it tested how top management's orientation mediated the link between SMU and B&Bs' performance (PP) in Southern Italy during a three-period of lockdown (from January to March 2020). The empirical findings depicted that SMU positively and significantly affected PP. Additionally, PP was significantly and positively impacted by OOP. Moreover, it is revealed that OOP partially mediates the connection between SMU and PP. Overall, all hypotheses were accepted. This study has various theoretical and managerial implications. To be more specific, this study contributes to the existing tourism and hospitality literature by indicating the crucial effect of SMU on OOP and PP within B&Bs sector in Italy. In addition, it is considered one of the limited attempts that examined the associations between SMU, OOP, and PP among B&Bs enterprises, particularly in Italy. Concerning the managerial implications, this research represents clear insights related to the benefits of using social media networks in tourism and hospitality enterprises. Furthermore, based on the empirical results, it is evident that top management orientation to use social media has a positive impact on the performance as well as mediates the association between SMU and the performance. That is, manager and/owners' orientation toward using or adopting social media has critical consequences on the enterprise' performance.

Appendix I

Constructs and sources

Construct and items		*References*
Social Media Usage		(Ghobakhloo et al., 2011; To & Ngai, 2006)
SMU 1	Social media is used for advertising and promotion	
SMU 2	Social media is used to search for competitor information	
SMU 3	Social media is used for getting referrals (e-WOM: likes, shares, and followers in Facebook, Instagram, etc.)	
SMU 4	Social media is used to communicate with customers	
SMU 5	Social media used for building customer relations	
SMU 6	Social media is used to analyse customer requirements more efficiently**	
SMU 7	Social media used for marketing and branding**	
Ownership/management orientation to apply a social media policy		(Liang et al., 2007; Teo & Pian, 2003; Wang et al., 2010)
OPI 1	Owners/top management considers social media adoption important to the organization	
OPI 2	Owners/top management is likely to invest funds in social media technology	
OPI 3	Owners/top management effectively communicates support for the use of social media	
OPI 4	Owners/top management had established goals and standards to monitor the benefits of social media usage in their organizations	

(continued)

(continued)

Construct and items		References
Performance in terms of profitability		(Yen & Tag, 2015; Watson, 2012)
PP1	Achieving firm profit goals over the past 3 years	
PP 2	Having a better return on investment over the past 3 years	
PP 3	Increase in total income over the past 3 years	

Note ** = removed item based on confirmatory factor analysis

References

Ahmad, S. Z., Bakar, A. R. A., & Ahmad, N. (2018). Social media adoption and its impact on firm performance: The case of the UAE. *International Journal of Entrepreneurial Behavior & Research, 25*(3).

Aichner, T., & Jacob, F. (2015). Measuring the degree of corporate social media use. *International Journal of Market Research, 57*(2), 257–275.

Ainin, S., Parveen, F., Moghavvemi, S., Jaafar, N. I., & Shuib, N. L. M. (2015). Factors influencing the use of social media by SMEs and its performance outcomes. *Industrial Management & Data Systems, 111*(3), 570–588.

Amaro, S., & Duarte, P. (2015). An integrative model of consumers' intentions to purchase travel online. *Tourism Management, 46*, 64–79.

Amichai-Hamburger, Y. (2008). Internet empowerment. *Computers in Human Behavior, 24*(5), 1773–1775.

Barney, J. B. (2001). Is the resource-based "view" a useful perspective for strategic management research? Yes. *Academy of Management Review, 26*(1), 41–56.

Barreda, A., Bilgihan, A., Nusair, K., & Okumus, F. (2015). Generating brand awareness in online social networks. *Computers in Human Behavior, 50*, 600–609.

Behera, M., Dash, M., Ayasa Kanta Mohanty, A. K., & Das, S. (2019). Entrepreneurial ecosystem: A geographical upliftment. *Revista Espacios, 40*, 26–36. http://www.revistaespacios.com/a19v40n01/19400126.html

Chiu, C. (2018). How can managerial efficiency be improved? Evidence from the bed and breakfast industry. *Tourism Management Perspectives, 27*, 111–124.

Cohen, J. (1988). *Statistical power analysis for the behavioral sciences* (2nd ed.). Lawrence Erlbaum Associates, Inc.

Colbert, B. (2004). The complex resource-based view: Implications for theory and practice in strategic human resource management. *The Academy of Management Review, 29*(3), 341–358.

Das, S. (2020). Innovations in digital banking service brand equity and millennial consumerism. In *Digital transformation and innovative services for business and learning* (pp. 62–79). IGI Global. https://doi.org/10.4018/978-1-7998-5175-2.ch004

Das, S. (2021a) A systematic study of integrated marketing communication and content management system for millennial consumers. In *Innovations in digital branding and content marketing* (pp. 91–112). IGI Global. https://doi.org/10.4018/978-1-7998-4420-4.ch005

Das, S. (2021b). Search Engine Optimization and Marketing: A Recipe for Success in Digital Marketing (1st ed.). CRC Press. https://doi.org/10.1201/9780429298509

David, M., Gilfoyl, D. M., & Jobs, C. (2012). Return on investment for social media: A proposed framework for understanding, implementing and measuring the return. *Journal of Business & Economics Research, 10*(4), 637–650.

Del Chiappa, G., & Presenza, A. (2013). The use of network analysis to assess relationships among stakeholders within a tourism destination: An empirical investigation on Costa Smeralda-Gallura. *Tourism Analysis, 18*(1), 1–13.

Demek, K. C., Raschke, R. L., Janvrin, D. J., & Dilla, W. N. (2018). Do organizations use a formalized risk management process to address social media risk? *International Journal of Accounting Information Systems, 28*, 31–34.

Devereux, L., Melewar, T., & Foroudi, P. (2017). Corporate identity and social media: Existence and extension of the organization. *International Studies of Management & Organization, 47*(2), 110–134.

Di Pietro, L., Di Virgilio, F., & Pantano, E. (2012). Social network for the choice of tourist destination: Attitude and behavioural intention. *Journal of Hospitality and Tourism Technology, 3*(1), 60–76.

Di Virgilio, F. (Ed.). (2018a). *Social media for knowledge management applications in modern organizations*. IGI Global.

Di Virgilio, F. (2018b). Exploring determinants of knowledge sharing: The role of social media in business organizations. Overview and new direction. In F. Di Virgilio, (Ed.), *Social media for knowledge management applications in modern organizations* (pp. 1–30). IGI Global.

Di Virgilio, F., & Antonelli, G. (2018). Consumer behavior, trust and electronic word-of-mouth communication: Toward a model of understanding of consumer's purchase intentions online. In F. Di Virgilio (Ed.), *Social media for knowledge management applications in modern organizations* (pp. 58–80). IGI Global.

Dua, S., Singh, I., & Das, S. (2021) Banking innovative service with digital brand equity for new age consumers: Internet banking and millennial consumerism. In *Innovations in digital branding and content marketing* (pp. 134–159). IGI Global. https://doi.org/10.4018/978-1-7998-4420-4.ch007

Duy, N. T., Mondal, S. R., Van, N. T. T., Dzung, P. T., Minh, D. X. H., & Das, S. (2020). A study on the role of Web 4.0 and 5.0 in the sustainable tourism ecosystem of Ho Chi Minh City, Vietnam. *Sustainability, 12*(17), 7140. https://doi.org/10.3390/su12177140

Fornell, C., & Larcker, D. F. (1981). Evaluating structural equation models with unobservable variables and measurement error. *Journal of Marketing Research, 18*(1), 39–50.

Gaál, Z., Szabó, L., Obermayer-Kovács, N., & Csepregi, A. (2015). Exploring the role of social media in knowledge sharing. *The Electronic Journal of Knowledge Management, 13*(3), 185–197.

Gannon, J. M., Roper, A., & Doherty, L. (2015). Strategic human resource management: Insights from the international hotel industry. *International Journal of Hospitality Management, 47*, 65–75.

Garcia-Morales, V., Martin-Rojas, R., & Lardòn-Lòpez, M. (2018). Influence of social media technologies on organizational performance through knowledge and innovation. *Baltic Journal of Management, 13*(3), 345–367.

Gensler, S., Volckner, F., Liu-Thompkins, Y., & Wiertz, C. (2013). Managing brands in the social media environment. *Journal of Interactive Marketing, 27*(4), 242–256.

Ghobakhloo, M., Arias-Aranda, D., & Benitez-Amado, J. (2011). Adoption of e-commerce applications in SMEs. *Industrial Management Data System, 111*(8), 1238–1269.

Gibbs, C., MacDonald, F., & MacKay, K. (2015). Social media usage in hotel human resources: Recruitment, hiring and communication. *International Journal of Contemporary Hospitality Management, 27*(2), 170–184.

Gupta, D. K., Jena, D., Samantaray, A. K., & Das, S. (2019). HRD climate in selected public sector banks in India. *Revista ESPACIOS, 40*(11).

Gursoy, D., & Chi, C. G. (2020). Effects of COVID-19 pandemic on hospitality industry: Review of the current situations and a research agenda. *Journal of Hospitality Marketing & Management, 29*(5), 527–529.

Hair, J. F., Howard, M. C., & Nitzl, C. (2020). Assessing measurement model quality in PLS-SEM using confirmatory composite analysis. *Journal of Business Research, 109*, 101–110.

Hajli, N. (2015). Social commerce constructs and consumer's intention to buy. *International Journal of Information Management, 35*(2), 183–191.

Harrigan, P., Evers, U., Miles, M., & Daly, T. (2017). Customer engagement with tourism social media brands. *Tourism Management, 59*, 597–609.

Harrington, R. J., & Ottenbacher, C. M. (2011). Strategic management: An analysis of its representation and focus in recent hospitality research. *International Journal of Contemporary Hospitality Management, 23*(4), 439–462.

Hassan, S., & Soliman, M. (2021). COVID-19 and repeat visitation: Assessing the role of destination social responsibility, destination reputation, holidaymakers' trust and fear arousal. *Journal of Destination Marketing & Management, 19,* 100495.

Jaafar, M., Abdul-Aziz, A. R., Maideen, S. A., & Mohd, S. Z. (2011). Entrepreneurship in the tourism industry: Issues in developing countries. *International Journal of Hospitality Management, 30*, 827–835.

Jeon, M. M., Lee, S. A., & Jong, M. (2017). E-social influence and customers' behavioral intentions on a bed and breakfast website. *Journal of Hospitality Marketing & Management*. https://doi.org/10.1080/19368623.2017.1367346

Jeong, M., & Jeon, M. M. (2008). Customer reviews of hotel experiences through consumer generated media (CGM). *Journal of Hospitality & Leisure Marketing, 17*(1–2), 121–138.

Kaplan, A. M., & Haenlein, M. (2010). Users of the world, unite! The challenges and opportunities of social media. *Business Horizons, 53*(1), 59–68.

Kim, W. G., Lim, H., & Brymer, R. A. (2015). The effectiveness of managing social media on hotel performance. *International Journal of Hospitality Management, 44*, 165–171.

Kock, N. (2020). *WarpPLS user manual: Version 7.0. Laredo, Texas USA: ScriptWarp Systems.* http://www.scriptwarp.com/warppls/UserManual_v_7_0.pdf

Ladkin, A., & Buhalis, D. (2016). Online and social media recruitment. *International Journal of Contemporary Hospitality Management, 28*(2), 327–345.

Laroche, M., Habibi, M. R., Richard, M. O., & Sankaranarayanan, R. (2012). The effects of social media-based brand communities on brand community markers, value creation practices, brand trust and brand loyalty. *Computers in Human Behavior, 28*(5), 1755–1767.

Leung, D., Lee, H. A., & Law, R. (2011). Adopting Web 2.0 technologies on chain and independent hotel websites: A case study of hotels in Hong Kong. In R. Law, M. Fuchs, & F. Ricci (Eds.), *Information and communication technologies in tourism* (pp. 229–240). Springer-Wien.

Lew, S., Tan, G. W.-H., Loh, X.-M., Hew, J.-J., & Ooi, K.-B. (2020). The disruptive mobile wallet in the hospitality industry: An extended mobile technology acceptance model. *Technology in Society, 63*, 101430.

Liang, H., Saraf, N., Hu, Q., & Xue, Y. (2007). Assimilation of enterprise systems: The effect of institutional pressures and the mediating role of top management. *MIS Quarterly, 31*(1), 59–87.

Lituchy, T. R., & Rail, A. (2000). Bed and breakfasts, small inns, and the Internet: The impact of technology on the globalization of small businesses. *Journal of International Marketing, 8*(2), 86–97.

López-Bolás, A., Valderrama-Santomé, M., & Di Virgilio, F. (2019). Claves del éxito para la viralización de contenidos de salud. El caso de las redes sociales del Hospital Povisa. *El profesional de la información, 28*(5), e280502.

Mathew, V., & Soliman, M. (2020). Does digital content marketing affect tourism consumer behavior? An extension of technology acceptance model. *Journal of Consumer Behaviour*. https://doi.org/10.1002/cb.1854

McCann, M., & Barlow, A. (2015). Use and measurement of social media for SMEs. *Journal of Small Business and Enterprise Development, 22*(2), 273–287.

McDonald, P., & Thompson, P. (2016). Social media (tion) and the reshaping of public/private boundaries in employment relations. *International Journal of Management Reviews, 18*(1), 69–84.

Mkono, M., & Tribe, J. (2016). Beyond reviewing: Uncovering the multiple roles of tourism social media users. *Journal of Travel Research*. http://dx.doi.org/0047287516636236. Article number: 0047287516636236.

Mohanty, P. C., Dash, M., Dash, M., & Das, S. (2019). A study on factors influencing training effectiveness. *Revista Espacios, 40*, 7–15. http://www.revistaespacios.com/a19v40n02/19400207.html

Mondal, S. (2021) A systematic study of new age consumer engagement and exploration for digital entertainment for over-the-top platforms in various digital media. In *Innovations in digital branding and content marketing* (pp. 113–133). IGI Global. https://doi.org/10.4018/978-1-7998-4420-4.ch006

Mondal, S. R. (2020). A systematic study for digital innovation in management education: An integrated approach towards problem-based learning in Vietnam. In *Digital innovations for customer engagement, management, and organizational improvement* (pp. 104–120). IGI Global. https://doi.org/10.4018/978-1-7998-5171-4.ch006

Mondal, S., & Sahoo, K. K. (2020). A study of green building prospects on sustainable management decision making. In *Green building management and smart automation* (pp. 220–231). IGI Global. https://doi.org/10.4018/978-1-5225-9754-4.ch011

Muntinga, D. G., Moorman, M., & Smit, E. G. (2011). Introducing COBRAs: Exploring motivations for brand-related social media use. *International Journal of Advertising, 30*(1), 13–46.

Nadanyiova, M., & Das, S. (2020). Millennials as a target segment of socially responsible communication within the business strategy. *Littera Scripta, 13*(1), 119–134. https://doi.org/10.36708/Littera_Scripta2020/1/8

Naudé, P., Zaefarian, G., Tavani, Z. N., Neghabi, S., & Zaefarian, R. (2014). The influence of network effects on SME performance. *Industrial Marketing Management, 43*(4), 630–641.

Nisar, T. M., & Whitehead, C. (2016). Brand interactions and social media: Enhancing user loyalty through social networking sites. *Computers in Human Behavior, 62*, 743–753.

Noone, B. M., McGuire, K. A., & Rohlfs, K. V. (2011). Social media meets hotel revenue management: Opportunities, issues and unanswered questions. *Journal of Revenue and Pricing Management, 10*(4), 293–305.

Núñez-Serrano, J. A., Turrión, J., & Velázquez, F. J. (2014). Are stars a good indicator of hotel quality? Assymetric information and regulatory heterogeneity in Spain. *Tourism Management, 42*, 77–87.

O'Connor, P. (2008). User-generated content and travel: A case study on Tripadvisor.Com. In P. O'Connor, Wolfram, H., & Ulrike, G. (Eds.), *Information and communication technologies in tourism 2008* (pp. 47–58). Springer.

O'Leary, D. E. (2011). The use of social media in the supply chain: Survey and extensions. *Intelligent System Accounting & Finance Management, 18*, 121–144.

O'Neil, J. (2014). An examination of Fortune 500 companies' and philanthropy 200 nonprofit organizations' relationship cultivation strategies on Facebook. *Public Relations Journal, 8*(1), 1–27.

Ouirdi, E. M., Ouirdi, A. E., Segers, J., & Pais, I. (2016). Technology adoption in employee recruitment: The case of social media in Central and Eastern Europe. *Computers in Human Behavior, 57*, 240–249.

Palacios-Marques, D., Merigo, J. M., & Soto-Acosta, P. (2015). Online social networks as an enabler of innovation in organizations. *Management Decision, 53*(9), 1906–1920.

Peters, M., & Kallmuenzer, A. (2018). Entrepreneurial orientation in family firms: The case of the hospitality industry. *Current Issues in Tourism, 21*(1), 21–40.

Ratten, V. (2020). Coronavirus and international business: An entrepreneurial ecosystem perspective. *International Business Review*, 1–6.

Regional Law n. 18/1997. https://www.gazzettaufficiale.it/eli/id/1997/11/22/097R0662/s3

Roberts, D. L., & Candi, M. (2014). Leveraging social network sites in new product development: Opportunity or hype? *Journal of Product Innovation Management, 31*(S1), 105–117.

Schaupp, L. C., & Bélanger, F. (2014). The value of social media for small businesses. *Information System, 28*(1), 187–192.

Scott, S. V., & Orlikowski, W. J. (2012). Reconfiguring relations of accountability: Materialization of social media in the travel sector. *Accounting, Organizations and Society, 37*(1), 26–40.

Sharma, E., & Das, S. (2020). Measuring impact of Indian ports on environment and effectiveness of remedial measures towards environmental pollution. *International Journal of Environment and Waste Management, 25*(3), 356–380. https://doi.org/10.1504/IJEWM.2019.10021787

Shih-Tse, E., & Jua, P.-Y. (2016). Entrepreneurial orientation and service innovation on consumer response: A B&B case. *Journal of Small Business Management, 54*(2), 532–545.

Siamagka, N.-T., Christodoulides, G., Michaelidou, N., & Valvi, A. (2015). Determinants of social media adoption by B2B organizations. *Industrial Marketing Management, 51*, 89–99.

Sigala, M., & Chalkiti, K. (2012). Knowledge management and web 2.0: Preliminary findings from the greek tourism industry. In M. Sigala, E. Christou, & U. Gretzel (Eds.), *Web 2.0 in travel, tourism and hospitality: Theory, practice and cases*. Ashgate Publishers.

Singh, L. B., Mondal, S. R., & Das, S. (2020). Human resource practices & their observed significance for Indian SMEs. *Revista ESPACIOS, 41*(7). http://www.revistaespacios.com/a20v41n07/20410715.html

Singh, S., Mondal, S., Singh, L. B., Sahoo, K. K., & Das, S. (2020). An empirical evidence study of consumer perception and socioeconomic profiles for digital stores in Vietnam. *Sustainability, 12*(5), 1716. https://doi.org/10.3390/su12051716

Siri R., Mondal S. R., Das, S. (2020). Hydropower: A renewable energy resource for sustainability in terms of climate change and environmental protection. In *The handbook of environmental Chemistry*. Springer. https://doi.org/10.1007/698_2020_635

Soliman, M. (2019). Extending the theory of planned behavior to predict tourism destination revisit intention. *International Journal of Hospitality & Tourism Administration*, 1–26.

Soliman, M., & Wahba, M. S. (2019). Investigating influencers of employee engagement in travel agents in Egypt. *Anatolia, 30*(1), 75–89.

Tajudeen, F. P., Jaafar, N. I., & Ainin, S. (2018). Understanding the impact of social media usage among organizations. *Information & Management, 55*, 308–321.

Tajvidi, R., & Karami, A. (2017). The effect of social media on firm performance. *Computers in Human Behavior*, 1–10.

Tajvidi, R., & Karami, A. (2021). The effect of social media on firm performance. *Computers in Human Behavior, 115*, 105174.

Teo, T. S., & Pian, Y. (2003). A contingency perspective on Internet adoption and competitive advantage. *European Journal of Information System, 12*(2), 78–92.

To, M. L., & Ngai, E. W. (2006). Predicting the organisational adoption of B2C e-commerce: An empirical study. *Industrial Management Data System, 106*(8), 1133–1147.

Trainor, K. J., Andzulis, J. M., Rapp, A., & Agnihotri, R. (2014). Social media technology usage and customer relationship performance: A capabilities-based examination of social CRM. *Journal of Business Research, 67*(6), 1201–1208.

Trunfio, M., Petruzzellis, L., & Nigro, C. (2006). Tour operators and alternative tourism in Italy Exploiting niche markets to increase international competitiveness. *International Journal of Contemporary Hospitality Management, 18*(5), 426–438.

Turkle, S. (2012). *Alone together: Why we expect more from technology and less from each other*. Basic Books.

Van, N. T. T., Vrana, V., Duy, N. T., Minh, D. X. H., Dzung, P. T., Mondal, S. R., & Das, S. (2020). The role of human–machine interactive devices for post-COVID-19 innovative sustainable tourism in Ho Chi Minh City, Vietnam. *Sustainability, 12*(22), 9523. https://doi.org/10.3390/su12229523

Wang, Y.-M., Wang, Y.-S., & Yang, Y.-F. (2010). Understanding the determinants of RFID adoption in the manufacturing industry. *Technology Forecasting Social Change, 77*(5), 803–815.

Watson, J. (2012). Networking: Gender differences and the association with firm performance. *International Small Business Journal, 30*(5), 536–558.

Xiang, Z., & Gretzel, U. (2010). Role of social media in online travel information search. *Tourism Management, 31*(2), 179–188.

Xiang, Z., Du, Q., Ma, Y., & Weiguo, F. (2017). A comparative analysis of major online review platforms: Implications for social media analytics in hospitality and tourism. *Tourism Management, 58*, 51–65.

Xiang, Z., Magnini, V. P., & Fesenmaier, D. R. (2015). Information technology and consumer behavior in travel and tourism: Insights from travel planning using the internet. *Journal of Retailing and Consumer Services, 22*, 244–249.

Xie, K. L., Xie, K. L., Zhang, Z., & Lee, S. K. (2016). Effects of managerial response on consumer eWOM and hotel performance: Evidence from TripAdvisor. *International Journal of Contemporary Hospitality Management, 28*(9), 2013–2034.

Xie, K. L., Zhang, Z., & Zhang, Z. (2014). The business value of online consumer reviews and management response to hotel performance. *International Journal of Hospitality Management, 43*, 1–12.

Yen, C. L. A., & Tag, C. H. H. (2015). Hotel attribute performance, eWom motivations, and media choice. *International Journal of Hospitality Management, 46*, 79–88.

Yoo, K. H., Sigala, M., & Gretzel, U. (2016). Exploring TripAdvisor. In R. Egger, I. Gula, & D. Walcher (Eds.), *Open tourism: Tourism on the verge*. Springer.

Zhang, M., Guo, L., Hu, M., & Liu, W. (2017). Influence of customer engagement with company social networks on stickiness: Mediating effect of customer value creation. *International Journal of Information Management, 37*(3), 229–240.

Zhang, Z., Zhang, Z., & Yang, Y. (2016). The power of expert identity: How website recognized expert reviews influence travelers' online rating behavior. *Tourism Management, 55*, 15–24.

Zyl, A. S. V. (2009). The impact of social networking 2.0 on organisations. *Electronic Library, 27*(6), 906–918.

CHAPTER 3

Effects of Covid-19 on Public Administration: Smart Working as an Organizational Revolution

Lucio Todisco, Gianluigi Mangia, Paolo Canonico, and Andrea Tomo

Introduction

The COVID-19 crisis has been a challenging test for public administrations, their widespread leadership styles and their organizational cultures. Thanks to digitisation processes, the emergency has made it

L. Todisco (✉) · G. Mangia · P. Canonico · A. Tomo
Department of Economics, Management, and Institutions, University of Naples Federico II, Naples, Italy
e-mail: lucio.todisco@unina.it

G. Mangia
e-mail: mangia@unina.it

P. Canonico
e-mail: paolo.canonico@unina.it

S. R. Mondal et al. (eds.), *HR Analytics and Digital HR Practices*,
https://doi.org/10.1007/978-981-16-7099-2_3

possible to accelerate organizational transformation processes that previously remained hidden and stopped by strong internal resistance. This has favored the diffusion of more flexible organizations able to be resilient, cushioning and facing the health emergency challenge. The massive spread of smart working (SW) is one of the modalities that most revolutionized work practices. SW is an entirely flexible way of conducting work activities that allow organizations to adapt to the context in which change emerges quickly (Sarti & Torre, 2017; Torre & Sarti, 2019). SW overcomes the Taylorism concept of organizational work by conquering the fragmentation of activities. "Smart workers" are those employees who agree with their managers to conduct work activities for a specific period outside the organization's physical workplace as per a schedule based on individual needs. During the activities of smart working, smart workers have no specific time or workplace constraints. Technologies represent a relevant factor for an organization that decides to implement smart working to create a resilient, flexible organization (Boin & Lodge, 2016). Thanks to technology, smart workers can perform the same tasks and activities as face-to-face workers and achieve the same goals and set results. Finally, temporal and spatial flexibility creates a new work organization based on results rather than physical presence in the workplace. As defined by De Masi (2020), most bureaucratic work has an intellectual nature. Consequently, it is more easily tele workable (Das, 2021a; Mondal, 2021). In a few weeks, smart working has transformed from an alternative way of working, seen "with suspicion" by public managers, into an excellent resource for public organizations to continue their activities (Dua et al., 2021; Duy et al., 2020; Van et al., 2020). This study, starting from an ongoing research initiative that focuses on the analysis of the SW phenomenon in public administration, seeks to understand and provide an interpretation of SW's impact on the flexibility of public organizations.

Accordingly, the first section of this work provides an overview of the impact of digitisation on organizational flexibility and how it has led to new ways of performing work activities (Sharma & Das, 2020; Singh et al., 2020a, 2020b; Siri et al., 2020). The second section explores SW as an organizational approach designed to make an organization flexible

---

A. Tomo
e-mail: andrea.tomo@unina.it

and how its constituent elements affect working conditions, surveillance and control mechanisms, the enhancement of knowledge and cooperation, and the achievement of individual and organizational objectives. Finally, in this section the author analyses SW in Italian public administration from a regulatory perspective. The fourth and fifth sections, through a qualitative methodological approach using semi-structured interviews with managers and public employees, aim to define SW's impact on the public sector before and during this emergency phase and its effect on organizational and individual flexibility as an emergency response. The last section outlines the implications of the research, limitations and avenues for further research. In detail, aims to provide the most significant actions public managers can take for a successful introduction of SW from the viewpoint of human resources management, the achievement of objectives and work-life balance and organizational flexibility. Finally, this study aims from a theoretical perspective to provide insight into the impact of SW's flexibility in the public sector.

The Role of Technology in Organizational Flexibility

The topic of technological transformation is closely connected to flexibility and has highlighted the evolution of the human operator's contribution to the production process and changes in organizational structures (Das, 2020; Mondal, 2020; Mondal & Sahoo, 2020; Nadanyiova & Das, 2020). Technological transformations are strictly connected to greater organizational flexibility and contribute to the evolution of work activities, the improvement of production processes and organizational structures (Di Virgilio et al., 2018; Hjelmar, 2019; Leonardi & Treem, 2020; Todisco et al., 2020; Torre & Sarti, 2020). However, technological transformations cannot be seen except through a relationship with the people who give them meaning (Butera, 2020). Already Touraine (1969, 1973), Bell (1976), and Toffler (1980), in contrast with the Taylorist-Fordist vision of the organization, highlighted how technologies had allowed the overcoming of production rigidities, allowing to create thanks to the experience of job design (e.g., job rotations and the enrichment of tasks) new human relationships in organizations and more flexible models. Furthermore, an increase in flexibility introduces the issue of trust between workers within an organization (Behera et al., 2019; Gupta et al., 2019; Mohanty et al., 2019). The topic of organizations in trust-based models has been extensively explored as one of the necessary conditions for improving an organization's effectiveness and efficiency (Kitchell, 1995; Morrison & Phelps, 1999; Williams, 2012).

Moreover, the phenomenon of organizational flexibility has become ever faster with the spread of increasingly innovative technologies capable of accelerating transformative processes (Sawyer & Tapia, 2005). With the spread of teleworking, for example, for the first time, we were faced with a work configuration created to make flexible organizations capable of improving both the work-family balance and creating greater organizational flexibility (Bailey & Kurland, 2002; Baruch, 2000; Nilles, 1998; Olsen & Dahl, 2010; Shockley & Allen, 2007). However, in the last two decades of the 2000s, thanks to new digital technologies, this work flexibility has further intensified. The spread of technological devices, the opportunities arising from data management and the development of the internet of things have profoundly transformed the relationship between production and consumption and between workforce and markets (Messenger & Gschwind, 2016; Schwab, 2016). Furthermore, new digital technologies have allowed organizations to leave the field of a single organizational model that can be easily framed, defined and structured, favoring the affirmation of a plurality of models whose common characteristic tends toward organizational change and the ability to adapt (Das, 2021b). The creation of a pluralistic and flexible organization made it possible to examine more closely how employees' work performance was evolving. This functional and organizational flexibility results in highly versatile skills for workers (Mascio et al., 2020).

Additionally, organizations push motivational levers for active employee involvement. It is in this scenario that smart working (SW) is established. The definition of SW's boundaries at an organized level is necessary to understand the differences from other ways of working, which risk being confused with SW. SW differs from teleworking. Teleworking is a contractual modality, not an additional and flexible way of carrying out work activities. Furthermore, unlike smart workers, teleworkers cannot choose the most comfortable workplace other than their home. SW also differs from remote working, which indicates the process of remote delocalization and dematerialization of work activities using technological tools that support remote workers in the realization of their actions. Thanks to new technologies, organizations have had the opportunity to offer ever-greater spaces of managerial autonomy to allow more excellent options for work-life balance, greater decentralization of decision making and more significant responsibilities for workers in the search for practical solutions. The flexibility required of workers implies a more remarkable ability to adapt to managing the necessary work, solving problems, sharing and continually updating knowledge. This greater flexibility enriches the working role, including in the public sector.

Furthermore, the sharing of clear and defined objectives favors the formation of increasingly effective and efficient organizations. In the public sector, since the early 1990s, essential digitalisation projects have been developed for public administrations to make them more flexible, modern, efficient, transparent and better respond to the needs of citizens and public employees. The role of technologies in transforming more flexible and adaptable public administrations can be framed through three factors on which digitisation is having a significant impact: planning and disseminating more immediate and easily accessible services to citizens, doing work activities of public employees and designing new flexible organizational models. In this scenario, since the early 2000s, SW has begun to spread throughout public administrations.

Smart Working: Constitutive Features

SW has revolutionized working methods and organizations, even though it is not a novelty in organizational contexts. As outlined in the previous paragraph, according to Sarti and Torre (2017) and Ellerton (2015), SW is a new managerial approach to the performance of work activities in organizations. It is based on redefining individuals' boundaries and social bonds in organizations with the introduction of greater flexibility and autonomy in the choice of spaces, times and technological tools (the so-called BYOD—"Bring Your Own Device"). Several researchers (e.g., Gastaldi et al., 2014; Riccò & Porta, 2007; Torre & Sarti, 2018) have identified three constitutive factors that characterize SW: *(i) the use of ICT tools*; *(ii) workplace redesign*, and *(iii) a new cultural approach to HR management*.

i. *Use of ICT Tools*

Building an organizational model focused on SW requires careful attention to processes' digitalisation and the use of new technologies, with investments linked to the organisation's technological improvement and personnel training in using new digital devices. SW is strictly connected to ICT solutions useful for reconfiguring and innovating organizational processes to make the performance of work flexible and innovate individual work behaviors. According to various researchers (Bednar & Welch, 2019; Sarti & Torre, 2017; Torre & Sarti, 2018) the change of individual behaviors in organizations is essential for the effective spread of SW. New digital technologies also play an essential role in simplifying the sharing of information and files and facilitating real-time interactions between employees (Alessandrini & Pignalberi, 2016; Riccò & Porta, 2017). Furthermore, given that SW operates along the logic of BYOD, an important training activity is necessary to improve workers' ability to use digital devices while carrying out work activities.

ii. *Workplace redesign*

The transition to more flexible organizational structures has impacted the workplace's traditional concept (Coenen & Kok, 2014). Implementing SW involves redesigning the organizational models and the offices' physical spaces and those at home (Raguseo et al., 2016; Tagliaro & Ciaramella, 2016). With the creation of coworking spaces, open space offices have become central in corporate offices. Furthermore, the COVID-19 pandemic has brought the reconfiguration of domestic environments to work in SW back to the center of attention, accelerating the home concept change (Molinari, 2020). Until the start of the COVID-19 pandemic, what remained unchanged was the home's role in people's lives. However, the change's acceleration due to the pandemic has put the house at the center of a real revolution. The workers' home becomes a new space that also impacts the life of the community. The home becomes a fluid and changing space that welcomes the complexity of people's lives: work, well-being, and socialization. Everything now takes place in a multitasking home environment, and SW represents an element that has redesigned the role of the home and the technological needs of occupants.

iii. *A new cultural approach to HR management*

Digital transformation has significantly affected organizational processes, transforming how management organizes, trains, and motivates employees (Ales et al., 2018; Stone et al., 2015). SW revolutionizes the classic concept of Tayloristic work. Thanks to spatiotemporal flexibility, employees can independently organize when and where to perform out work activities. This represents a significant challenge for management to increase employee empowerment and adapt to a goal-based organization (Riccò & Porta, 2017; Stone et al., 2015; Tiraboschi, 2017; Wrzesniewski & Dutton, 2001; Zappalà, 2017). Furthermore, the SW turns the lights on the relationship between leadership and technology and how it requires new knowledge and skills to respond to digital challenges (Kahai, 2012; Torre & Sarti, 2020).

Smart working in the Italian regulatory context was defined as a way of performing work activities with the support of technological tools, without the limitations of the time and place of work, freeing employees maximally from the limitations of a physical presence in the workplace (Article 18.1 of Law 81/2017). In the Italian public sector, the regulatory framework on SW was initially defined by:

a. *Law n. 124/2015 (art. 14) "Delegation to the Government regarding the reorganisation of public administrations".*
b. *Law n. 81/2017 (articles 18–24): "Measures for the protection of self-employed non-entrepreneurs and measures to promote flexibility in the times and places of subordinate work".*
c. *Directive of the Presidency of the Council of Ministers (PCM) n. 3/2017: "Directive of the President of the Council of Ministers containing guidelines for implementing paragraphs 1 and 2 of article 14 of the Law of 7 August 2015, n. 124 and the guidelines concerning the organisation of work aimed at promoting the employees' work-life balance".*

It is with Directive n. 3/2017 that SW in the Italian public administration is starting to take root. The directive clarifies objectives of a more innovative way of organizing work, based on the attempt to achieve greater working flexibility, the evaluation of work performance based on the achievement of objectives and recognizing public employees' needs to reconcile work-life. Furthermore, the Directive was introduced as an evaluation parameter for Italian public administrations to achieve at least 10% of public employees who had requested it. Adopting these organizational measures is subject to an individual written agreement between the public manager responsible for the administration and the public employee

(Tiraboschi, 2017). Among the European countries, in February 2020, Italy was the first to challenge the health emergency due to COVID-19. Therefore, it was the country that first had to introduce a series of actions to ensure public administrations continued to operate remotely. The COVID-19 health crisis intervened in the SW pilot projects' activation phase, requiring all public administrations, in a short time, to adopt SW for all public employees and offices, changing the original formulation. The circular of 4 March 2020 of the Ministry for Public Administration has made SW structural as the primary modality of work performance. This study, starting an ongoing research initiative analysing the SW phenomenon in public administration, aims to understand the impact of SW on flexible organizations. A qualitative methodology was chosen and conducted through semi-structured interviews. The following paragraph describes the methodological choices that have shaped the research process.

Methods

This research focused on SW experiences originating in Italian public administration at the local level. More precisely, public employees who already had a sufficiently long knowledge background were considered to analyse the introduction of SW with a critical approach (Jeyasingham, 2016). The use of a qualitative methodology was considered adequate by the authors, considering the evidence present in an increasingly complex society in which iterative processes may provide an authentic interpretation of the meaning of individuals' actions in organizations (Cassell et al., 2006; Denzin & Lincoln, 1995). Indeed, a qualitative methodology, according to many researchers (Gentles et al., 2015; Kvale, 1983; Richards, 2005; Roulston, 2010) gives the possibility of filling words with meaning, providing, in the analysis phase, a greater understanding of the constraints and opportunities of a given phenomenon. The researchers considered this aspect relevant to understanding the strengths and weaknesses of SW in local public administrations before and after the COVID-19 emergency.

Consequently, this study is based on semi-structured interviews with 25 public employees of local public administrations who had applied to participate in pilot SW projects started in Italian public administrations before the health emergency. Public employees had already been contacted to answer on SW, given the relevance of this topic to public administrations. For this study, besides semi-structured interviews (telephone conversations and emails), other data sources such as reports, documents, and internal regulations were used to understand respondents' organizational contexts in more detail. The interviews took place in two phases: the first occurred between April 2018 and June 2019. The second took place between September and November 2020. Anonymity was ensured to encourage the completeness, clarity, and transparency of data and information. All interviews, lasting 30 minutes, were introduced by presenting the research topic and thanking the interviewees for their willingness to participate.

Results and Discussion

From the analysis of the interviews, it was possible to identify similar aspects regarding SW in public administrations and the interesting differentiations illustrated below. The following section is structured in a paragraph concerning interviews before the COVID-19 health emergency and a subsequent paragraph with interviews during the health emergency.

Smart Working Pilot Project Before Covid-19 Health Emergency

First, the interviews highlight how SW, thanks to technology, is seen as strictly connected to a change of cultural approach in the public organization, which must be understood as more flexible and more participatory. The interviews highlighted how technologies, both before and during the emergency phase, favored their work activities' effectiveness. However, one of the most critical aspects concerns training. Both before and during the emergency phase, in the interviewees' public organizations, no technological training activities happened in the organization of SW and work by objectives. The technological adaptation emerged from the interviews with public employees. Both the technological devices made available by one's administration and personal ones are considered adequate for activities to be conducted in SW. This aspect is important since the centrality of technologies in a modern organization is relevant to being flexible, resilient, and useful. Moreover, according to Kvaløy and Schöttner (2015), the correct and consistent use of technologies in organizations creates technical support for employees in carrying out their work performance and motivation in achieving personal and organizational goals more than economic incentives. The answers of some public employees are particularly interesting, such as the ones below:

> *ICT devices have allowed us to improve the entire work process, accelerating our way of carrying out work activities. Today, thanks to ICT technologies, we can carry out work activities more quickly and effectively, which is what we make, particularly in the workplace.*

Technologies cannot, in any way, be irrelevant to today's organizational planning. It creates the conditions for planning ever more significant improvements and shapes organizational cultures. Technologies enable the creation of new requirements for working remotely or for using spaces not in one's structure. However, the positive impact it can have on an organisation's flexibility can affect internal relationships among colleagues. The public employees' interviews highlighted this relevance.

> *The risk I see is not so much the use of technologies to achieve the result linked to aspects of responsibility that an official must possess and who accepts the challenge of working in a new way in his organisation. Instead, I believe that the reliance on technology can lead to an effect of individual isolation, creating dynamics of distancing from the office.*

The SW pilot projects consciously use technologies to increase temporal and spatial flexibility, which have led to a redefinition of organizational models in public administration. As we have already highlighted above, the debate on the spread of well-being in organizations has become relevant in recent decades (Janssen, 2000; Janssen et al., 2004; Morrison, 2011). The public employees' interviews highlighted this relevant aspect.

> *Operating in smart working is an opportunity for everyone because it allows everyone to meet the personal needs a person has to face in a given period of his life.*

According to Golden (2001), work autonomy through the introduction of personalized working hours is an excellent opportunity for workers to accept the challenges of change in their organization, including improving individual health conditions. The answers of some public employees are particularly interesting, such as the ones below:

I asked to work in smart working mode because I could finally organise some days of the week in which I need to be closer to my children.
Having flexible hours allows me to be able at this moment to be able to dedicate myself to small children, but at the same time always feel operational and central in my administration.

Another element highlighted concerns about the positive evaluation of the relationship between flexibility, work-life balance, and organizational results.

For a public employee, flexibility becomes a consolidation of his work which already, many times, takes place in different hours and places from the office. Flexibility is just another way of imagining an organisation more effectively to achieve the required goals.

However, the execution of flexible work performances may not always lead to advantages in the medium to long term but have a marginal impact. Particularly interesting is the following answer from one of the public employees:

I find doing my work in the office stimulating and not impactful negatively on my relationship with the family. To the opposite, carrying out the work activity this way, I feel more responsible than everyone, and I don't feel the burden of not having more time at home. This aspect is one of the reasons why I would not apply for the smart working pilot project.

This limited impact appears to be due to the perception of an increase in smart workers' family responsibilities. Therefore, the effect is that SW can increase the conflict between family and work and decrease work efficiency. Finally, the transition to work activities to be performed no longer exclusively in the office and the absence of physical control in the presence by public managers introduces an additional element of flexibility, highlighted in the interviews regarding establishing fiduciary relationships between managers and public employees.

Smart Working During Covid-19 Health Emergency

The spread of what can be called "emergency smart working" during the pandemic crisis caused by COVID-19 has highlighted how a flexible way of work is possible in public organizations. The smart workers interviewed highlighted how public administrations have shown considerable organizational flexibility and a high degree of response and resilience to the health emergency. In this phase, the investments aimed at increasing the technological equipment and digital skills of public employees, after an initial adjustment phase, have made it possible to improve internal organizational processes and to maintain constant productivity and the provision of services. The answers of some public employees are particularly interesting, such as the ones below:

> *In recent months, IT devices have been distributed to thousands of public employees.*

> *At the beginning, digitalisation was improvised, despite the existence of new tools and methodologies. Necessarily, with the health emergency, forcibly, there was an improvement in digital processes.*

Furthermore, the importance of technologies is being highlighted by interviewees, where the emergency situations are better handled now as compared to previously in the field of smart working. Particularly interesting is the following answer from one of the public employees:

> *I have always considered the emergence of a hybrid organisation to be significant: half in presence, half in smart working. Yes, technically, I wanted it, but I didn't think it was possible in such a short time.*

Compared to the SW pilot projects' experience, although the use of technologies has been more significant and there has been improved digital processes, critical issues have been found in interactions at a communicative and relational level. Particularly relevant are the answers of some public employees, as follows:

> *Absolutely not. Smart working was pure isolation. Mainly because the public manager prefers to use email and instant messaging. Relationships could also occur through other IT tools (i.e., Zoom meeting for a week).*

> *One of the problems I encountered was the lack of collaboration between colleagues and the fact that there was no possibility of meeting, even remotely, with public managers. Communication was, therefore, penalised.*

These critical considerations show an aspect of the rigidity of SW that may have been caused precisely by the connotation of emergency that has made it no longer a work option chosen by the individual with greater flexibility but an imposition due to the current situation, perhaps more to be considered as "homework". Regarding the balance between private life and work life, public employees perceived the impact of emergency SW discordantly. One of the most highlighted aspects is that of an excessive mix and overlap between professional and personal life and, in particular, of a contraction of the right to disconnect. Particularly relevant are the answers of some public employees, as follows:

> *Difficult to give a correct answer for all public employees. Regarding the employees' level of responsibility and the ability to carry out all activities remotely, the answer changes significantly. Unfortunately, I believe that the right to disconnect has not been respected for all, with a significant increase in effective working hours for a few.*

> *I don't think the hours have increased, but there has certainly been a mix between working hours and time dedicated to personal life.*

> *No right to disconnect. WhatsApp notifications have been constant and pounding and working hours have increased.*

As during SW pilot projects and the health emergency, the theme of the impact of this organizational model emerged for a more effective achievement of organizational objectives and the central role that public managers have toward a perspective of the more relevant sharing of information and effective identification of clear objectives and strategies for an increasingly flexible organization. Of great interest are the answers of some public employees, as follows:

> *So far, public managers have immediately seized this new opportunity, even if the change has come in a short and sudden time.*

> *Yes, we have established a work plan with clear and convincing objectives to be achieved.*

Although SW will not maintain the characteristics assumed in the emergency phase, the public employees interviewed believe that this experience, with the necessary mitigation of the critical issues highlighted, is not a lost organizational experience but one to be enhanced, transforming it into a future resource.

Conclusion, Limitations, and Future Research Directions

The COVID-19 emergency has made SW obligatory for Italian public administrators that only a year ago were still contemplating experimental dissemination and the gradual introduction of SW within organizational contexts. Overall, according to the SW observatory of Politecnico di Milano, in November 2020, smart workers in the Italian public administration increased about 17 times compared to before the COVID-19 health emergency. The smart workers interviewed highlighted the opportunities that SW has generated within organizations with some critical issues that have impacted the effectiveness and flexibility of SW before and during the health emergency (as summarized in Table 3.1). One of the main drivers of SW, that is digital technologies, has played a central role in facilitating and making possible an immediate response of public organizations to the emergency challenge, favoring the emergence of more flexible organizations, guaranteeing new ways of working and allowing expanding and making the workspace virtual, creating a workplace in the process of implementing work, relational and organizational methods in a non-chosen context and for an indefinite duration (Allen et al., 2015). The interviews highlighted how technologies have provided practical support for participatory involvement within the offices and made it possible to digitize processes previously considered not transformable. In the interviews conducted both before and after the health emergency, another element of reflection is the actual transition to an increasingly "task-oriented" public organization. This represents a leadership challenge for public managers who must be increasingly "relationship-oriented" by increasing smart workers' empowerment and promoting training on soft-skill issues. Concerning work-life balance, the results before the health emergency highlighted the positive impact of SW on work-life balance. As De Masi (2020) states, SW allows for a radical shift in the relationship

Table 3.1 Summary table of the relevant aspects highlighted in the Italian local public employees on Smart Working in public administration before and during COVID-19 health emergency

Smart working before COVID-19 health emergency	*Smart working during COVID-19 health emergency*
• Improvement of organizational processes • Greater attention to the personal needs of public employees • The relevant role of time flexibility in improving family relationships • The central role of ICT in improving work activities and organizational flexibility • Consolidation of public administration's goals and improvement of organizational efficiency • Risk of isolation from office colleagues who carry out work in the physical presence • Public employees' de-responsibility respect other colleagues that work in presence in the workplace	• The key role of technologies in responding effectively to health emergencies • The ability of public administrations to start the SW in a short time • Clarity of the objectives set by public managers and improvement of public administration's efficiency • Capacity thanks to the support of technologies to improve organizational processes previously considered impossible to modify • Contraction of work–life balance and right to disconnect • Reduction of collaboration between colleagues

Source EDITED BY THE AUTHORS, 2020

between life and work, with integration focused on the needs of the individual rather than, as in industrial society, operating as a stone angular and the needs of the organization. However, in this emergency phase, some critical issues were highlighted regarding an excessive mix of professional and private life and a lack of flexibility in working hours (Chiaro et al., 2015). This study has some limitations. First, the choice of a single analysis context and the methodology of the semi-structured interviews could limit the results' generalisability. However, the Italian context is experiencing significant growth of SW in public organizations, and this provides a valuable context for in-depth qualitative research (Das, 2021b; Yin, 2017). A second limitation concerned the need to carry out semi-structured interviews during the emergency phase exclusively in virtual mode due to the restrictions linked to the COVID-19 pandemic. This potential limitation can also be seen as an interesting perspective on the changes that virtual methodologies can bring in research (Dodds & Hess, 2021). Finally, based on the results obtained in this study, it would be useful for future research to examine further the best way to implement SW in the public administration considering the critical issues that have emerged. In an era in which digitalisation has become increasingly important in public administrations, it is essential to capitalize on the experience gained in this emergency and bring what has emerged into what is called "new normal," in which public organizations must keep this approach flexible and goal oriented (Bonacini et al., 2020; Marcuccio, 2020; Välikangas & Lewin, 2020; Yang, 2020). It will be interesting to understand what impact training will have, which represents a significant opportunity to increase public employees' skills in the use of information systems and multimedia communication skills. These training activities should be added to vocational and managerial training focused on soft skills and evaluating online work results for groups and time management. Finally, a further research reflection may concern how public organizations will manage the transition from the physical to the virtual office space instead of the idea that work activities in presence are the only possibility for public employees' work. This aspect would allow public organizations to reduce their costs and reorient the purpose of physical spaces on what they can offer uniquely, favoring social interaction and promoting public employees' empowerment.

References

Ales, E., Curzi, Y., Fabbri, T., Rymkevich, O., Senatori, I., & Solinas, G. (2018). Working in digital and smart organizations. In *Legal, economic and organizational perspectives on the digitalization of labour relations*. Palgrave Macmillan.

Alessandrini, G., & Pignalberi, C. (2016). Smart working: nuovi modelli di lavoro e di formazione sostenibili nella città in evoluzione. In *Dialoghi sulla Sostenibilità* (pp. 207–208). RomaTre Press.

Allen, T. D., Golden, T. D., & Shockley, K. M. (2015). How effective is telecommuting? Assessing the status of our scientific findings. *Psychological Science in the Public Interest, 16*(2), 40–68.

Bailey, D. E., & Kurland, N. B. (2002). A review of telework research: Findings, new directions, and lessons for the study of modern work. *Journal of Organizational Behavior: The International Journal of Industrial, Occupational and Organizational Psychology and Behavior, 23*(4), 383–400.

Baruch, Y. (2000). Teleworking: Benefits and pitfalls as perceived by professionals and managers. *New Technology, Work and Employment, 15*(1), 34–49.

Bednar, P. M., & Welch, C. (2019). Socio-technical perspectives on smart working: Creating meaningful and sustainable systems. *Information Systems Frontiers, 22*, 1–18.

Behera, M., Dash, M., Mohanty, A. K., & Das, S. (2019). Entrepreneurial ecosystem: A geographical upliftment. *Revista Espacios, 40*, 26–36. http://www.revistaespacios.com/a19v40n01/19400126.html

Bell, D. (1976). *The coming of post-industrial society: A venture in social forecasting*. Basic Books.

Boin, A., & Lodge, M. (2016). Designing resilient institutions for transboundary crisis management: A time for public administration. *Public Administration, 94*(2), 298–298.

Bonacini, L., Gallo, G., & Scicchitano, S. (2020). Working from home and income inequality: Risks of a 'new normal' with COVID-19. *Journal of Population Economics, 34*(1), 303–360.

Butera, F. (2020). Dallo Smart Working al lavoro ubiquo di qualità: una opportunità per cambiare il lavoro e le organizzazioni. *Harvard Business Review*. https://www.hbritalia.it/speciale-gestire-le-crisi/2020/09/30/news/dallo-smart-working-al-lavoro-ubiquo-di-qualita-unopportunita-per-cambiare-il-lavoro-e-le-organizzazioni-1-14869/

Cassell, C., Symon, G., Buehring, A., & Johnson, P. (2006). The role and status of qualitative methods in management research: An empirical account. *Management Decision, 44*(2), 290–303.

Chiaro, G., Prati, G., & Zocca, M. (2015). Smart working: dal lavoro flessibile al lavoro agile. *Sociologia del lavoro, 138*(2015), 69–87.

Coenen, M., & Kok, R. A. W. (2014). Workplace flexibility and new product development performance. *European Management Journal, 32*(4), 564–576.

Das, S. (2020). Innovations in digital banking service brand equity and millennial consumerism. In *Digital transformation and innovative services for business and learning* (pp. 62–79). IGI Global. https://doi.org/10.4018/978-1-7998-5175-2.ch004

Das, S. (2021a). A systematic study of integrated marketing communication and content management system for millennial consumers. In *Innovations in digital branding and content marketing* (pp. 91–112). IGI Global. https://doi.org/10.4018/978-1-7998-4420-4.ch005

Das, S. (2021b). *Search engine optimization and marketing: A recipe for success in digital marketing* (1st ed.). CRC Press. https://doi.org/10.1201/9780429298509

De Masi, D. (2020). *Smart working: La rivoluzione del lavoro intelligente*. Marsilio Editori.

Denzin, N. K., & Lincoln, Y. S. (1995). Transforming qualitative research methods: Is it a revolution? *Journal of Contemporary Ethnography, 24*(3), 349–358.

Di Virgilio, F., Valderrama, M., & Lopez Bolas, A. (2018). Social media strategy within organizational communication: Major open issues and challenges. In F. Cantoni & G. Mangia (Eds.), *Human resource management and digitalization* (pp. 207–227). Routledge.

Dodds, S., & Hess, A. C. (2021). Adapting research methodology during COVID-19: Lessons for transformative service research. *Journal of Service Management, 32*(2), 203–217. https://doi.org/10.1108/JOSM-05-2020-0153

Dua, S., Singh, I., & Das, S. (2021). Banking innovative service with digital brand equity for new age consumers: Internet banking and millennial consumerism. In *Innovations in digital branding and content marketing* (pp. 134–159). IGI Global. https://doi.org/10.4018/978-1-7998-4420-4.ch007

Duy, N. T., Mondal, S. R., Van, N. T. T., Dzung, P. T., Minh, D. X. H., & Das, S. (2020). A study on the role of web 4.0 and 5.0 in the sustainable tourism ecosystem of Ho Chi Minh City, Vietnam. *Sustainability, 12*(17), 7140. https://doi.org/10.3390/su12177140

Ellerton, S. (2015). Smart working—Creating the next wave. *Leadership & Organization Development Journal, 36*(7), 903–904.

Gastaldi, L., Corso, M., Raguseo, E., Neirotti, P., Paolucci, E., & Martini A. (2014). Smart working: Rethinking work practices to leverage employees' innovation potential. In *Proceedings of the 15th International CINet Conference, Operating Innovation—Innovating Operations* (pp. 337–347). Budapest.

Gentles, S. J., Charles, C., Ploeg, J., & McKibbon, K. (2015). Sampling in qualitative research: Insights from an overview of the methods literature. *The Qualitative Report, 20*(11), 1772–1789.

Golden, L. (2001). Flexible work schedules: Which workers get them? *American Behavioral Scientist, 44*(7), 1157–1178.

Gupta, D. K., Jena, D., Samantaray, A. K., & Das, S. (2019). HRD climate in selected public sector banks in India. *Revista ESPACIOS, 40*(11), 14–20.

Hjelmar, U. (2019). The institutionalization of public sector innovation. *Public Management Review, 23*, 1–17.

Janssen, O. (2000). Job demands, perceptions of effort-reward fairness, and innovative work behavior. *Journal of Occupational and Organizational Psychology, 73*(3), 287–302.

Janssen, O., Van de Vliert, E., & West, M. (2004). The bright and dark sides of individual and group innovation: A special issue introduction. *Journal of Organizational Behavior, 25*(2), 129–145.

Jeyasingham, D. (2016). Open spaces, supple bodies? Considering the impact of agile working on social work office practices. *Child & Family Social Work, 21*(2), 209–217.

Kahai, S. S. (2012). Leading in a digital age: What's different, issues raised, and what we know. In *Exploring distance in leader-follower relationships* (pp. 83–128). Routledge.

Kitchell, S. (1995). Corporate culture, environmental adaptation, and innovation adoption: A qualitative/quantitative approach. *Journal of the Academy of Marketing Science, 23*(3), 195–205.

Kvale, S. (1983). The qualitative research interview: A phenomenological and a hermeneutical mode of understanding. *Journal of Phenomenological Psychology, 14*(2), 171.

Kvaløy, O., & Schöttner, A. (2015). Incentives to motivate. *Journal of Economic Behavior & Organization, 116*, 26–42.

Leonardi, P., & Treem, J. W. (2020). Behavioral visibility: A new paradigm for organization studies in the age of digitization, digitalization, and datafication. *Organization Studies*. https://doi.org/10.1177/0170840620970728

Marcuccio, G. (2020). Smart working o lavoro smart? La leadership alla prova dell'etica. *Harvard Business Review*. https://www.hbritalia.it/speciale-gestire-le-crisi/2020/10/05/news/smart-working-o-lavoro-smart-la-leadership-alla-prova-delletica14881/?fbclid=IwAR0B8X1C6g2rCRLJ2jtJLwhkWmWRscclGdyp267dnhJ7BQVg24c6js1STKQ

Mascio, F. D., Natalini, A., & Cacciatore, F. (2020). Public administration and creeping crises: Insights from COVID-19 pandemic in Italy. *The American Review of Public Administration, 50*(6–7), 621–627.

Messenger, J. C., & Gschwind, L. (2016). Three generations of telework: New ICT s and the (R)evolution from home office to virtual office. *New Technology, Work and Employment, 31*(3), 195–208.

Mohanty, P. C., Dash, M., Dash, M., & Das, S. (2019). A study on factors influencing training effectiveness. *Revista Espacios, 40*, 7–15. http://www.revistaespacios.com/a19v40n02/19400207.html

Molinari, L. (2020). *Le case che saremo. Abitare dopo il lockdown*. Nottetempo Editori.

Mondal, S. (2021). A systematic study of new age consumer engagement and exploration for digital entertainment for over-the-top platforms in various digital media. In *Innovations in digital branding and content marketing* (pp. 113–133). IGI Global. https://doi.org/10.4018/978-1-7998-4420-4.ch006

Mondal, S. R. (2020). A systematic study for digital innovation in management education: An integrated approach towards problem-based learning in Vietnam. In *Digital innovations for customer engagement, management, and organizational improvement* (pp. 104–120). IGI Global. https://doi.org/10.4018/978-1-7998-5171-4.ch006

Mondal, S., & Sahoo, K. K. (2020). A study of green building prospects on sustainable management decision making. In *Green building management and smart automation* (pp. 220–234). IGI Global. https://doi.org/10.4018/978-1-5225-9754-4.ch011

Morrison, E. W. (2011). Employee voice behavior: Integration and directions for future research. *The Academy of Management Annals, 5*(1), 373–412.

Morrison, E. W., & Phelps, C. C. (1999). Taking charge at work: Extrarole efforts to initiate workplace change. *Academy of Management Journal, 42*(4), 403–419.

Nadanyiova, M., & Das, S. (2020). Millennials as a target segment of socially responsible communication within the business strategy. *Littera Scripta, 13*(1), 119–134. https://doi.org/10.36708/Littera_Scripta2020/1/8

Nilles, J. M. (1998). *Managing telework: Strategies for managing the virtual workforce* (Vol. 6). Wiley.

Olsen, K. M., & Dahl, S. (2010). Working time: Implications for sickness absence and the work–family balance. *International Journal of Social Welfare, 19*(1), 45–53.

Raguseo, E., Gastaldi, L., & Neirotti, P. (2016). Smart work: Supporting employees' flexibility through ICT, HR practices and office layout. *Evidence-Based HRM: A Global Forum for Empirical Scholarship, 4*(3), 1–19.

Riccò, R. (2007). *Gestione della diversità: sfida presente e futura per le imprese.*

Riccò, R., & Porta, S. (2017). Smart working, agili si diventa Basta porsi le giuste domande. *Sviluppo & Organizzazione*, 34–38.

Richards, L. (2005). *Handling qualitative data: A practical guide.* Sage.

Roulston, K. (2010). Considering quality in qualitative interviewing. *Qualitative Research, 10*(2), 199–228.

Sarti, D., & Torre, T. (2017). Is smart working a win-win solution? First evidence from the field. *Well-Being at and Through Work, 9*, 231.

Sawyer, S., & Tapia, A. (2005). The sociotechnical nature of mobile computing work: Evidence from a study of policing in the United States. *International Journal of Technology and Human Interaction, 1*(3), 1–14.

Schwab, K. (2016). *La quarta rivoluzione industrial.* Franco Angeli.

Sharma, E., & Das, S. (2020). Measuring impact of Indian ports on environment and effectiveness of remedial measures towards environmental pollution. *International Journal of Environment and Waste Management, 25*(3), 356–380. https://doi.org/10.1504/IJEWM.2019.10021787

Shockley, K. M., & Allen, T. D. (2007). When flexibility helps: Another look at the availability of flexible work arrangements and work–family conflict. *Journal of Vocational Behavior, 71*(3), 479–493.

Singh, L. B., Mondal, S. R., & Das, S. (2020). Human resource practices & their observed significance for Indian SMEs. *Revista ESPACIOS, 41*(7). http://www.revistaespacios.com/a20v41n07/20410715.html

Singh, S., Mondal, S., Singh, L. B., Sahoo, K. K., & Das, S. (2020). An empirical evidence study of consumer perception and socioeconomic profiles for digital stores in Vietnam. *Sustainability, 12*(5), 1716. https://doi.org/10.3390/su12051716

Siri, R., Mondal, S. R., & Das, S. (2020) Hydropower: A renewable energy resource for sustainability in terms of climate change and environmental protection. In *The handbook of environmental Chemistry*. Springer. https://doi.org/10.1007/698_2020_635

Stone, D. L., Deadrick, D. L., Lukaszewski, K. M., & Johnson, R. (2015). The influence of technology on the future of human resource management. *Human Resource Management Review, 25*(2), 216–231.

Tagliaro, C., & Ciaramella, A. (2016). Experiencing smart working: A case study on workplace change management in Italy. *Journal of Corporate Real Estate, 18*(3), 194–208.

Tiraboschi, M. (2017). Il lavoro agile tra legge e contrattazione collettiva: la tortuosa via italiana verso la modernizzazione del diritto del lavoro. *WP CSDLE "Massimo DAntona", IT*, 335.

Todisco, L., Tomo, A., Canonico, P., Mangia, G., & Sarnacchiaro, P. (2020). Exploring social media usage in the public sector: Public employees' perceptions of ICT's usefulness in delivering value added. *Socio-Economic Planning Sciences, 73*, 100858.

Toffler, A. (1980). *The third wave*. Sperling & Kupfer.

Torre, T., & Sarti, D. (2018). Into smart work practices: Which challenges for the HR department? In E. Ales, Y. Curzi, T. Fabbri, O. Rymkevich, I. Senatori, & G. Solinas (Eds.), *Working in digital and smart organizations*. Palgrave Macmillan. https://doi.org/10.1007/978-3-319-77329-2_12

Torre, T., & Sarti, D. (2019). Themes and trends in smart working research: A systematic analysis of academic contributions. In *HRM 4.0 for human-centered organizations*. Emerald Publishing Limited.

Torre, T., & Sarti, D. (2020). Innovative approaches to work organization and new technologies: First insight from the Italian context. In *ICT for an inclusive world* (pp. 133–145). Springer.

Touraine, A. (1969). *La société post-industrielle [The Post Industrial Society]*. Denoel-Gonthier.

Touraine, A. (1973). Production de la socrete. Paris, Seuil. 1974 Pour la socrologre. Paris, Seuil. 1975 "Les nouveaux conflits sociaux", Sociologie du Travail 1.

Välikangas, L., & Lewin, A. Y. (2020). The lingering new normal. *Management and Organization Review, 16*(3), 467–472.

Van, N. T. T., Vrana, V., Duy, N. T., Minh, D. X. H., Dzung, P. T., Mondal, S. R., & Das, S. (2020). The role of human–machine interactive devices for post-COVID-19 innovative sustainable tourism in Ho Chi Minh City, Vietnam. *Sustainability, 12*(22), 9523. https://doi.org/10.3390/su12229523

Williams, M. (2012). Building and rebuilding trust: Why perspective taking matters. In R. M. Kramer & T. L. Pittinsky (Eds.), *Restoring trust in organizations and leaders: Enduring challenges and emerging answers* (pp. 171–184). Oxford University Press.

Wrzesniewski, A., & Dutton, J. E. (2001). Crafting a job: Revisioning employees as active crafters of their work. *Academy of Management Review, 26*(2), 179–201.

Yang, K. (2020). Unprecedented challenges, familiar paradoxes: COVID-19 and governance in a new normal state of risks. *Public Administration Review, 80*, 657–664

Yin, R. K. (2017). *Case study research and applications: Design and methods*. SAGE.

Zappalà. S. (2017). Smart working e fattori psico-sociali. In M. Neri (Ed.), *Smart working: una prospettiva critica* (pp. 15–22). TAO Digital Library.

CHAPTER 4

Digitalize Work in Pandemic Time: Practices for Remote Working and Job Redesign in Public Organization

Rocco Reina, Marzia Ventura, Concetta L. Cristofaro, and Walter Vesperi

Introduction

The global pandemic (Covid-19)—in a short time—has profoundly changed the expectations, perspectives, and behaviors of individuals, organizations, and even countries. If the context influences the achievement of the organizations' objectives, our case study shows that the new context created by Covid-19 has generated new scenarios for them. Taleb (2010) analyzed and discussed a series of past events capable of generating sudden shocks in society and the economic system. In the study conducted by

R. Reina · C. L. Cristofaro
Department of Law, Economics and Sociology, University of Catanzaro, Catanzaro, Italy
e-mail: rreina@unicz.it

C. L. Cristofaro
e-mail: concetta.cristofaro@unicz.it

S. R. Mondal et al. (eds.), *HR Analytics and Digital HR Practices*,
https://doi.org/10.1007/978-981-16-7099-2_4

Taleb (2010), major events (such as the crisis of September 11 and 29) had repercussions on organizations' strategic actions. Among these events, we can add the Covid-19 pandemic, which represents a sudden and unpredictable external change for all organizations, affecting all business activities incisively. Covid-19 brings new hindrances concerning the profound alteration of interactions and interpersonal relationships. Individual employees have had to adapt to new ways of working. Organizations' speedy response and adaptation to environmental change is an element of survival. Holling (1996) observed how organizations' functional capacity to adapt and survive the rapidly changing environment and extraordinary challenges can be defined as "resilience." Therefore, resilience represents the ability of an organization to adapt. This line of study highlights how the inability to manage resources according to principles of effectiveness and efficiency or the reduction in the quality of relationships—during phases of external chaos (Lengnick-Hall et al., 2011)—represent sure signs of organizational decline.

Another field of research focuses on companies' ability to adapt to rapidly changing environments through organizational improvisation (Ciborra, 1996; Hadida et al., 2015; Verjans, 2005). The prime obstacle for any organization is to find ways to manage and implement processes using digital platforms. In fact, one of the main effects that the current Covid-19 pandemic context has generated is an acceleration of the process of the digitization of work processes (Das, 2021a; Mondal, 2021). According to the principles of effectiveness and efficiency, the digitization of work processes generates an increasing complexity of organizational aspects. The evolution and change induced by the Covid-19 pandemic (Korunka, 2017; Mondal & Das, 2021) requires workers to update and enrich their knowledge and skills and take ample benefit of advanced technologies in the new normal design of workplace (Das, 2021b; Dua et al., 2021; Sharma & Das, 2021).

M. Ventura (✉)
Department of Health of Science, University of Catanzaro, Catanzaro, Italy
e-mail: marziaventura@unicz.it

W. Vesperi
Department of Economics, University of Messina, Messina, Italy

From these premises, new reflections on the change imposed by the current context concerning the design of work processes and human resource management are needed (Duy et al., 2020; Siri et al., 2020; Van et al., 2020). This chapter aims to examine the design of work by digital platforms along with public administration. The digitization of work processes is currently an important driver of change in the public sector (Duman & Das, 2021; Ravi & Mondal, 2021; Siri & Das, 2021).

Public organizations' significant investments in digital technologies fall under different perspectives of analysis (Mondal, 2020; Watts, 2016; Yegen & Mondal, 2021). Few studies have addressed the reconfigurations of work in public organizations heavily affected by digitization (Behera et al., 2019; Gupta et al., 2019; Singh et al., 2020). Using digital platforms, the evolution of remote work is based on the definition of an integrated system (Mondal & Sahoo, 2020; Nadanyiova & Das, 2020; Sharma & Das, 2020; Singh, Mondal, & Das, 2020). The orientation in the design of remote work, through platforms, must be consistent with the company's information system, technological level, and organizational-management design, which should be oriented toward flexibility and results (Das, 2020a; Mohanty et al., 2019; Mondal, 2020, February).

This research is determined by the influence that the recent and unforeseeable pandemic crisis is having on organizations and human resource management in public administrations (Das, 2020b). The chapters target to identify the changes that have taken place in public organizations that have initiated the digitization of production processes, this chapter aims to offer an overview of the main theoretical references on the phenomena of the digitalization of work processes and remote work in public organizations by analyzing the remote working scenario in form of a case. The case study concerning the Chamber of Commerce of Catanzaro (CCIAA) allowed us to analyze the nature and scope along with various dynamics of digital platform-based remote working.

The chapter caricature flows in a sequential hierarchy. Firstly, it describes the detailed literature review of related analysis on digitization in public organizations and new forms of work. Subsequently, the methodology and the chapter's objective are illustrated; then, a case study is presented, followed by discussion. Finally, conclusions and future research areas are suggested.

Review of Literature

Digitalization and ICT for Public Organizations

Nowadays due to rapid innovation coming into information and associated communication technologies, organizations are bringing new changes within themselves. This combined technological revolution is known as Information and Communications Technology (ICT. It modifies management practices, modes of communication, methods, the internal workings of the organization, and relations with the environment and local communities (Pupion, 2010, p. 2). The model by Bozeman (2000) expressed the reciprocal relationship between ICT and red tape bureaucratic involvement as "*rules, regulations, and procedures that remain in force and entail a compliance burden but do not advance the legitimate purposes the rules were intended to serve.*" On the contrary, ICT can help in reducing the red tape by streamlining the organizational processes (Moon & Bretschneider, 2002). Subsequently the analysis of Garicano and Heaton (2010) "*found that IT investments would reflect an effect on organizational measures*" (p. 10). Kallinikos (2006), Orlikowski (2007), Harris (2006, 2008), Introna (2009), Hung et al. (2009), Pors and Andersen (2015), Yeo and Marquardt (2015), Hussenot (2008), Arellano-Gault et al. (2013), rethink on the concept of technology in organization studies. According to the studies, the disruptive new dynamic technologies have completely brought forced changes in the public sector around the world by continuously challenging the administrative landscapes of major organizations (Decastri et al., 2020). Governments are ready to embrace these new disruptive technologies at all possible levels to get a facelift for delivering sustainable growth and streamline their inner processes to adjust with the dynamism of the technology-driven market (Gil-Garcia, 2012). Digitalization is the core of all the possible technological changes (Das, 2020a). Ejersbo and Greve (2017) definition of digitization, "*focuses on digital change and digitized interactions with citizens and businesses*" (p. 269). Therefore "*it is a new form of automated processes, which facilitates isocratic administration to improve the public sector*" (Dunleavy et al., 2006, p. 481). This change needs the innovation specifically driven toward sustainable goals within the system which should be supportive of organizational structure. Korunka (2017) shows that "*the technologies can have a substantial impact even to a relatively small degree*" (p. 132). As Morgan (2013) notes, technology impacts our work. Lindgren and

Jansson (2013) define public organizations "*as the formal public entities that decide on and organize public administration of different sorts, e.g., state authorities, ministries, municipalities or regional authorities*" (p. 167). Government reforms are digitalization driven as it brings multifaceted operation stability and flexibility Digitization has become an essential component of most government reforms. The OECD (2009) identified "*that digitization is viewed as a solution to big issues, such as high public expenditures, ineffectiveness, user involvement, and the need for transparency in public administration*" (OECD, 2009). Bekkers and Homburg (2005) and Marhetts (2009) refer digitalization as a core essential for "*digital-era governance*" (Dunleavy et al., 2006, p. 471). The organization theory builds the theoretical structure for digitalization at every levels. According to Barley and Kunda (2001) "digital technologies are used in a variety of ways and have a variety of effects on the way firms organize themselves" (p. 76). Yeo and Marquardt (2015) emphasized on the diffusion of organizational boundaries due to digitalization. Following these lines of reasoning, Plesner et al. (2018) "*if we want to improve our understanding of how work transforms in the digitized age is important to turn to organizational studies*" (p. 6).

The New Forms of Work: Remote vs Smart

ICT brings out wholesome changes by innovating the process of work in altering the dynamics of how, where, and when to work (Harvey, 2010). Cantoni and Mangia (2018) see ICTs as one component of the work system and are important tools for completing work and outcomes of change processes, at the same time. According to Boundreau et al. (2014) "*ICT driven changes in work practices can be greatly influenced by the sensemaking process that organizational members go through as they appropriate new information technologies or digital work environments*" (p. 2). The widespread use of ICT also serves as challenges in modern workplaces. The revolution in the fields of ICT does not only influence people's daily lives but the interactions between public administration and citizens (Bargsted et al., 2019).

Over the last few decades, the rapid advance in the field of ICTs has tremendously contributed to transforming traditional workplaces and work practices (Boudreau et al., 2014). Today, in this pandemic era, we are assisting in a changing scenario within the business landscape. Indeed, innovative ways of working among organizations are increased.

Employees are benefiting from growth opportunities thanks to remote work outside of the traditional office buildings (Errichiello & Pianese, 2016; Martinez-Sanchez et al., 2007; Nilles, 1998; Sullivan, 2008). According to Kurland and Bailey (1999) and Martinez-Sanchez et al. (2007) "*the remote work is a form of flexible working that has attracted a great deal of attention because of its multifaceted implications for individuals, organizations, and society to work anywhere and at any time*" (p. 10). As a result, there has been an increase in interest shown by both scholars and policymaker regarding "*the different typologies of flexible work arrangements, including remote work, home-based telework, mobile work, virtual teams and, more recently, smart working*" (Decastri et al., 2020, p. 345). Remote smart working needs a blend of primary requirements (smart devices like phones, internet, laptops, etc.) and secondary establishments (empty spaces, halls, etc.) (Errichiello & Pianese, 2016). Due to Covid-19, there is a surge in remote working requirements (Eurofound, 2020; Working, 2019). New demands show a complex challenge. The perfect mixture of proper job design and job fit conditions for an employee is very essential (Parker et al., 2017a). Wrzesniewski and Dutton (2001) argued for the idea of "*job crafting to capture the actions employees take to shape, mold, and redefine their jobs*" (p. 180). However, the implementation of ICT redefines the pivotal role of employees (Alvarez, 2002; Lamb & Davidson, 2005). Due to Covid-19, employees prefer to work remotely to avoid physical transmission of the virus. So, they prefer to work from home (WFH), remote offices, even on the road too (Parker et al., 2017b). So, we can safely say Covid-19 is rapidly changing the dynamics of work culture with the closure of business and smart remote working. Remote work refers to a set of flexible working models that, exploiting the potential of ICT, offer employees the opportunity to carry out their activities at a distance from their organization's central offices (Errichiello & Pianese, 2016). In recent years, a growing interest has been expressed about the so-called remote working—a way of working through ICT, which makes it possible to work outside the central office (Burns, 2006; Cascio, 2000; Kurland & Bailey, 1999).

In the context of organizational and managerial literature, in particular, considerable attention has been of institutional, cultural, and technological variables capable of favoring or hindering the adoption of remote work models as well as the multiple benefits that they can generate for the workers, organization and, more broadly, the community (Bélanger et al., 2016; Illegems & Verbeke, 2004; Kurland & Bailey, 1999; Martin & MacDonnel, 2012; Moktarian & Salomon, 1993, 1997; Neirotti et al., 2014; Pérez et al., 2005; Peters et al., 2005, 2010; Siha & Monroe, 2006).

The wide variety of ICT tools that can be used makes it possible to prepare very large remote working plans, extending their application to a wide range of activities. In this regard, in fact, many studies agree that the nature of the duties does not constitute an obstacle to the adoption of remote working (Campo dell'Orto, 2000; Daniels et al., 2001; Pérez et al., 2002; Errichiello & Pianese, 2014, p. 18). Remote tasks are numerous and heterogeneous, and, except for those involving the physical manipulation of an object, they range from simple tasks (e.g., secretarial, data upload) to more complex activities with professional and/or managerial content (e.g., programmers, consultants), regardless of the level of operational or informational interdependence. Alternatively, remote work is influenced by the degree of adequacy of managerial practices and the ICT tools and technologies used for its development and management. The more advanced the level of technologies available, the greater the opportunities to extend the remote work to many workers. Remote work refers to employees who work at home, though not necessarily every day. An individual can be a remote worker if their telecommunications link to the office using electronic mail and personal computer links to office servers. Remote management is characterized by the inability of a manager to observe their employees' work processes.

Based on Mann's research (2012), taken up by Decastri et al. (2020, p. 349), an adaptation is reported by relating the constituent elements of remote work with smart working (Table 4.1).

Recently (Errichiello & Pianese, 2018; Versteegh, 2010), "*a holistic approach in managing workplace flexibility, known as smart working, is spreading throughout many organizations worldwide*" (p. 15). Smart working extends the remote working concept by adding more autonomy to the employees along with empowering them for the overall mutual benefit of organization and themselves (Clapperton & Vanhoutte, 2014; De Kok, 2016; Hartog et al., 2015).

The smart implementation of remote smart working culture stands on 3Bs like integrated remodified physical space (Bricks), combination of

Table 4.1 Remote and smart working elements

Elements	*Dimension*	*References*
Remote working		
ICT	"*Use of ICTs that enable employees and managers to get access to their labor activities from remote locations*"	Nilles (1998), Sullivan (2008)
HR	"*Reconfigure resources and activities in response to environmental demands* *Workplace flexibility, making work more portable and ubiquitous*"	Wright and Snell (1998), Pérez et al. (2002)
Layout	"*Flexible workspace practices that need the implementation of human resource (HR) development practices to create an organizational climate of trust and commitment*"	Martinez-Sanchez et al. (2007)
Smart working		
ICT	"*Extent to which employees telework* *Use of ICT personal devices and\or external ICT Services*"	Martinez-Sanchez et al. (2007)
HR	"*Extent to which employees can manage their working hours in a flexible way* *Change-Management Actions implemented in the organization and new HRM practice\tools developed*"	Coenen and Kok (2014)
Layout	"*Adoption of initiatives for the redesigning of the physical workspace for creating environments that are more flexible and oriented to collaboration*"	Elsbach and Pratt (2007)

Source Authors' Adaptation from Mann (2012), Decastri et al. (2020, p. 349)

information and communication technologies (Bytes) and human activities (Behaviors) (Clapperton & Vanhoutte, 2014; De Kok, 2016; Hartog et al., 2015): "*Bricks refer to new office space designs so that smart workers have different typologies of working areas (e.g., open spaces, meeting rooms, concentration areas) suitable for concentration and/or interaction with colleagues* (Greene & Myerson, 2011; Hartog et al., 2015). *Bytes refer to the design of simple and sophisticated ICT (collaborative tools, videoconference system) to enable smart workers to perform activities whenever and wherever, thus creating a virtual work environment*" (p. 15) (Errichiello & Pianese, 2018; Johns & Gratton, 2013). These changes in the workplace have immediate effects on the economy and may transform the business scenarios beyond post-Covid-19 (Brynjolfsson et al., 2020).

Objective of Chapter

The rapid change of context—caused by Covid-19—and the rapid spread of new technologies have generated new reflections in human resource management. Human resource management seems to be particularly complex in bureaucratic and large organizations such as public organizations. The implication of new managerial practices in public administrations, especially in HR, appears to be a complex and contradictory phenomenon. With the aim of identifying the changes that have taken place in public organizations that have begun the digitization processes, this chapter aims to offer an overview of the main theoretical references on the phenomena of digitalization processes of work and remote work in public organizations through the analysis of one case study. By observing the case study of the Chamber of Commerce of Catanzaro (CCIAA), we have focused to investigate the nature and dynamics of remote work through digital platforms.

Method

The study has adopted a qualitative/inductive approach based on one case study, according to the methods and instructions suggested by Yin (2013). This approach involved collecting data through semi-structured interviews and desk research. "*Privileged access to relevant information allowed authors to collect data from different sources, increasing the quality of the information obtained*" (Benbasat et al., 1981; Zardini et al., 2016, p. 67).

A qualitative study seemed particularly suited to the purpose of the research and the complexity of the phenomenon since it allows us to consider the specific characteristics of the public organizations (Bamberger, 2000) and also explore the process of implementing new technologies in human resource management, in response to the Covid-19 emergency, to learn about the potential solutions adopted.

In this research, a case study was used because it is particularly favorable when an inductive approach is adopted, and theory is used to explain empirical observations. The case study proposed in this chapter will allow us to understand better the implementation of new technologies in human resource management during the pandemic. An analysis of a case study was developed because it was considered useful for the analysis of real-life events in organizations and understanding the meaning of people's experiences. The subject of our case study is the Chamber of Commerce of the province of Catanzaro, a public organization that represents the general interests of small and medium-sized enterprises. Its main activities include the promotion of study paths and data analysis of the local economy, the implementation of interventions aimed at favoring the internationalization of businesses, innovation, and technology transfer, the development of infrastructures, environmental performance in business activity, and access to credit. Since 2016, new strategic functions have been added in terms of digitization, job orientation, and professions.

The information for this research was collected in November 2020. From the methodological point of view, the time frame in which the data collection was developed is important for our analysis because it offers us the possibility to define the relevance and nature of information collection. The data and information useful for this work were collected through semi-structured interviews and questionnaires to ensure conclusions based on specific observations (Das, 2021c; Van Dijk et al., 2007). The interview was done with the strategic top of the organization, the Secretary General, while the questionnaire was given to all the organization's employees.

Context

The Italian central government has launched a series of initiatives to encourage the promotion of digital transformation in Public Administrations (PA). The most recent initiative launched by the Italian government is the 2020–2022 Three-Year Plan.

On this premises, we have considered the case study of the Chamber of Commerce of Catanzaro (CCIAA) like a public organization that offers services through digitized processes to companies in its provincial territory. In fact, its mission is to play a propulsive role in local development through careful administrative simplification processes, protection of legality, company and product qualification, internationalization, tourism incentives, protection of the environment, and cultural heritage.

The organizational structure represented in the organization chart below (Fig. 4.1) is divided into two management areas, one with competence on all processes relating to institutional and support activities, and one with competence on all services of direct contact with the external users, such as personal data—certification and supervisory and control

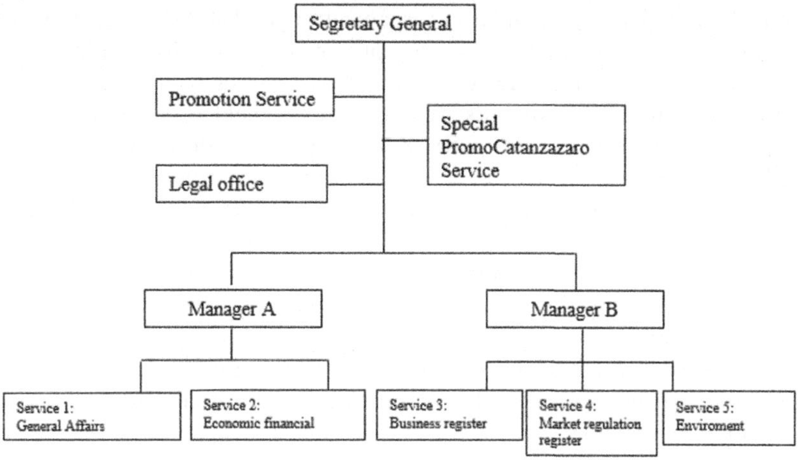

Fig. 4.1 Organizational chart of Commerce of Catanzaro (CCIAA) (*Source* Website Chamber of Commerce of Catanzaro [CCIAA])

Table 4.2 Personnel distribution of the Chamber of Commerce of Catanzaro

Category	*Full-time*	*Part-time*
Manager	1	0
Officials	9	0
Technicians	7	2
Collaborators	8	0
Manual workers	3	0
Total	28	2

Source Performance Plan for Chamber of Commerce of Catanzaro, 2020

services. These areas, coordinated at the top by the Secretary General, are in turn divided into Services and Offices.

The Chamber of Commerce of Catanzaro currently employs 30 employees, of whom 28 are permanent (full-time) and 2 are temporary (part-time). Table 4.2 summarizes the distribution of personnel by category and type of contract.

Due to the rules introduced by Covid-19, which have limited mobility, initiated social distancing measures, banned travel, meetings, and prevented the participation/organization of fairs, the Chamber of Commerce of Catanzaro was promptly rescheduled to continue the work remotely. In this regard, the telematic services continued working remotely; however, as regards the work in the field of supervision and inspections, it suffered many setbacks during the lockdown, which persist today despite the new methods of remote working. Finally, the promotion activity of companies and the territory has been completely transformed; in fact, remote training, management of tenders, and remote assistance have replaced the initiatives in various ways because they have been prohibited by the rules regarding Covid-19. They have also been profoundly expanded, requiring a considerable financial commitment of the Chamber, which had to draw on its own capitalized resources, as well as a strong professional commitment of the entire administrative bureaucratic structure.

Case Study: The Interview

Consistent with the purpose of our chapter, we conducted our first interview with a privileged observer of this phenomenon—the Secretary General of the Chamber of Commerce of Catanzaro. The first part of the interview focused on managing change in public administration. The second part of the interview focused on understanding the phenomenon of "remote working" and "smart working" in the PA considered. The questions of the second section are presented in tabular form with the relative answers.

The Chamber of Commerce of Catanzaro was already a digitized organization before Covid-19 came about. The change process began in 2017. The information system the Chamber uses is InfoCamere, one in-house company of the Chamber system. InfoCamere has activated private telematic connections (technically the so-called VPNs, secure digital channels between remote locations and the workstations or office networks) for the chamber staff. In addition, there are connections with VDI technology (an even more advanced way to access all the office resources from a remote location) so that the people from the chamber system can work easily with different technologies during the Covid-19 era.

Since March 10, 2020, employees have had no difficulty in managing the services from home electronically (e.g., e-mail and related services). 100% of the workers were required to do teleworking, which proved proactive in emergency management. The workers were willing to

continue their work from home using and in some cases purchasing (84%) a digital tool (PC) themselves.
Second Part of the Interview:
Focus: the new forms of work in the Chamber of Commerce

Question: What is, in your opinion and based on your experience, the meaning of remote working?	Secretary General: An instrument provided for by the legislation; the office is reproduced by the same organization in the employee's home, remotely creating the employee's work room
Question: What is, in your opinion and based on your experience, the meaning of smart working?	Secretary General: A mere technical distinction from teleworking The two different forms are necessarily going to "mix" the tendency to work toward goals; tending toward the result is something we were already used to as an administration. The performance cycle has led us to think about objectives for some time; therefore, it is a question of strengthening that concept of management through objectives
Question: What is the percentage of staff who used this modality pre-pandemic?	Secretary General: None The National Chamber system had foreseen and tested this new form of work in large Chambers of Commerce to meet the needs of employees and reconcile work times with family time (WLB)
Question: What is the percentage of personnel who have used this modality during the pandemic phase?	Secretary General: 100%
Question: Has the Chamber of Commerce defined the activities that cannot be done remotely?	Secretary General: Yes. In presence, mediation has continued to take place and/or been suspended due to the emergency; the management of business crises; some promotional activities and inspections In the public sector, there was a need to provide a continuous service to users, as well as the time and time slot to be contacted\available on the phone, leading to the replacement of the traditional counter with the telematic one

(continued)

(continued)

Question: Has the Chamber of Commerce encountered difficulties with its staff adapting to the new form of work?	Secretary General: No. In teleworking, employees and service heads have been in continuous, direct connection with the office (through the Google meet platform). The services have been continuous, and the employees have given the possibility to connect to the office's switchboard through their mobile phones, to be available from home, proving the great availability of all chamber employees
Question: What training interventions have the organization put in place to implement and guarantee the new forms of work?	Secretary General: The Chamber of Commerce already relied on the InfoCamere system in the pre-Covid 19 phase, which has been implemented to assist employees from a technical-IT point of view in the Covid 19 era
Question: An analysis on the well-being and organizational climate in the Covid-19 era regarding the new forms of work was carried out: Do workers feel more motivated—satisfied? Have the workers performed better?	Secretary General: Yes. The well-being of employees was the organization's priority, which was analyzed through a purely qualitative analysis to monitor their status The employees were enthusiastic about working from home. They all guarantee working hours and also work on Saturdays and Sundays (when requested). Employees have greatly appreciated the fact that they can "do public work with the logic of private work" without being tied to the logic of a time card or making up time during working hours. However, they did report the negative aspect of a lack of social and relational exchanges with colleagues. They requested the possibility to work in person (a few days a week) to meet with colleagues, so they were not subjected to and dominated by automation. The workers felt motivated and satisfied, achieving better performance than in previous months; the percentage amounted to 98% of the working practices processed
Question: Has the organization monitored and assessed the performance of workers in the Covid-19 era?	Secretary General: Yes. Through the InfoCamere System, thus being able to keep an eye on the situation and monitor the practices processed daily, while always respecting their privacy

(continued)

(continued)

Question: Can the use of these new forms of work be a means of reducing stress and anxiety levels in the worker?	Secretary General: Yes Employees greatly appreciate the fact that they can "do public work with the logic of private work" without being tied to the logic of a time card or making up time during working hours
Question: Can the use of these new forms of work be a means to reduce absenteeism?	Secretary General: Yes, especially for those with family problems related to the health and care of relatives with disabilities or other pathologies, for those with small children or for those who more generally have problems in reconciling working hours with family time
Question: The use of these new forms of work has reduced the possibility of visually checking employees, how can this difficulty be overcome, if an issue?	Secretary General: Before Covid-19, there was a direct, daily relationship that allowed us to check employees. Today, it is done through the InfoCamere system for the cases processed by each employee and through telephone contact or video calls
Question: Have differences been found between pre-Covid-19 and post-Covid-19 workers?	Secretary General: Yes I found that some workers performed better. As I said before, 98% of the cases were processed, and they were more motivated and eager to serve the community
Question: Could you indicate the strengths and weaknesses that may be related to the implementation of new forms of work?	Weaknesses The working distance The transfer of knowledge Employee monitoring The reduction of economic spin-offs from employees on the local context The layout of the office The availability and use of technological tools Security of chamber data on employees' personal PCs Strengths Reconciliation of work and family times Improvement of individual and organizational performance Cultural change

(continued)

(continued)

Question: Could the new forms of work represent a new way of work to be implemented and\or developed even in the post-Covid-19 era?	Secretary General: Only in part The idea that these new forms of work (teleworking or\and smart working) are the turning point for success, "the panacea" to all problems of the public administration, is madness, as if this change will not be programmed and planned. Rather than leading to a real change, it will be the death of the public sector and PAs
Question: What are the implications of the use of new forms of work?	Secretary General: Definitely from a socio-economic point of view on the environment and mobility

Source Interview of The Secretary General of The Chamber of Commerce

Solutions and Recommendations

Catanzaro's Chamber System's response to the emergency was compact (with respect to the staff employed) and responsible (working beyond working hours, on Saturdays and Sundays), as required by the seriousness of the moment, both toward users, from the perspective of quality, and toward companies guaranteeing services through digital platforms.

Therefore, this contribution responds to the working needs that are emerging. It is a vision linked to tools and organization resulting from a perspective vision and linked to smart working in terms of sustainability, efficiency, and quality of service. Enhancing human capital means growing the entire organization by increasing the well-being of those who live it daily (direct interviews with employees on well-being and organizational climate). Teleworking, Smart working, and flexible working hours go in the direction of greater harmonization between private and professional life, improving the organization's ability to respond to the needs of its internal stakeholders quickly and optimally. Organizations are trying to spread a sense of cultural change to develop a responsible and proactive attitude, to guarantee productivity (98% of working practices processed) and higher levels of quality in services for its users.

This emergency can be transformed into opportunities through the organization and planning of these new forms of work; only in this way will it be possible to talk about the adoption of more virtuous behaviors (elimination of the crafty time card) by developing new tools to restart and successfully face the challenges that await us from tomorrow.

Future Research Directions

Covid-19 has impacted many aspects of daily life. The behaviors of organizations had to adopt this evolution. In particular, this study highlighted the impact that Covid-19 has had on job design. The planning of post-Covid-19 work—especially in public organizations, as emerged from the analysis of the case study—must take into consideration elements capable of increasing the quality of working life and productivity. The new basic elements to consider are reduction of physical needs (through the use of digital platforms), increase in workplace and data safety. On these considerations, future studies—in the field of HR and work planning—must focus on ergonomic approaches, on the reconciliation of work-family times and well-being of workers. The relationship between work through digital platforms and remote control appears to be an emerging issue that needs further development and analysis. At present, some aspects are not investigable. Some effects of Covid-19 on organizations take additional time to become apparent. At the same time, the rapid development of ICTs will represent a further element of change for the coming decades (Korunka, 2017) in public organizations.

Conclusion

Digitization will be the main driver of innovation and change in all sectors of our economy. In the face of exponential digitization, to meet new technological and social requirements, the Chamber of Commerce of Catanzaro has continued its digitization process. Public administrations—in order to respond to the changing context—had to increase their organizational flexibility and reduce response times.

Covid 19 has forced workers and administrations to work from home, making remote work and the use of digital tools necessary (and to a certain extent mandatory). The emergency has made it clear that it is possible to work from places other than the office, but, to be effective, this practice must be consolidated. If the emergency and consequent blockade favor the adoption of remote working practices, the workers of the PA and beyond could take advantage of them, making the care of children or other relatives simple.

The Chamber of Commerce we have taken into consideration has demonstrated how, in an emergency like Covid-19, they guaranteed their service in continuity and with quality, placing at the center not only the employees but also the citizens\users (individual and\or company). During the pandemic, the InfoCamere system has allowed its employees to work remotely and interact flexibly and effectively with colleagues and citizens/users.

The changes introduced in the HR practices concern the reorganization of processes and the redesign of work which has led to new forms of communication and information sharing. The layout of the office, designed primarily as a home space to increase productivity and communication between colleagues, has been rethought both in terms of numbers and distancing. The methodology of the single case study has the limit of offering a simplified representation of reality. Despite these limitations, the results achieved in this study represent an important starting point for the analysis of the PA and its evolution in the era Covid-19. The discussion on the reorganization of work and the new forms of work that are increasingly being implemented during the Covid-19 era, provides some useful ideas to set the path out of this health emergency.

References

Alvarez, R. C. (2002). The promise of e-Health—A Canadian perspective. *Ehealth International, 1*(4).

Arellano-Gault, D., Demortain, D., Rouillard, C., & Thoenig, J. C. (2013). Bringing public organization and organizing back in. *Organization Studies, 34*(2), 145–167.

Bamberger, M. (Ed.). (2000). *Integrating quantitative and qualitative research in development projects: Lessons from the field*. The World Bank.

Bargsted, M., Ramírez-Vielma, R., & Yeves, J. (2019). Professional self-efficacy and job satisfaction: The mediator role of work design. *Journal of Work and Organizational Psychology, 35*(3), 157–163.

Barley, S. R., & Kunda, G. (2001). Bringing work back in. *Organization science, 12*(1), 76–95.

Behera, M., Dash, M., Ayasa Kanta Mohanty, A. K., & Das, S. (2019). Entrepreneurial ecosystem: A geographical upliftment. *Revista Espacios, 40*, 26–36. http://www.revistaespacios.com/a19v40n01/19400126.html

Bekkers, V. J., & Homburg, V. (Eds.). (2005). *The information ecology of e-government: E-government as institutional and technological innovation in public administration* (Vol. 9). IOS press.

Bélanger, V., Kergosien, Y., Ruiz, A., & Soriano, P. (2016). An empirical comparison of relocation strategies in real-time ambulance fleet management. *Computers & Industrial Engineering, 94*, 216–229.

Benbasat, I., Dexter, A. S., Drury, D. H., & Goldstein, R. C. (1984). A critque of the stage hypothesis: Theory and empirical evidence. *Communications of the ACM, 27*(5), 476–485.

Benbya, H., & Leidner, D. (2017). *Harnessing employee innovation in idea management platforms: Lessons from Allianz UK.*

Boudreau, J., & Lawler III, E. E. (2014). Stubborn traditionalism in HRM: Causes and consequences. *Human Resource Management Review, 24*(3), 232–244.

Boudreau, M.-C., Serrano, C., & Larson, K. (2014). IT-driven identity work: Creating a group identity in a digital environment. *Information and Organization, 24*(1), 1–24. https://doi.org/10.1016/j.infoandorg.2013.11.001

Bozeman, B. (2000). Technology transfer and public policy: A review of research and theory. *Research Policy, 29*(4–5), 627–655.

Brynjolfsson, E., Horton, J. J., Ozimek, A., Rock, D., Sharma, G., & TuYe, H. Y. (2020). COVID-19 and remote work: An early look at US data (No. w27344). National Bureau of Economic Research.

Burns, M. (2006). Essential components of human resources practices and management. *Managing Human Resources in Health Care Organizations, 51.*

Campo dell'Orto, S. M. G. (2000). *Conoscere il telelavoro. Caratteristiche, esperienze, guida all'utilizzo.* Franco Angeli.

Cantoni, F., & Mangia, G. (Eds.). (2018). *Human resource management and digitalization.* Routledge.

Cascio, W. F. (2000). Managing a virtual workplace. *Academy of Management Perspectives, 14*(3), 81–90.

Ciborra, C. (1996). Improvisation and information technology in organizations. In *ICIS 1996 Proceedings* (p. 26).

Clapperton, G., & Vanhoutte, P. (2014). *The Smarter Working Manifesto: When, where and how do you work best?* Sunmakers.

Coenen, M., & Kok, R. A. (2014). Workplace flexibility and new product development performance: The role of telework and flexible work schedules. *European Management Journal, 32*(4), 564–576.

Criado, J. I., & Villodre, J. (2018, May). Breaking through government digital communities in social media: A comparative analysis at the local level in Spain. In *Proceedings of the 19th Annual International Conference on Digital Government Research: Governance in the Data Age* (pp. 1–2).

Cunha, M. A. V., Coelho, T. R., & Pozzebon, M. (2013). The use of ICT in public decision-making participation.

Daniels, K., Lamond, D., & Standen, P. (2001) Teleworking: Frameworks for organizational research. *Journal of Management Studies, 38*(8), 1151–1185. https://doi.org/10.1111/1467-6486.00276

Das, S. (2020a). Innovations in digital banking service brand equity and millennial consumerism. In *Digital transformation and innovative services for business and learning* (pp. 62–79). IGI Global. https://doi.org/10.4018/978-1-7998-5175-2.ch004

Das, S. (2020b, February). *Media impact of advertising on consumer buying behaviour a comparative study of different media*. Shiksha o Anusandhan University. http://hdl.handle.net/10603/273691

Das, S. (2021a) A systematic study of integrated marketing communication and content management system for millennial consumers. In *Innovations in digital branding and content marketing* (pp. 91–112). IGI Global. https://doi.org/10.4018/978-1-7998-4420-4.ch005

Das, S. (2021b). *Digital entertainment: The next evolution in service sector*. Springer Nature. https://doi.org/10.1007/978-981-15-9724-4. Print ISBN978-981-15-9723-7. Online ISBN978-981-15-9724-4

Das, S. (2021c). *Search engine optimization and marketing: A recipe for success in digital marketing* (1st ed.). CRC Press. https://doi.org/10.1201/9780429298509

De Kok, A. (2016). The new way of working: Bricks, bytes, and behavior. In *The impact of ICT on work* (pp. 9–40). Springer.

Decastri, M., Gagliarducci, F., Previtali, P., & Scarozza, D. (2020). Understanding the use of Smart Working in Public Administration: The experience of the Presidency of the Council of Ministers. In *Exploring digital ecosystems* (pp. 343–363). Springer.

Du Gay, P., & Vikkelsø, S. (2016). *For formal organization: The past in the present and future of organization theory*. Oxford University Press.

Dua, S., Singh, I., & Das, S. (2021) Banking innovative service with digital brand equity for new age consumers: Internet banking and millennial consumerism. In *Innovations in digital branding and content marketing* (pp. 134–159). IGI Global. https://doi.org/10.4018/978-1-7998-4420-4.ch007

Duman, Ü. O., & Das, S. (2021). The dynamic rise of digital brands' market mavens in digital entertainment: A complete know how for curious customers. In *Digital entertainment* (pp. 147–172). Palgrave Macmillan. https://doi.org/10.1007/978-981-15-9724-4_8

Dunleavy, P., Margetts, H., Bastow, S., & Tinkler, J. (2006). New public management is dead—Long live digital-era governance. *Journal of Public Administration Research and Theory, 16*(3), 467–494.

Duy, N. T., Mondal, S. R., Van, N. T. T., Dzung, P. T., Minh, D. X. H., & Das, S. (2020). A study on the role of Web 4.0 and 5.0 in the sustainable tourism ecosystem of Ho Chi Minh City, Vietnam. *Sustainability*, *12*(17), 7140. https://doi.org/10.3390/su12177140

Ejersbo, N., & Greve, C. (2017). Digital era governance reform and accountability. The case of Denmark. In T. Christensen & P. Lægreid (Eds.), *The Routledge handbook to accountability and welfare state reforms in Europe* (Chapter 19, pp. 267–279). Routledge.

Elsbach, K. D., & Pratt, M. G. (2007). 4 the physical environment in organizations. *Academy of Management Annals, 1*(1), 181–224.
Erickson, L. B., Trauth, E. M., & Petrick, I. (2012). *Getting inside your employees' heads: Navigating barriers to internal-crowdsourcing for product and service innovation.*
Errichiello, L., & Pianese, T. (2014). Ripensare il remote working: le opportunità degli Smart Work Center. *Economia dei Servizi, 9*(3), 305–328.
Errichiello, L., & Pianese, T. (2016, December). Transforming the workplace: Smart Work Centers as the new frontier of remote work arrangements. In *First RGCS Symposium, 'Work and Workplace Transformations: Between Communities, Doing, and Entrepreneurship'*. Université EM-Lyon, Paris.
Errichiello, L., & Pianese, T. (2018). Smart Work Centers as "creative workspaces" for remote employees. *CERN IdeaSquare Journal of Experimental Innovation, 2*(1), 14–21.
Eurofound. (2020, December 12). Working anytime, anywhere: The effects on the world of work [online]. Available at: https://www.ilo.org/wcmsp5/groups/public/---dgreports/---dcomm/---publ/documents/publication/wcms_544151.pdf
European Journal of Information Systems, 14(5), 504–506.
Garicano, L., & Heaton, P. (2010). Information technology, organization, and productivity in the public sector: Evidence from police departments. *Journal of Labor Economics, 28*(1), 167–201.
Gil-Garcia, J. R. (2012). *Enacting electronic government success: An integrative study of government-wide websites, organizational capabilities, and institutions* (Vol. 31). Springer Science & Business Media.
Grant, A. M., Fried, Y., & Juillerat, T. (2010). Work matters: Job design in classic and contemporary perspectives. In S. Zedeck (Ed.), *APA handbook of industrial and organizational psychology* (Vol. 1, pp. 417–453). American Psychological Association.
Grant, A. M., & Parker, S. K. (2009). Redesigning work design theories: The rise of relational and proactive perspectives. *Academy of Management Annals, 3*(1), 317–375.
Greene, C., & Myerson, J. (2011). *Space for thought: Designing for knowledge workers*. Facilities.
Gupta, D. K., Jena, D., Samantaray, A. K., & Das, S. (2019). HRD climate in selected public sector banks in India. *Revista ESPACIOS, 40*(11).
Hadida, A. L., Tarvainen, W., & Rose, J. (2015). Organizational improvisation: A consolidating review and framework. *International Journal of Management Reviews, 17*(4), 437–459.
Harvey, D. (2010). *A Companion to Marx's Capital*. Verso.
Harris, R. (2006). *New ethnicities and language use*. Springer.

Harris, A. (2008). Distributed leadership: According to the evidence. *Journal of Educational Administration*.

Hartog, K. L., Solimene, A., & Tufani G. (2015). *The smart working book, Seedble*. http://www.thesmartworkingbook.com/downloads/the-smart-working-book/

Haynes, B. P., Greene, C., & Myerson, J. (2011). Space for thought: Designing for knowledge workers. *Facilities, 29*, 19–30.

Holling, C. S. (1996). Engineering resilience versus ecological resilience. *Engineering Within Ecological Constraints, 31*(1996), 32.

Hung, A., Parker, A. M., & Yoong, J. (2009). *Defining and measuring financial literacy*.

Hussenot, A. (2008). Between structuration and translation: An approach of ICT appropriation. *Journal of Organizational Change Management*.

Illegems, V., & Verbeke, A. (2004). Telework: What does it mean for management? *Long Range Planning, 37*(4), 319–334.

Introna, L. D. (2009). Ethics and the speaking of things. *Theory, Culture & Society, 26*(4), 25–46.

Jansen, A., & Ølnes, S. (2016). The nature of public e-services and their quality dimensions. *Government Information Quarterly, 33*(4), 647–657.

Johns, T., & Gratton, L. (2013). The third wave of virtual work. *Harvard Business Review, 91*(1), 66–73. https://hbr.org/2013/01/the-third-wave-of-virtual-work

Kallinikos, J. (2006). The institution of bureaucracy: Administration, pluralism, democracy. *Economy and Society, 35*(4), 611–627.

Korunka, C. (2017). Challenges for job design. In *Job demands in a changing world of work* (pp. 131–151). https://doi.org/10.1007/978-3-319-54678-0_8

Korunka, C., & Kubicek, B. (2017). Job demands in a changing world of work. In *Job demands in a changing world of work* (pp. 1–5). Springer.

Kurland, N. B., & Bailey, D. E. (1999). Telework: The advantages and challenges of working here, there, anywhere, and anytime. *Organizational Dynamics, 28*(2), 53–68.

Lamb, R., & Davidson, E. (2005). Information and communication technology challenges to scientific professional identity. *The Information Society, 21*(1), 1–24.

Landsbergen, D., Jr., & Wolken, G., Jr. (2001). Realizing the promise: Government information systems and the fourth generation of information technology. *Public Administration Review, 61*(2), 206–220.

Lengnick-Hall, C. A., Beck, T. E., & Lengnick-Hall, M. L. (2011). Developing a capacity for organizational resilience through strategic human resource management. *Human Resource Management Review, 21*(3), 243–255.

Lindgren, I., & Jansson, G. (2013). Electronic services in the public sector: A conceptual framework. *Government Information Quarterly, 30*(2), 163–172.

Lindgren, I., & Melin, U. (2017, September). Time to refuel the conceptual discussion on public e-services–revisiting how e-services are manifested in practice. In *International Conference on Electronic Government* (pp. 92–101). Springer.

Maciejewski, M. (2017). To do more, better, faster and more cheaply: Using big data in public administration. *International Review of Administrative Sciences, 83*(1, suppl), 120–135.

Mann, J. (2012). Transform the workplace with focus on bricks, behaviors and bits. *Gartner Report* (G0021229).

Margetts, H. (2009). Public management change and e-government: The emergence of digital-era governance. *Routledge Handbook of Internet Politics*, 119–131.

Martin, B. H., & MacDonnell, R. (2012). Is telework effective for organizations? A meta-analysis of empirical research on perceptions of telework and organizational outcomes. *Management Research Review.*

Martínez-Sánchez, A., Pérez-Pérez, M., De-Luis-Carnicer, P., & Vela-Jiménez, M. J. (2007). Telework, human resource flexibility and firm performance. *New Technology, Work and Employment, 22*(3), 208–223.

Mohanty, P. C., Dash, M., Dash, M., & Das, S. (2019). A study on factors influencing training effectiveness. *Revista Espacios, 40*, 7–15. http://www.revistaespacios.com/a19v40n02/19400207.html

Mondal, S. (2021). A systematic study of new age consumer engagement and exploration for digital entertainment for over-the-top platforms in various digital media. In *Innovations in digital branding and content marketing* (pp. 113–133). IGI Global. https://doi.org/10.4018/978-1-7998-4420-4.ch006

Mondal, S., & Sahoo, K. K. (2020). A study of green building prospects on sustainable management decision making. In *Green building management and smart automation* (pp. 220–234). IGI Global. https://doi.org/10.4018/978-1-5225-9754-4.ch011

Mondal, S. R. (2020). A systematic study for digital innovation in management education: An integrated approach towards problem-based learning in Vietnam. In *Digital innovations for customer engagement, management, and organizational improvement* (pp. 104–120). IGI Global. https://doi.org/10.4018/978-1-7998-5171-4.ch006

Mondal, S. R. (2020, February). *Factors influencing store image loyalty and satisfaction from customer perspective an empirical study in retail sector*. Shiksha o Anusandhan University. http://hdl.handle.net/10603/273688

Mondal, S. R., & Das, S. (2021). Examining diabetic subjects on their correlation with TTH and CAD: A statistical approach on exploratory results. In

Machine learning and the internet of medical things in healthcare (pp. 153–177). Academic Press. https://doi.org/10.1016/B978-0-12-821229-5.00007-0

Moon, M., & Bretschneider, S. (2002). Does the perception of red tape constrain IT innovativeness in organizations? Results from simultaneous equation model and implications. *Journal of Public Administration Research and Theory, 11*(3), 327–352.

Morgan, G. (2013). *Riding the waves of change*. Imaginization Inc.

Nadanyiova, M., & Das, S. (2020). Millennials as a target segment of socially responsible communication within the business strategy. *Littera Scripta, 13*(1), 119–134. https://doi.org/10.36708/Littera_Scripta2020/1/8

Neirotti, P., De Marco, A., Cagliano, A. C., Mangano, G., & Scorrano, F. (2014). Current trends in smart city initiatives: Some stylised facts. *Cities, 38*, 25–36.

Nevo, S., & Wade, M. R. (2010). The formation and value of IT-enabled resources: Antecedents and consequences of synergistic relationships. *MIS Quarterly, 34*, 163–183.

Nilles, J. M. (1998). *Managing telework: Strategies for managing the virtual workforce*. John Wiley & Sons.

OECD. (2009). Rethinking E-government services. *User-Centred Approaches*. OECD. https://www.oecd.org/gov/digital-government/

Orlikowski, W. J. (2007). Sociomaterial practices: Exploring technology at work. *Organization Studies, 28*(9), 1435–1448.

Parker, S. K., Morgeson, F. P., & Johns, G. (2017a). One hundred years of work design research: Looking back and looking forward. *Journal of Applied Psychology, 102*(3), 403.

Parker, S. K., Van den Broeck, A., & Holman, D. (2017b). Work design influences: A synthesis of multilevel factors that affect the design of jobs. *Academy of Management Annals, 11*(1), 267–308.

Peters, M. (2005). *Entrepreneurial skills in leadership and human resource management evaluated by apprentices in small tourism businesses*. Education + Training.

Peters, D. H., Chakraborty, S., Mahapatra, P., & Steinhardt, L. (2010). Job satisfaction and motivation of health workers in public and private sectors: Cross-sectional analysis from two Indian states. *Human Resources for Health, 8*(1), 1–11.

Pérez, M. P., Sánchez, A. M., & de Luis Carnicer, M. P. (2002). Benefits and barriers of telework: Perception differences of human resources managers according to company's operations strategy. *Technovation, 22*(12), 775–783.

Pérez, M. P., Sánchez, A. M., de Luis Carnicer, P., & Jiménez, M. J. V. (2005). The differences of firm resources and the adoption of teleworking. *Technovation, 25*(12), 1476–1483.

Plesner, U., Justesen, L., & Glerup, C. (2018). The transformation of work in digitized public sector organizations. *Journal of Organizational Change Management, 31*, 1176–1190.

Power, M. (2000). The audit society—Second thoughts. *International Journal of Auditing, 4*(1), 111–119.

Pors, J. G., & Andersen, N. Å. (2015). Playful organisations: Undecidability as a scarce resource. *Culture and Organization, 21*(4), 338–354.

Pupion, P. C. (2010). Tourisme durable et valorisation de l'environnement du littoral aquitain: diversité et stratégies des acteurs. *Management Avenir*, (4), 289–305.

Ravi, S., & Mondal, S. R. (2021). Digital entertainment based do it yourself content & advertisement as a factor of driving force for trust & customer patronage. In *Digital entertainment* (pp. 127–146). Palgrave Macmillan. https://doi.org/10.1007/978-981-15-9724-4_7

Reina, R., & Scarozza, D. (2020). Human resource management in the public administration. In *Organizational development in public administration* (pp. 61–101). Palgrave Macmillan.

Rodrigues, M., Machado, R., Costa, R., & Gonçalves, S. (2020, July). Smart cities: Using gamification and emotion detection to improve citizens well fair and commitment. In *Science and Information Conference* (pp. 426–442). Springer.

Scholta, H., & Lindgren, I. (2019). The long and winding road of digital public services-one next step: Proactivity. In *ICIS*.

Sharma, E., & Das, S. (2020). Measuring impact of Indian ports on environment and effectiveness of remedial measures towards environmental pollution. *International Journal of Environment and Waste Management, 25*(3), 356–380. https://doi.org/10.1504/IJEWM.2019.10021787

Sharma, E., & Das, S. (2021). Integrated model for women empowerment in rural India. *Journal of International Development*, 1–18. https://doi.org/10.1002/jid.3539

Sharma, E., Nigam, N., & Das, S. (2020). Measuring gap in expected and perceived quality of ICT enabled customer services: A systematic study of top ten retailers of India. *International Journal of Applied Systemic Studies, 9*(2), 159–184. https://doi.org/10.1504/ijass.2020.113260

Siha, S. M., & Monroe, R. W. (2006). Telecommuting's past and future: A literature review and research agenda. *Business Process Management Journal.*

Singh, L. B., Mondal, S. R., & Das, S. (2020). Human resource practices & their observed significance for Indian SMEs. *Revista ESPACIOS, 41*(7). http://www.revistaespacios.com/a20v41n07/20410715.html

Singh, S., Mondal, S., Singh, L. B., Sahoo, K. K., & Das, S. (2020). An empirical evidence study of consumer perception and socioseconomic profiles for digital stores in Vietnam. *Sustainability, 12*(5), 1716. https://doi.org/10.3390/su12051716

Siri, R., & Das, S. (2021). A study on processing of information storage & use of new age consumers in digital wellness sector through story telling anda creating interest. In *Digital entertainment* (pp. 45–63). Palgrave Macmillan. https://doi.org/10.1007/978-981-15-9724-4_3

Siri, R., Mondal, S. R., & Das, S. (2020). Hydropower: A renewable energy resource for sustainability in terms of climate change and environmental protection. In *The handbook of environmental chemistry*. Springer. https://doi.org/10.1007/698_2020_635

Soukhoroukova, M. S., & Skiera, B. (2012). Sourcing, filtering, and evaluating new product ideas: An empirical exploration of the performance of idea markets. *Journal of Product Innovation Management, 29*(1), 100–112.

Sullivan, J. X. (2008). Borrowing during unemployment unsecured debt as a safety net. *Journal of Human Resources, 43*(2), 383–412.

Taleb, N. N. (2010). *Why did the crisis of 2008 happen?* Available at SSRN 1666042.

Toapanta, S. M. T., Diaz, A. F. G., Subia, D. F. H., & Gallegos, L. E. M. (2019). Proposal for a security model for a popular voting system process in Latin America. *Advances in Science, Technology and Engineering Systems, 4*(5), 53–60.

Valcárcel Dueñas, M., & Solórzano García, M. (2019). Digitalización, monitorización y evaluación del impacto de la Economía Social. Análisis en el Tercer Sector de Acción Social español: el caso de Juntos por el Empleo.

Van, N. T. T., Vrana, V., Duy, N. T., Minh, D. X. H., Dzung, P. T., Mondal, S. R., & Das, S. (2020). The role of human-machine interactive devices for post-COVID-19 innovative sustainable tourism in Ho Chi Minh City, Vietnam. *Sustainability, 12*(22), 9523. https://doi.org/10.3390/su12229523

Van Dijk, G., Minocha, S., & Laing, A. (2007). Consumers, channels and communication: Online and offline communication in service consumption. *Interacting with Computers, 19*, 7–19.

Vargo, S. L., & Lusch, R. F. (2004). The four service marketing myths: Remnants of a goods-based, manufacturing model. *Journal of Service Research, 6*(4), 324–335.

Verjans, S. (2005). Bricolage as a way of life–Improvisation and irony in information systems. *European Journal of Information Systems, 14*(5), 504–506.

Versteegh, R. (2010). Smart Work Centers: Improve collaboration and productivity while reducing ecological footprint. http://www.slideshare.net/Ray1961/cisco-smart-work-center

Watts, S. (2016). *The Internet of Things (IoT): Applications, technology, and privacy issues*. Nova Science Publishers, Inc.

Working, O. S. (2019). *Smart working really: Flexibility is not enough*. Milan Report.

Wright, P. M., & Snell, S. A. (1998). Toward a unifying framework for exploring fit and flexibility in strategic human resource management. *Academy of Management Review, 23*(4), 756–772.

Wrzesniewski, A., & Dutton, J. E. (2001). Crafting a job: Revisioning employees as active crafters of their work. *Academy of Management Review, 26*(2), 179–201.

Yegen, C., & Mondal, S. R. (2021). Sharenting: A new paradigm of digital entertainment of new age parenting and social media. In *Digital entertainment* (pp. 213–231). Palgrave Macmillan. https://doi.org/10.1007/978-981-15-9724-4_11

Yeo, R. K., & Marquardt, M. J. (2015). (Re) interpreting action, learning, and experience: Integrating action learning and experiential learning for HRD. *Human Resource Development Quarterly, 26*(1), 81–107.

Yin, R. K. (2013). Validity and generalization in future case study evaluations. *Evaluation, 19*(3), 321–332.

Yin, R. K. (2009). *Case study research: Design and methods* (Vol. 5). Sage.

Zardini, A., Rossignoli, C., & Ricciardi, F. (2016). A bottom-up path for IT management success: From infrastructure quality to competitive excellence. *Journal of business research, 69*(5), 1747–1752.

CHAPTER 5

Effective Management of a Remote Workforce for Covid-19: A Proposed Research Model Toward Smart Working Adoption Within Organizations

Concetta Metallo, Rocco Agrifoglio, and Ferrara Maria

Introduction

The lockdown caused by the COVID-19 epidemic has encouraged the widespread use of smart working (SW) for all activities that can be carried out remotely within organizations (Das, 2021a; Duy et al., 2020; Mondal, 2021; Van et al., 2020). This experience has shown that SW can be applied on a large scale by organizations and that it could continue

C. Metallo · F. Maria
Department of Sciences and Technology, University of Naples Parthenope, Naples, Italy
e-mail: metallo@uniparthenope.it

F. Maria
e-mail: maria.ferrara@uniparthenope.it

S. R. Mondal et al. (eds.), *HR Analytics and Digital HR Practices*,
https://doi.org/10.1007/978-981-16-7099-2_5

to be used as an organizational practice in the future when the emergency period will be overcome (Dua et al., 2021; Siri et al., 2020; Singh, Mondal, & Das, 2020; Singh et al., 2020).

SW was defined as a flexible form of work where workers doing a part of their working activities out of the organizational workspace thanks to new technologies usage. It could be defined as a flexible form of work where workers doing a part of their working activities out of the organizational workspace thanks to new technologies usage (Das, 2020; Mondal, 2020; Nadanyiova & Das, 2020; Sharma & Das, 2020). Building upon the telework's concept, SW was recognized as a new model of work that adds greater mobility, autonomy, and versatility to workers in the choice of working places, times, and ways. It also allows organizations to generate savings, useful for further investment, as well as to reduce traffic emissions and traffic-related air pollution (Behera et al., 2019; Gupta et al., 2019; Mohanty et al., 2019; Mondal & Sahoo, 2020). On the basis of these reasons, some Northern European Countries are changing their legislation plans to make the option to work from home mandatory. In this regards, numerous academicians, managers, and politics look at SW as a disruptive innovation that is changing the organizational working ways.

Although there are widespread advantages for individual, firms, and society, SW adoption is not an organizational innovation that organizations can introduce inside easily and without problems. For instance, IS research has shown that teleworkers, such as smart workers, are more prone to problems of social and professional isolation that could lead them to organizational issues in terms of motivation, satisfaction, and job performance. Since not all individuals are suited to remote work, organizations should firstly select smart workers who have personality traits consistent with remote work, as well as manage them properly afterward. Moreover, the adoption of SW also requires a rethinking of current human resource management practices that in most companies have been designed to manage traditional workers, rather than smart workers.

The research aims to investigate the HRM practices enabling organizations to manage effectively smart workers. Linking the HRM literature

---

R. Agrifoglio (✉)
Department of Business and Economics, University of Naples Parthenope, Naples, Italy
e-mail: rocco.agrifoglio@uniparthenope.it

and the IS research, we will propose an integrated research model based on three HRM systems (mobility and development, evaluation, and rewards) that could be adopted by organizations to effectively manage the smart workers workforce.

The book chapter will be articulated as follow.

First, the section "Smart Working Within Organizations" will provide an overview of smart working by focusing on main advantages and disadvantages for individuals, firms, and society. The section "Designing Smart Working and HRM Within Organizations" will present the proposed research model (Fig. 5.1) and will focuses on HRM systems and practices for designing SW in organizations. Moreover, the section "The Mobility and Development HRM System" will focus on mobility and development HRM system, the section "The Evaluation HRM System" will focus on

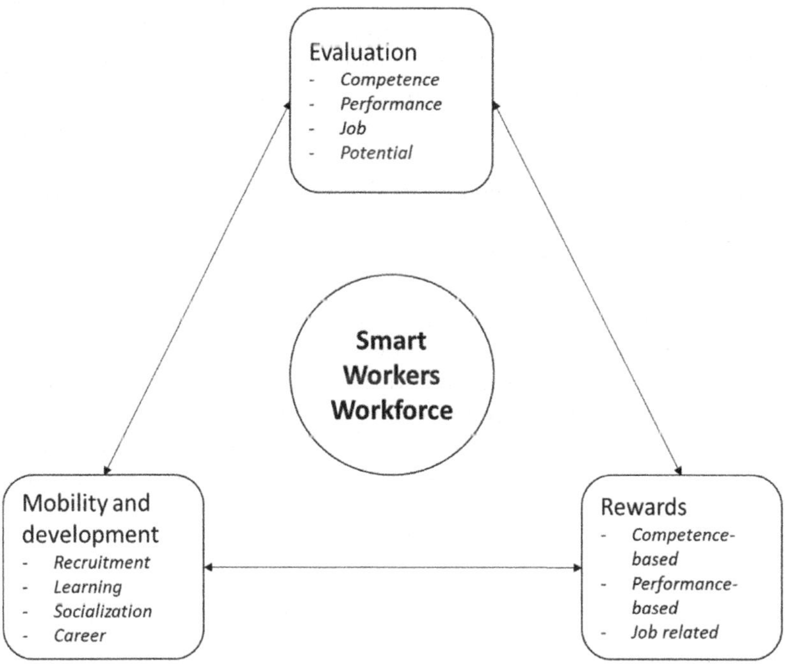

Fig. 5.1 A proposed research model for effective management of a remote workforce

evaluation HRM system and, finally, the section "The Rewards HRM System" will focus on rewards ones.

Smart Working Within Organizations

Smart working is a very interesting topic that has been studied in many disciplinary areas. Its theoretical importance to organizational literature derives from its diffusion in real-world business as well as its profound implications for a company's operations.

The topic of smart working can be placed in the wider debate on flexible working. It is well-established that an increase in work flexibility is the result of the diffusion of new technologies, their applications, and organizational and managerial implications that derive from them. In fact, technological advances have led to an increase in synchronous and asynchronous communication channels that allow information to be available and transferred between users operating in different workplaces.

These new digital tools have favored the diffusion of distinct forms of work organization based on remote work, whereby several actors can work in different places and times, even within a group. Over time, the concept of smart working has evolved from a synonym of telework to include any work carried out and/or shared in a remote location through the use of computer and telematic technologies.

Telework was certainly the first and most widespread form of smart working, in which an individual (self-employed or employee) carries out a work activity using a computer and telematic tools in a place separate and remote from the company headquarters. However, smart working is much broader than telework. Telework focuses on the location, and the main types of telework found in literature and empirical evidence distinguish between (Bailey & Kurland, 1999) home-based telecommuting,[1] satellite offices, tele cottages or neighborhood work centers,[2] and mobile working.

[1] In particular, work at home is "a general term which refers to any employment related work performed at home, regardless of whether the individual who is performing the work is an employee of an organization or is self-employed" (Venkatesh & Vitalari, 1992). Kraut (1989) also distinguishes four types of home-based workers: workers who operate from home, moonlighters, the self-employed, and professionals who do not usually work at a fixed office location.

[2] Telecentres can be urban or rural, like the one in Castelnuovo nei Monti, which opened in 1997 and was the first in Italy. Rural telecentres represent a peculiar typology

The advent of digital technologies has made this conceptualization of smart working obsolete, shifting attention to the digital environment where work can not only be done, but also shared. This results in new forms of work that emphasize cooperative work, such as co-working. On the one hand, smart working helps repopulate areas of the South, lake and mountain regions, and internal areas that are likely to decline in population: For instance, In Italy, several people who work for Northern organizations are joining a cultural movement named South working aimed to improve the economy of the Southern regions of Italy by moving to the cities and villages they are from.

On the other hand, it helps satisfy the needs of workers who would like to live elsewhere because they are not satisfied with their everyday life. Accordingly, this study adopts the broader meaning of smart working, which includes telework and all forms of virtual work with central knowledge sharing and cooperation between remote workers.

The growing attention paid by scholars to the phenomenon of smart working is often the result of an underlying economic trend that emphasizes the use of more flexible working relationships. However, this trend cannot be considered the main reason for the attention to the issue in question.

The multi-disciplinarity of the object of investigation has resulted in numerous theoretical contributions that have occasionally emphasized different aspects with respect to which the phenomenon of remote working has been analyzed.

The present work focuses on the feasibility and effectiveness of smart working. It is believed that the success of any remote working initiative is closely related to the ability of the organization that implements it to manage it effectively. The effective management of smart working can be understood in terms of the effective management of remote workers, since it is precisely in the methods of governance of work relations and human resources management (HRM) that companies encounter the greatest difficulties (O'Neill et al., 2009).

of telework centers, generally called telecottages. The first telecottages were built in Scandinavia and later spread to Ireland, France, England, Wales, and Scotland. Usually, such centers involve the reconversion of country houses and farms, with the main purpose of encouraging the development of technological knowledge and high professional profiles in remote areas, allowing residents to find a job.

The criticality of the management aspects, as determining factors in favoring a wide diffusion of smart working, has already been emphasized by previous research, in particular, by studies focusing on telecommuting (DeSanctis, 1984; Duxbury et al., 1987). However, the definition of the effective management of remote workers is a question that has not received an exhaustive answer.

Advantages and Disadvantages of Remote Working

The use of various forms of remote working has significant consequences both for the individual workers involved in the project and for the organization that implements it. In this sense, numerous studies have been conducted to highlight how the organization is impacted, and the advantages and disadvantages associated with smart working. The impact on the organization depends on the specific situations that characterize the actors involved (Boell et al., 2016; Dima et al., 2019; Leonardi et al., 2010). The main advantages and disadvantages associated with remote working have traditionally been distinguished using three levels of analysis: organization, worker, and society. Many scholars agree that smart working leads to an increase in workers' productivity because working at home involves fewer distractions than the traditional workplace (Olson, 1989). At the same time, the spatial and temporal flexibility that can be associated with some forms of smart working is often interpreted by the worker in terms of autonomy to choose the most appropriate workplace and plan the working day according to his or her needs and preferences (Olson, 1982; Salomon & Salomon, 1984; Venkatesh & Vitalari, 1992).

The main benefits for smart workers are as follows (Becker, 1986; Hill et al., 1996; Kurland & Egan, 1999; Mokhtarian & Salomon, 1997; Teo & Lim, 1998): an increase in flexibility, autonomy, and control of work activity leading to increased motivation to work; a reduction in mobility costs and stress due to travelling time and traffic; improved work/life balance; the free choice of a place to live; strengthening of ties with the local community; possibility of continuous training and refresher courses that improve the cultural level of the smart worker; as well as the propensity to develop and maintain his or her learning ability.

In addition, smart working allows companies to benefit from a reduction in office costs and company size (Kurland & Egan, 1999), greater organizational flexibility, low absenteeism, and turnover (Kraut, 1989), improved attractiveness during recruitment and hiring, and greater ability to retain talent and high professional profiles (Kurland & Egan, 1999; Olson, 1982; Salomon & Salomon, 1984; Stone & Colella, 1996).

However, literature also highlights non-linear relationships between smart working, productivity, and job performance. There are numerous studies that emphasize an increase in productivity and job performance as the main positive consequences of smart working, even compared to traditional working methods (Hill et al., 1998; Neal et al., 1993). By contrast, a reduction in job performance (Bailey & Kurland, 1999; Suh & Lee, 2017) negatively impacts the smart workers' motivation and job satisfaction. In fact, smart working (Albano et al., 2019) is believed to hinder the development of social relationships and networks, lead to a decrease in teamwork, and cause conflicts and resentments with fellow workers of the traditional type. It is clear that all these implications derive essentially from the "distance" between the smart worker and organization (Müller & Niessen, 2018). Therefore, it is a common opinion that the main consequences of this "distance" can be traced to the problem of the social and professional isolation of the smart worker (Even, 2020; Golden et al., 2008; Orhan et al., 2016).

Social isolation manifests itself in the disappearance of informal interactions between the worker and colleagues, supervisors, and friends within the organization. Of course, for the smart worker who works remotely, the possibilities for face-to-face social interactions with colleagues and supervisors are greatly reduced (e.g., Feldman & Gainey, 1997). However, it should be noted that social isolation tends to manifest mainly in teleworking at home rather than in other types of smart working. The absence of social relationships and social networks results in a lack of informal learning, less non-verbal communication, and difficulty creating and supporting a shared organizational culture, which negatively affect job performance (Bailey & Kurland, 1999). It has been observed (Pinsonneault & Boisvert, 2001) that social isolation generates non-uniform reactions from individuals and is perceived differently by teleworkers.

In addition to social isolation, smart working sometimes results in professional isolation, which is the fear that the remote worker will not receive career advancement opportunities, benefit from promotions, or receive other organizational awards (Bailey & Kurland, 1999; Kurland & Egan, 1999). Professional isolation is closely related to the way the worker perceives the relationship between himself and his organization. Numerous studies show that workers believe that "out of sight" equals "out of mind," when it comes to the relationship between the organization and smart workers (Alexander, 1999; Watad & DiSanzo, 2000). This belief emphasizes the ambiguities and distortions that characterize the perceptive process of the organization's smart workers. This results in dynamics that are similar to professional isolation, the loss of the sense of belonging to the company, and a decrease in work motivation and performance (Hartman & Hasher, 1991; Kurland & Egan, 1999; Olson, 1982; Wright & Oldford, 1993).

In general, literature shows that social and professional isolation have significant implications for employees in terms of their identification with the workplace, organizational citizenship behavior, organizational commitment, career advancement opportunities, and increased stress due to a lack of work–life balance (Feldman & Gainey, 1997; Hilbrecht et al., 2008; Weinert et al., 2014).

It should also be noted that supervisors usually do not trust this form of organizational flexibility due to the difficulty of directly observing the work performance of the smart worker, thus generating problems related to the control and measurement of performance (Brunelle, 2013; Collins et al., 2016; Konradt et al., 2003; Kurland & Egan, 1999; Salomon & Salomon, 1984; Wright & Oldford, 1993).

From these considerations it emerges that smart working has many problematic aspects as it has significant implications for the company and the worker, which need to be properly managed. In particular, a company opting for smart working is involved in a radical process of change that involves the reorganization of business processes, organizational culture, and human resources management policies (Kwon & Jeon, 2020).

In fact, the availability of technological tools alone is not sufficient to guarantee the satisfaction of organizational efficiency requirements. First, the knowledge of how to use the tools to support communication, rather than the availability of technologies, is important. Technological knowledge among remote workers is a critical and fundamental requirement for the optimal use of IT tools, which relates to work performance. Moreover, the development of technological knowledge is important for remote worker, traditional colleagues, and supervisors in order to allow effective communication and interaction between the remote worker and the organization. The effective use of technology in virtual communication processes requires governance rules in work processes and communication methods to establish shared languages, message content, frequency of responses, quality and correctness of communications, and so on.

In virtual communication, the cognitive distortions that typically characterize traditional communication and decision-making processes tend to be accentuated. The perception and interpretation of the message by the receiver and sender are different, and this results in recurrent cases of ambiguity. There is an increased likelihood of misunderstandings, conflicts, construction of false stereotypes, and false impressions of the other actors involved in the interaction. Therefore, it is necessary to develop a set of rules and standards for interactions, communication protocols, and terminology, which explicitly define behaviors that must be adopted by remote workers to achieve effective communication.

Therefore, the company's ability to properly manage smart working becomes critical (i.e., to provide adequate tools and mechanisms to govern the consequences resulting from the "distance" between the smart worker and the organization).

Hence, there is a need to identify the main implications of the use of remote working on human resources management, in order to highlight those areas that are most critical and, consequently, to envisage more efficient solutions in terms of human resources management policies.

Designing Smart Working & HRM Within Organizations

Although remote working enables organizations greater organizational flexibility, with considerable advantages for the company and the workers, it has not had the expected diffusion over the years. Many scholars have tried to provide an explanation for this situation, highlighting how, in many cases, the idea prevails that "out of sight is out of mind" led the management's decisions (Sewell & Taskin, 2015).

In fact, the problems related to remote working and the difficulties that the actors involved encounter have been widely highlighted.[3] These problems include how to manage perceived social and professional isolation and encourage the identification and development of feelings of organizational citizenship, such as "how to design career paths," "how

[3] For a review of the psychological consequences of remote working, see Leonardi and Harrison (2007).

to design control systems and with which techniques to evaluate performance," and "how to favor the management of times and places of work and non-work."

These problems, combined with a managerial culture in several countries that does not promote organizational innovation, have certainly slowed down the spread of remote working in favor of more centralized organizational models characterized by greater rigidity. The COVID-19 health emergency has pushed states to put restrictive measures in place that limit or prohibit mobility and access to the workplace. Traditional forms of work organization have proved to be unsuitable for the performance of work activities, pushing managers and entrepreneurs to approach more flexible and remotely oriented configurations such as for example, smart working. Many organizations have been forced to implement smart working to allow their workers to perform their work at home. This experience has shown that smart working can be applied on a large scale and could continue to function as an organizational practice in the future after the pandemic. The future of smart working and the effectiveness of new forms of organizational requires the design and implementation of an HRM model that covers the organizational and individual needs of smart workers.

Accordingly, it is necessary to analyze the three HRM systems (mobility and development, evaluation, and rewards[4]) that could be adopted by organizations to effectively manage their remote workforce. Figure 5.1 shows the proposed research model.

The Mobility and Development HRM System

The main area of human resources management that is particularly critical for remote working is staff mobility and development systems.

Numerous studies (e.g., Feldman & Gainey, 1997; Raghuram et al., 2001; Venkatesh & Vitalari, 1992) have shown that individual characteristics such as age, experience, and gender, can influence an individual's predisposition to work remotely and determine the success of a telework initiative. In operational terms, this tends to be a guiding element in smart worker recruitment and selection policies.

[4] For an in-depth analysis of HRM systems, see Grandori (1999, 2001).

In particular, the most relevant implications for personnel selection tend to be closely linked to social and professional isolation, which is the main consequence of teleworking as noted in the literature (e.g., Hartman & Hasher, 1991; Kurland & Egan, 1999; Olson, 1982, 1989; Wright & Oldford, 1993).

The use of different forms of remote working, which includes smart working, requires a careful analysis of workers' personalities in order to understand their adaptation to work and career. Therefore, the use of techniques aimed at analyzing personality in the selection of smart working personnel tends to be particularly important.

A technique generally used for personality analysis, based essentially on the study of personality traits, is represented by the Big Five (e.g., Barrick & Mount, 1991; Liu & Campbell, 2017; McCrae & Costa, 1987; Smith et al., 2018). Through this technique, it is possible to detect the personality traits of workers, in order to highlight the individual profiles most suitable for remote working, with the aim of minimizing the implications related to both social and professional isolation (Feldman & Gainey, 1997). In this sense, building upon previous research (Barrick & Mount, 1991; Digman, 1990), it is possible to assume that HRM managers should use the Big Five technique in the workers' selection phase to select smart workers who are less likely to be affected by distance and isolation.

With reference to telework, some research (e.g., Baumeister & Leary, 1995; Clark et al., 2012) has shown that social isolation negatively influences individuals' ability to satisfy their need for affiliation. For example, it has been hypothesized that workers with certain personality traits, such as extroversion and amiability, are less suitable for telework because they would be greatly affected by isolation. At the same time, it is assumed that a greater predisposition to telework can be found in the presence of traits such as openness to experience (Feldman & Gainey, 1997). Other scholars (e.g., Rabbie, 1963) have observed that anxious and depressed workers generally prefer to interact constantly with others, in order to acquire greater security; a low level of emotional stability (tendency to be self-confident and poised) is not compatible with telework opportunities (Feldman & Gainey, 1997). Moreover, literature indicates that working with other people can influence individual work effort due to silent competition in productivity (Zajonc, 1965); therefore, low levels of conscientiousness (understood as the propensity to be organized and self-disciplined) is more likely to result in isolation being connected to telework (Feldman & Gainey, 1997).

In addition to social isolation, telework also tends to generate professional isolation, that is, the perceived fear of the teleworker not advancing in their careers, and not benefiting from promotions or other organizational awards (Bailey & Kurland, 1999; Kurland & Egan, 1999). The study conducted by Wiesenfeld and colleagues (2001) identifies individual attributes and employment relationships as determinants of professional isolation.

With regard to individual attributes, it should be noted that the need for affiliation, understood as an attribute of personality, positively influences the organizational identification of the worker. Therefore, individuals with different levels of this attribute will present different levels of organizational identification and predisposition to smart working. Emphasis is therefore once again placed on the importance of the phase of search and selection of individuals for smart working and analysis of the worker's personality as a central element for the success of this form of work flexibility.

However, the same research (Wiesenfeld et al., 2001) shows the presence of a further determinant of identification—the perceived work-based social support (i.e., signals to which smart workers are exposed), which indicate their belonging to the organization. In other words, perceived work-based social support refers to the degree to which individuals perceive that they are socially integrated with other members of the organization (Aspinwall & Taylor, 1992; Dormann & Zapf, 1999; Wanberg & Banas, 2000). Social support positively influences organizational identification. Social support is generally provided by colleagues and supervisors (i.e., by those members of the organization who are in constant contact with the teleworker) (Wiesenfeld et al., 1998; Sproull & Kiesler, 1991). The level of social support depends on how these individuals (colleagues and supervisors) perceive smart working, depending on whether they give it a positive or negative value.

Perceived social support also plays a role in moderating the effects of the need for affiliation; that is, the positive relationship between the need for affiliation and identification is attenuated when the perceived social support is relatively high (Wiesenfeld et al., 2001).

It is believed that the results of such research can also be extended to smart working, which, unlike teleworking, allows workers to work remotely without space–time limitations. However, although smart working allows the worker to decide the place (where) and time (when) of work, working from home could encourage the emergence of problems relating to social and professional isolation. The results of Wiesenfeld and colleagues (2001) are of considerable significance in terms of the management implications they generate. In fact, they place emphasis on those situational factors that allow to organizations overcome the differences between individuals related to their need for affiliation and organizational identity. Moreover, if personality attributes constitute a determinant of identification—which can be a little influenced by human resources management policies, if not through selection- work-based social support certainly represents a factor that can be more easily managed by the organization through the use of special socialization methods. It is possible, for example, to create preparatory courses for virtual interactions between teleworkers and their supervisors, organize periodic meetings between teleworkers and supervisors/traditional workers, promote the company strategy remotely through press releases, invest in new technologies to support electronic communication with training for workers, and encourage traditional workers to interact with virtual workers. Therefore, it becomes essential for managers to communicate frequently by phone or email with individual smart workers to reduce the feeling of isolation and promote feelings of identification. Staff training is another critical area in mobility and development systems with regard to smart working. In this sense, training involves not only the smart worker but traditional workers and supervisors.

First, training must be aimed at the development of technological knowledge, necessary both for the use of IT tools to support the performance of work remotely and to enable effective communication and interaction between smart workers and the organization to which they belong (colleagues and supervisors). Therefore, training policies place particular emphasis on technological knowledge. A training "expert" is usually included, who is a resource whose task is to provide assistance in the presence of technical problems and to facilitate interaction if necessary. With this type of support, the smart worker will be able to focus on the objectives to be pursued, rather than on technical problems (Metallo, 2007).

Moreover, the training policies to be used in relation to a telework project should favor the development of certain skills in the actors involved, aiming at fostering collaboration, socialization, and communication. For example, with reference to virtual teams, the skills needed for an effective functioning of the group have been highlighted (Cascio, 2000): virtual-collaborative skill, virtual-socialization skill, and virtual-communication skill. The virtual-collaborative skills refer to the ability of members to exchange opinions and ideas freely without fear of receiving criticism, summarize and share opinions and ideas in a written text, write down in a special document the initial comments and subsequent agreements on work activities, and respect deadlines. Virtual-socialization skills refer to the ability of members to communicate with others in real time, solicit feedback from the team during the performance of their activities, share personal information, express opinions on ideas and tasks carried out by others, apologize for mistakes made, and spontaneously offer to fill roles. Virtual-communication skills refer to members' ability to rephrase sentences more clearly so that all members can understand what they are saying and respond to messages within the same working day.

In other words, training policies must be able to direct the behavior of actors toward the development of a common culture, trust, shared values, and languages. Therefore, training, as a human resources management system, becomes critical in increasing the success of a telework initiative and must involve not only teleworkers, but also supervisors and managers, traditional workers, and, therefore, the whole organization that has decided to implement this form of remote working (Cascio, 2000; Das, 2021b).

The Evaluation HRM System

The assessment of human resources focuses on the following four dimensions: potential, position, skills, and performance. With regard to smart working, the potential and performance of workers are more relevant in terms of the personnel management system in organizations.

The assessment of potential aims to understand whether a worker has the skills and aptitude to remotely perform a part of his or her work. As noted above, this dimension is more critical as time spent working remotely increases. It is therefore essential for organizations to be able to assess the potential of workers who will be employed as smart workers in order to avoid or limit individual problems typical of working remotely (see section "The Mobility and Development HRM System" for more details). The evaluation of potential is an activity closely linked to the recruitment and selection of personnel to be employed in organizations.

It is precisely at this stage that the human resources manager or organizational manager is called upon to assess the potential of the smart worker in terms of skills, aptitude, and personality. For more information on the assessment techniques identified in the managerial and organizational literature for the selection of remote workers, see section "The Mobility and Development HRM System".

The evaluation of the performance of remote workers is particularly critical for organizations that are less innovative in personnel management. One of the main difficulties of remote working relates to the control and measurement of performance, trust, and management of remote workers (Kurland & Egan, 1999; Metallo, 2007; Salomon & Salomon, 1984; Wright & Oldford, 1993): "How do you measure productivity, build trust, and manage people who are physically out of sight?" (Mason, 1993). It is an established view that the control of smart worker performance should be based on results rather than on observation of behavior (Olson, 1989). Therefore, the basis of the assessment ("what" is assessed) is the result (i.e., the individual's contribution through a comparison of expected and achieved results). In this sense, in contexts where distance work is preferred, it is considered necessary to move from a "face-time culture" to a "results-oriented culture" and placing emphasis on the result rather than behavior.

According to Grandori (1999), the following issue related to the design of an evaluation system based on results tends to arise: "the further one moves away from the characteristics and attributes of the actors (the skills) and moves towards the results, the less what is evaluated can be attributed in a deterministic way to the actor being evaluated, especially in activities subject to uncertainty" (p. 341).

In addition, another problem relates to methods of measuring performance results ("how" it is assessed). The method of evaluation by objectives, particularly suitable in the presence of high decisional autonomy and discretion of the assessor, tends to be a valid reference model in the context of smart working, where the worker enjoys wide autonomy in relation to the manner in which his or her performance is carried out. It was noted, however, that the main consequence of a results-based assessment system is a greater formalization of job characteristics, performance standards, and communication. Therefore, in a remote working context, performance evaluation, since it cannot be based on direct supervision, determines the institutionalization of rules that clearly specify the job description and expectations regarding results (Olson, 1982; Zuboff, 1982). At the same time, the distance between the supervisor and worker determines the prevalence of formal communication models (Sundstrom et al., 1990). In this sense, it is necessary to define communication protocols and message content, in order to make clear the behaviors and actions to be taken by remote workers.

The formalization and standardization of rules reduce the prejudices and distortions that typically characterize the perceptual process of the worker concerning his/her relationship with the organization and the evaluation system (Thibaut & Walker, 1975). In fact, there is a general consensus that the evaluation process, in order to be effective and valid, must be perceived as fair by the actors involved. Some scholars (e.g., Kurland & Egan, 1999; Skarlicki & Folger, 1997) use the concept of "organizational justice" and recognize that the presence of some elements is considered relevant (adequate communication, impartial listening, and evidence-based judgements) can guarantee the fairness of the evaluation process. It follows that a fair valuation system should be matched by a fair reward system.

In the context of smart working, the need for the worker to perceive assessment systems as fair and equitable tends to become more important. In line with some organizational justice studies, according to which the level of acceptance and perceived fairness of the remuneration system increases as the transparency of the system increases (Folger & Greenberg, 1985), the formalization, clear communication, and stability of the evaluation criteria represent mechanisms that tend to guarantee teleworkers consistency and fairness of treatment in the evaluation of their performance compared to that of traditional workers (Hartman & Hasher, 1991).

However, in relation to the measurement of performance results, difficulties may arise from interdependence on other actors, if the smart worker is part of a virtual team and what is evaluated is the result of the working group. In this case, it also becomes problematic to observe, evaluate, and measure the result of the individual worker's performance. The main ways, suggested by the literature (e.g., Grandori, 1999, 2001; Metallo, 2007), to overcome these difficulties are essentially to use group or company performance indicators (evaluating the collective results of the interdependent actors), widen the range of parameters of evaluation of the results considered, and combine the evaluation of results with some parameters of evaluation of behavior. Indeed, "under conditions of high interdependence, the most effective evaluation systems will be mixed and composite, rather than unilaterally based on the evaluation of inputs or outputs" (Grandori, 1999, p. 345). Therefore, with respect to performance evaluation, it can be effective to combine the evaluation of results with some parameters of behavior evaluation.

The evaluation of behaviors consists in "measuring how objectives have been achieved by comparing expected and implemented performance behaviors" (Tosi et al., 2004, p. 339). In a remote working context, the technologies used for interaction also represent a means to support supervision and control (e.g., Kirkman et al., 2002; Townsend et al., 2012). It is possible to control the data present in the databases; the communications and information exchanged during virtual meetings, stored in special servers; the reports and all the documentation produced; and to supervise the electronic discussions, emails, and other activities. In addition, it is possible to use not only objective evaluation parameters but also more subjective ones such as, for example, the ability to be proactive in virtual meetings or to suggest strategies for improving the effectiveness of the work.

In traditional work contexts, individual performance evaluation is carried out by the direct supervisor or manager. In the case of smart working, instead, the manager-assessor is distant and is not able to grasp all the aspects that characterize the worker's behavior and his or her ability to interact and dynamically assume roles. For this reason, in such contexts, it is preferable to integrate the evaluation of the manager with that of other sources, using multi-source-feedback evaluation systems or the so-called "360-degree evaluation." With this system, the worker is also evaluated by his colleagues (i.e., employees, internal and external clients).

The Rewards HRM System

The assessment of position and performance forms the basis for the definition of workers' remuneration. Specifically, the evaluation of the position allows the identification of a remuneration commensurate with the time spent and the specific task of the worker, while the evaluation of performance refers to a remuneration commensurate with the objectives that the company has agreed with the worker. The evaluation of the position makes it possible to define the fixed part of the remuneration, while the evaluation of performance refers to the variable part. In the case of smart working, evidently, the evaluation of performance is the most feasible option.

Among the various purposes of performance evaluation, the main one is to "establish an information base to which to link rewards (monetary and non-monetary) according to contributions" (Grandori, 1999, p. 341). There is, therefore, a close relationship between the evaluation of contributions and rewards, which can be monetary and non-monetary.

With reference to non-monetary rewards, "social exchanges" inevitably take place in the working groups that have as their object "social rewards" such as status, power, esteem, and membership (Grandori, 1999, 2001). Social rewards are particularly important not only for traditional workers but especially for those who work outside the company boundaries. Specifically, defining a system of personnel evaluation that allows workers to obtain social rewards for the achievement of objectives established a priori can be particularly useful for smart workers, who, compared to workers physically present in offices, suffer more from problems related to commitment and organizational identification. To this end, organizations should design and formalize a system for evaluating non-monetary rewards that allow workers, especially remote workers, to feel as though they are an integral part of the organization based on the rewards they receive.

With reference to monetary rewards, it should be noted that they are related to different forms of variable remuneration. In this way, it is possible to link remuneration to the achievement of certain objectives through different formulas, which favors social control and cooperative behavior. There are different forms of variable remuneration that could be applied to smart workers, which are Management by Objectives (MBO) and Management by Performance (MBP).

The MBO is an approach to goal management introduced in 1954 by Peter Drucker, which allows the employee to agree on their work objectives with the company. It is a systematic approach because it allows top management to break down a long-term objective into short-term objectives and then assign them to the lowest levels through a process of delegation and organizational decentralization.

> The system of management by objectives can be described as a process whereby the superior and subordinate jointly identify common goals, define each individual's major areas of responsibility in terms of the results

> expected of him or her, and use these measures as guides for operating the unit and assessing the contribution of each of its members. (Odiorne, 1970)

A possible disadvantage of the MBO system is the lack of long-term attention. In fact, focusing on the short term, guides the company with a very narrow vision, oriented to ordinary business, preventing the pursuit of strategic objectives. To overcome the critical issues inherent in the MBO, a new model was developed, Management by Performance. This makes it possible to define a long-term strategic vision and operational activities useful for achieving it. It allows results to be measured by aligning them with the company's vision. The identification of performance measures, both financial and non-financial, supports the decision-making process, in line with pre-established strategic objectives and all improvement initiatives to be launched to achieve the strategies themselves.

Piecework is a form of remuneration in which the worker is remunerated according to the result obtained, rather than according to the duration of the work. Originally a form of remuneration designed for self-employment, piecework subsequently spread within industrial companies, where it was applied to pay for subordinate work. In fact, while in self-employment, piecework is characterized by the fact that it specifically considers the result of the work done, in subordinate work, the determination of the remuneration through this system uses the worker's performance more properly as a parameter. Therefore, piecework is currently used by organizations to remunerate professional and subordinate remote workers who carry out professional or executive activities, respectively. This is the case, for example, of call center employees who carry out their work outside the company boundaries. Recent evidence from companies, also closely linked to the management of the COVID-19 pandemic, has revealed that piecework is being used to pay smart workers who have worked from home. Although piecework pay is characterized as a fair way of rewarding remote workers, it is also true that the use of this form of remuneration presupposes that the company adopts a "scientific" organization of work, characterized by a high standardization of work activities, to achieve greater efficiency and better control. The adoption of a Tayloristic model of work organization also represents a limit to the use of piecework pay, as workers are not only motivated by pay but also interested in the work they do.

References

Albano, R., Parisi, T., & Tirabeni, L. (2019). Gli smart workers tra solitudine e collaborazione. Cambio. *Rivista sulle Trasformazioni Sociali, 9*(17).

Alexander, G. (1999). Is telecommuting right for you. *Black Enterprise, 29*(11), 61–62.

Aspinwall, L. G., & Taylor, S. E. (1992). Modeling cognitive adaptation: A longitudinal investigation of the impact of individual differences and coping on college adjustment and performance. *Journal of Personality and Social Psychology, 63*(6), 989.

Bailey, N. B. K. D. E., & Kurland, N. B. (1999). The advantages and challenges of working here, there, anywhere, and anytime. *Organizational Dynamics, 28*(2), 53–68.

Barrick, M. R., & Mount, M. K. (1991). The big five personality dimensions and job performance: A meta-analysis. *Personnel Psychology, 44*(1), 1–26.

Baumeister, R. F., & Leary, M. R. (1995). The need to belong: Desire for interpersonal attachments as a fundamental human motivation. *Psychological Bulletin, 117*(3), 497.

Becker, F. D. (1986). Loosely-coupled settings: A strategy for computer-aided work decentralization. *Research in Organizational Behavior, 8*, 199–231.

Behera, M., Dash, M., Ayasa Kanta Mohanty, A. K., & Das, S. (2019). Entrepreneurial ecosystem: A geographical upliftment. *Revista Espacios, 40*, 26–36. http://www.revistaespacios.com/a19v40n01/19400126.html

Boell, S. K., Cecez-Kecmanovic, D., & Campbell, J. (2016). Telework paradoxes and practices: The importance of the nature of work. *New Technology, Work and Employment, 31*(2), 114–131.

Brunelle, E. (2013). Leadership and mobile working: The impact of distance on the superior-subordinate relationship and the moderating effects of leadership style. *International Journal of Business and Social Science, 4*(11), 1–14.

Cascio, W. F. (2000). Managing a virtual workplace. *Academy of Management Perspectives, 14*(3), 81–90.

Clark, L. A., Karau, S. J., & Michalisin, M. D. (2012). Telecommuting attitudes and the 'big five' personality dimensions. *Journal of Management Policy and Practice, 13*(3), 31–46.

Collins, A. M., Hislop, D., & Cartwright, S. (2016). Social support in the workplace between teleworkers, office-based colleagues and supervisors. *New Technology, Work and Employment, 31*(2), 161–175.

Das, S. (2020). Innovations in digital banking service brand equity and millennial consumerism. In *Digital transformation and innovative services for business and learning* (pp. 62–79). IGI Global. https://doi.org/10.4018/978-1-7998-5175-2.ch004

Das, S. (2021a). A systematic study of integrated marketing communication and content management system for millennial consumers. In *Innovations in digital branding and content marketing* (pp. 91–112). IGI Global. https://doi.org/10.4018/978-1-7998-4420-4.ch005

Das, S. (2021b). Search engine optimization and marketing: A recipe for success in digital marketing (1st ed.). CRC Press. https://doi.org/10.1201/978042929850

DeSanctis, G. (1984). Attitudes toward telecommuting: Implications for work-at-home programs. *Information & Management, 7*(3), 133–139.

Digman, J. M. (1990). Personality structure: Emergence of the five-factor model. *Annual Review of Psychology, 41*(1), 417–440.

Dima, A. M., Ţuclea, C. E., Vrânceanu, D. M., & Ţigu, G. (2019). Sustainable social and individual implications of telework: A new insight into the Romanian labor market. *Sustainability, 11*(13), 3506.

Dormann, C., & Zapf, D. (1999). Social support, social stressors at work, and depressive symptoms: Testing for main and moderating effects with structural equations in a three-wave longitudinal study. *Journal of Applied Psychology, 84*(6), 874.

Dua, S., Singh, I., & Das, S. (2021) Banking innovative service with digital brand equity for new age consumers. Internet banking and millennial consumerism. In *Innovations in digital branding and content marketing* (pp. 134–159). IGI Global. https://doi.org/10.4018/978-1-7998-4420-4.ch007

Duxbury, L., Higgins, C., & Irving, R. (1987). Attitudes of managers and employees to telecommuting. *INFOR: Information Systems and Operational Research, 25*(3), 273–285.

Duy, N. T., Mondal, S. R., Van, N. T. T., Dzung, P. T., Minh, D. X. H., & Das, S. (2020). A study on the role of Web 4.0 and 5.0 in the sustainable tourism ecosystem of Ho Chi Minh City, Vietnam. *Sustainability, 12*(17), 7140. https://doi.org/10.3390/su12177140

Even, A. (2020, February 23). The evolution of work: Best practices for avoiding social and organizational isolation in telework employees. Available at SSRN: https://ssrn.com/abstract=3543122 or https://doi.org/10.2139/ssrn.3543122

Feldman, D. C., & Gainey, T. W. (1997). Patterns of telecommuting and their consequences: Framing the research agenda. *Human Resource Management Review, 7*(4), 369–388.

Folger, R., & Greenberg, J. (1985). Procedural justice: An interpretive analysis of personnel systems. In K. M. Rowland & G. R. Ferris (Eds.), *Research in Personnel and Human Resource Management, 3*, 141–183. JAI Press.

Golden, T. D., Veiga, J. F., & Dino, R. N. (2008). The impact of professional isolation on teleworker job performance and turnover intentions: Does time spent teleworking, interacting face-to-face, or having access to communication-enhancing technology matter? *Journal of Applied Psychology, 93*(6), 1412.

Grandori, A. (1999). *Organizzazione e comportamento economico*. Il Mulino.

Grandori, A. (2001). *Organization and economic behavior*. Psychology Press.

Gupta, D. K., Jena, D., Samantaray, A. K., & Das, S. (2019). HRD climate in selected public sector banks in India. *Revista Espacios, 40*(11).

Hartman, M., & Hasher, L. (1991). Aging and suppression: Memory for previously relevant information. *Psychology and Aging, 6*(4), 587.

Hilbrecht, M., Shaw, S. M., Johnson, L. C., & Andrey, J. (2008). 'I'm home for the kids': Contradictory implications for work–life balance of teleworking mothers. *Gender, Work & Organization, 15*(5), 454–476.

Hill, E. J., Hawkins, A. J., & Miller, B. C. (1996). Work and family in the virtual office: Perceived influences of mobile telework. *Family Relations, 45*(3), 293–301.

Hill, E. J., Miller, B. C., Weiner, S. P., & Colihan, J. (1998). Influences of the virtual office on aspects of work and work/life balance. *Personnel Psychology, 51*(3), 667–683.

Kirkman, B. L., Rosen, B., Gibson, C. B., Tesluk, P. E., & McPherson, S. O. (2002). Five challenges to virtual team success: Lessons from Sabre, Inc. *Academy of Management Perspectives, 16*(3), 67–79.

Konradt, U., Hertel, G., & Schmook, R. (2003). Quality of management by objectives, task-related stressors, and non-task-related stressors as predictors of stress and job satisfaction among teleworkers. *European Journal of Work and Organizational Psychology, 12*(1), 61–79.

Kraut, R. E. (1989). Telecommuting: The trade-offs of home work. *Journal of Communication, 39*(3), 19–47.

Kurland, N. B., & Egan, T. D. (1999). Telecommuting: Justice and control in the virtual organization. *Organization Science, 10*(4), 500–513.

Kwon, M., & Jeon, S. H. (2020). Do leadership commitment and performance-oriented culture matter for federal teleworker satisfaction with telework programs? *Review of Public Personnel Administration, 40*(1), 36–55.

Leonardi, P. M., Treem, J. W., & Jackson, M. H. (2010). The connectivity paradox: Using technology to both decrease and increase perceptions of distance in distributed work arrangements. *Journal of Applied Communication Research, 38*(1), 85–105.

Leonardi, R. S., & Harrison, D. A. (2007). The good, the bad, and the unknown about telecommuting: Meta-analysis of psychological mediators and individual consequences. *Journal of Applied Psychology, 92*(6), 1524.

Liu, D., & Campbell, W. K. (2017). The Big Five personality traits, Big Two metatraits and social media: A meta-analysis. *Journal of Research in Personality, 70*, 229–240.

Mason, J. C. (1993). Working in the family way. *Management Review, 82*(7), 25.

McCrae, R. R., & Costa, P. T. (1987). Validation of the five-factor model of personality across instruments and observers. *Journal of Personality and Social Psychology, 52*(1), 81.

Metallo, C. (2007). *L'organizzazione del lavoro a distanza*. Giappichelli.

Mohanty, P. C., Dash, M., Dash, M., & Das, S. (2019). A study on factors influencing training effectiveness. *Revista Espacios, 40*, 7–15. http://www.revistaespacios.com/a19v40n02/19400207.html

Mokhtarian, P. L., & Salomon, I. (1997). Modeling the desire to telecommute: The importance of attitudinal factors in behavioral models. *Transportation Research Part A: Policy and Practice, 31*(1), 35–50.

Mondal, S. (2021). A systematic study of new age consumer engagement and exploration for digital entertainment for over-the-top platforms in various digital media. In *Innovations in digital branding and content marketing* (pp. 113–133). IGI Global. https://doi.org/10.4018/978-1-7998-4420-4.ch006

Mondal, S., & Sahoo, K. K. (2020). A study of green building prospects on sustainable management decision making. In *Green building management and smart automation* (pp. 220–234). IGI Global. https://doi.org/10.4018/978-1-5225-9754-4.ch011

Mondal, S. R. (2020). A systematic study for digital innovation in management education: An integrated approach towards problem-based learning in Vietnam. In *Digital innovations for customer engagement, management, and organizational improvement* (pp. 104–120). IGI Global. https://doi.org/10.4018/978-1-7998-5171-4.ch006

Müller, T., & Niessen, C. (2018). Self-leadership and self-control strength in the work context. *Journal of Managerial Psychology, 33*, 74–92.

Nadanyiova, M., & Das, S. (2020). Millennials as a target segment of socially responsible communication within the business strategy. *Littera Scripta, 13*(1), 119–134. https://doi.org/10.36708/Littera_Scripta2020/1/8

Neal, M. B., Chapman, N. J., Ingersoll-Dayton, B., & Emlen, A. C. (1993). *Balancing work and caregiving for children, adults, and elders*. Sage.

O'Neill, T. A., Hambley, L. A., Greidanus, N. S., MacDonnell, R., & Kline, T. J. (2009). Predicting teleworker success: An exploration of personality, motivational, situational, and job characteristics. *New Technology, Work and Employment, 24*(2), 144–162.

Odiorne, G. S. (1970). How to implement management by objectives. *Industry Week, 166*(18), 40.

Olson, M. H. (1982). New information technology and organizational culture. *MIS Quarterly, 6*, 71–92.

Olson, M. H. (1989). Work at home for computer professionals: Current attitudes and future prospects. *ACM Transactions on Information Systems (TOIS), 7*(4), 317–338.

Orhan, M. A., Rijsman, J. B., & Van Dijk, G. M. (2016). Invisible, therefore isolated: Comparative effects of team virtuality with task virtuality on workplace isolation and work outcomes. *Revista De Psicología Del Trabajo y De Las Organizaciones, 32*(2), 109–122.

Pinsonneault, A., & Boisvert, M. (2001). The impacts of telecommuting on organizations and individuals: A review of the literature. In *Telecommuting and virtual offices: Issues and opportunities* (pp. 163–185). IGI Global.

Rabbie, J. M. (1963). Differential preference for companionship under threat. *The Journal of Abnormal and Social Psychology, 67*(6), 643.

Raghuram, S., Garud, R., Wiesenfeld, B., & Gupta, V. (2001). Factors contributing to virtual work adjustment. *Journal of Management, 27*(3), 383–405.

Salomon, I., & Salomon, M. (1984). Telecommuting: The employee's perspective. *Technological Forecasting and Social Change, 25*(1), 15–28.

Sewell, G., & Taskin, L. (2015). Out of sight, out of mind in a new world of work? Autonomy, control, and spatiotemporal scaling in telework. *Organization Studies, 36*(11), 1507–1529.

Sharma, E., & Das, S. (2020). Measuring impact of Indian ports on environment and effectiveness of remedial measures towards environmental pollution. *International Journal of Environment and Waste Management, 25*(3), 356–380. https://doi.org/10.1504/IJEWM.2019.10021787

Singh, L. B., Mondal, S. R., & Das, S. (2020). Human resource practices & their observed significance for Indian SMEs. *Revista ESPACIOS, 41*(7). http://www.revistaespacios.com/a20v41n07/20410715.html

Singh, S., Mondal, S., Singh, L. B., Sahoo, K. K., & Das, S. (2020). An empirical evidence study of consumer perception and socioeconomic profiles for digital stores in Vietnam. *Sustainability, 12*(5), 1716. https://doi.org/10.3390/su12051716

Siri, R., Mondal, S. R., & Das, S. (2020). Hydropower: A renewable energy resource for sustainability in terms of climate change and environmental protection. In *The handbook of environmental chemistry*. Springer, Berlin, Heidelberg. https://doi.org/10.1007/698_2020_635

Skarlicki, D. P., & Folger, R. (1997). Retaliation in the workplace: The roles of distributive, procedural, and interactional justice. *Journal of Applied Psychology, 82*(3), 434.

Smith, S. A., Patmos, A., & Pitts, M. J. (2018). Communication and teleworking: A study of communication channel satisfaction, personality, and job satisfaction for teleworking employees. *International Journal of Business Communication, 55*(1), 44–68.

Sproull, L., & Kiesler, S. (1991). Computers, networks and work. *Scientific American, 265*(3), 116–127.

Stone, D. L., & Colella, A. (1996). A model of factors affecting the treatment of disabled individuals in organizations. *Academy of Management Review, 21*(2), 352–401.

Suh, A., & Lee, J. (2017). Understanding teleworkers' technostress and its influence on job satisfaction. *Internet Research, 27*(1), 140–159.

Sundstrom, E., De Meuse, K. P., & Futrell, D. (1990). Work teams: Applications and effectiveness. *American Psychologist, 45*(2), 120.

Teo, T. S., & Lim, V. K. (1998). Factorial dimensions and differential effects of gender on perceptions of teleworking. *Women in Management Review, 113*(7), 253–263.

Thibaut, J., & Walker, L. (1975). *Procedural justice: A psychological analysis*. Erlbaum.

Tosi, H. L., Misangyi, V. F., Fanelli, A., Waldman, D. A., & Yammarino, F. J. (2004). CEO charisma, compensation, and firm performance. *The Leadership Quarterly, 15*(3), 405–420.

Townsend, K., Wilkinson, A., Allan, C., & Bamber, G. (2012). Mixed signals in HRM: The HRM role of hospital line managers 1. *Human Resource Management Journal, 22*(3), 267–282.

Van, N. T. T., Vrana, V., Duy, N. T., Minh, D. X. H., Dzung, P. T., Mondal, S. R., & Das, S. (2020). The role of human-machine interactive devices for post-COVID-19 innovative sustainable tourism in Ho Chi Minh City, Vietnam. *Sustainability, 12*(22), 9523. https://doi.org/10.3390/su12229523

Venkatesh, A., & Vitalari, N. P. (1992). An emerging distributed work arrangement: An investigation of computer-based supplemental work at home. *Management Science, 38*(12), 1687–1706.

Wanberg, C. R., & Banas, J. T. (2000). Predictors and outcomes of openness to changes in a reorganizing workplace. *Journal of Applied Psychology, 85*(1), 132.

Watad, M. M., & DiSanzo, F. J. (2000). Case study: The synergism of telecommuting and office automation. *MIT Sloan Management Review, 41*(2), 85.

Weinert, C., Maier, C., Laumer, S., & Weitzel, T. (2014, May). Does teleworking negatively influence IT professionals? An empirical analysis of IT personnel's telework-enabled stress. In *Proceedings of the 52nd ACM Conference on Computers and People Research* (pp. 139–147).

Wiesenfeld, B. M., Raghuram, S., & Garud, R. (1998). Communication patterns as determinants of organizational identification in a virtual organization. *Journal of Computer-Mediated Communication, 3*(4), JCMC344.

Wiesenfeld, B. M., Raghuram, S., & Garud, R. (2001). Organizational identification among virtual workers: The role of need for affiliation and perceived work-based social support. *Journal of Management, 27*(2), 213–229.

Wright, P. C., & Oldford, A. (1993). Telecommuting and employee effectiveness: Career and managerial issues. *International Journal of Career Management, 5*, 4–9.

Zajonc, R. B. (1965). Social facilitation. *Science, 149*(3681), 269–274.

Zuboff, S. (1982). *Comment computer-mediated work: The emerging managerial challenge*. Office Technology and People.

CHAPTER 6

Remote Work at the Time of COVID-19 Pandemic and Beyond: A Scoping Review

Aizhan Tursunbayeva, Stefano Di Lauro, and Gilda Antonelli

Introduction

According to the United Nations (2020), "2020 has been a year like no other in recent memory." The ongoing COVID-19 pandemic is considered to be the worst health issue the world has faced since the 1918 Spanish flu pandemic (Saplakoglu & Writer, 2020). Its outbreak originated in China in December 2019. Only after a month (in January 2020), the World Health Organization (WHO, 2020) declared its outbreak a

A. Tursunbayeva
University of Naples Parthenope, Naples, Italy
e-mail: a.tursunbayeva@uniparthenope.it

S. Di Lauro (✉)
University of Sannio, Benevento, Italy
e-mail: stefano.dilauro@unisannio.it

G. Antonelli
University of Sannio, Benevento, Italy
e-mail: gilda.antonelli@unisannio.it

S. R. Mondal et al. (eds.), *HR Analytics and Digital HR Practices*,
https://doi.org/10.1007/978-981-16-7099-2_6

Public Health Emergency of International Concern, and on March 11, 2020, it was declared a pandemic.

COVID-19 has brought many changes to our daily life, thus impacting the ways in which work is organized and where it is performed (Das, 2021a; Dua et al., 2021; Duy et al., 2020; Mondal, 2021; Van et al., 2020). Indeed, the social distancing response to COVID-19 aimed at flattening the curve has shifted portions of the workforce from the work-places to home environments (Sharma & Das, 2020; Singh et al., 2020; Singh, Mondal, & Das, 2020; Siri et al., 2020). Overall, remote work is not something revolutionary, but it (frequently) became mandatory or recommended for health reasons ("The Case of Remote Work," 2020). In the U.K., for example, the percentage of employees working from home in April reached 47%, of whom 86% did so due to COVID-19 (Office for National Statistics, 2020). The overall increase in remote work is also evident from the impressive transformation of companies and employees to virtual settings instead of physical workplaces (Das, 2020; Mondal, 2020; Mondal & Sahoo, 2020; Nadanyiova & Das, 2020; Schawbel, 2020, March). Indeed, Zoom, a video-conferencing company, reported an increase in their regular users by 67% in March 2020 (Behera et al., 2019; Gupta et al., 2019; Leonardi, 2020; Mohanty et al., 2019); moreover, LinkedIn data suggested that the use of their "remote" job filter has increased by 43% since March. The latter also implies a notable surge in the demand for remote jobs (Das, 2021b; Seaman, 2020).

This "biggest (forced) experiment in history" (Green, 2020) has created debates in academic and business circles that are watching closely and trying to understand what kind of potential benefits and unintended consequences can be generated for the organizations, individuals involved, and the society in general. However, this is not an easy task because individual examples of remote work during COVID-19 are spread between interdisciplinary scholarly and practitioner literature. This scoping review addresses this gap by identifying and synthesizing existing international evidence on the adoption and spread of remote work practices during the pandemic. In particular, this review explores the benefits/opportunities and challenges/dangers that are created or could be potentially created by this style of working for all stakeholders. Moreover, it provides insights and recommendations that may help organizations, employees, work consultants, and policymakers to develop or implement evidence-based remote work strategies.

Background

Remote Work Definition

Remote work does not have a universally accepted definition. Recognizing that the COVID-19 pandemic has significantly influenced how work is organized and where it is performed, the International Labour Organization (ILO, 2020a) divided this "new normal" work arrangement into four categories, namely, teleworking, remote work, working at home, and home-based work. Remote work and telework or distance work are related to situations where work is conducted outside the default workplace. Moreover, telework also implies the use of information and communication technologies (ICT) (e.g., smartphones, tablets, and computers). Meanwhile, working at home and home-based work are related to situations where work is conducted from the employee's residence. Despite these differences in the terminology, several authors use these terms interchangeably (ILO, 2020b). Accordingly, this approach is followed in this chapter. Thus, "remote work" hereinafter is used as an umbrella term that implies any arrangement of work outside the usual workplace, irrespective of whether this is performed with the help of any ICT.

Generic Research on Remote Work

Remote work, as a research topic, has been studied from diverse angles often separately for employers (Farrer, 2020) and employees (Baruch & Nicholson, 1997). For employers, remote work has been studied for organizations from diverse sectors; thus, the existence of benefits (e.g., availability of data) and limits (e.g., lack of trust) of remote work in a bureaucratic environment (Taskin & Edwards, 2007) or the public sector (De Vries et al., 2019) is already known. However, overall, it seems to be a favored way of working for startups and tech conglomerates (e.g., Facebook and Twitter) (Hopwood, 2019). For employees, previous studies revealed some categories of workers who could benefit from remote work the most. Moreover, these studies demonstrated that as of today, the applicability and diffusion of remote work vary between employees from different sectors (Yuhan et al., 2020). Thus, overall, only a few employees from selected sectors worked completely from home. For example, remote work has frequently been mentioned to be practiced by self-employed employees, managers, and more broadly white-collar professionals, but it was uncommon among those employed in the health sector. Moreover, remote work was found to be usually part-time, incidental (Parent-Thirion et al., 2017), or related to shifting work.

Previous relevant research often studied the antecedents of remote work such as factors that can affect its adoption or successful use. Thus, Baruch and Nicholson (1997) identified the following factors that need to be fulfilled for remote work to become feasible and effective: individual (e.g., individual traits of remote workers), job (e.g., type of jobs fit with remote working), organizational (e.g., supportive culture and appropriate systems), and family/home (e.g., the boundary between work and home). This framework was further enriched recently by Belzunegui-Eraso and Erro-Garcés (2020) with technological (e.g., available ICT instruments), environmental (i.e., environmental impact of the travel to the workplace), safety, and legal factors.

Finally, previous studies have also explored the implications of remote work. For instance, several studies revealed the impact of remote work on employees' health and well-being (Crawford et al., 2011), productivity (Whiting, 2020), or engagement (Beheshti, 2020). Thus, employees who worked remotely reported greater flexibility of their work schedules, although they also acknowledged professional isolationism (Cooper et al., 2020) and blurring of the line between their professional and private lives. Organizations using remote work reported lowered real estate or utility costs (e.g., electricity) while noting higher potential risks (e.g., risks related to cybersecurity) of working from home compared with working from the office. Thus, the existing corpus of research on implications of remote work presents some positive and negative consequences separately for employees and organizations, not considering that these stakeholders can share some of these outcomes (Vega et al., 2015). Moreover, most of these studies were published before the COVID-19 pandemic, and thus, they were conducted in a situation wherein the companies and employees could choose whether and how to adopt remote working. Therefore, although this research enriches our understanding of the impacts of remote work for organizations and employees, it does not provide a complete picture or a common framework on the benefits and challenges that organizations and employees can encounter or share during large-scale remote work roll-out that occurred during COVID-19. This study aimed to bridge this literature gap.

COVID-19 and Remote Work

During the COVID-19 restrictions and lockdown, the remote work assumed a different perspective (Iqbal et al., 2020). The pandemic shifted remote work from an incidental work arrangement to a main or any work arrangement. Indeed, within several months, COVID-19 has realized the "future of work" that experts were predicting to happen in a couple of years (McGowan, 2020). However, due to the emergency, most of the companies had little time to organize or develop strategies for introducing or normalizing remote work practices (Carroll & Conboy, 2020). Thus, many questions regarding this unplanned global experiment, including its effects on the labor market (Bonacini et al., 2021), workplace, and organizational practices (Carroll & Conboy, 2020), remain unanswered. This review addressed these knowledge and literature gaps. To the best of our knowledge, this is one of the first literature reviews to have specifically investigated the benefits and challenges of remote work during COVID-19 in various sectors that draw on scholarly and gray literature sources. Moreover, this is one of the few studies that explores the benefits and challenges of large-scale remote work for organizations and their employees. Based on the analysis results, recommendations for future research, policy, and practice are proposed.

Methodology

Literature Review Approach

Drawing on the methodology proposed by Arksey and O'Malley (2005), this present study undertook a scoping review of academic and gray literature. This approach is often used to study emerging topics where research is at a nascent stage or where the relevant evidence is being mostly produced in business circles (Tursunbayeva et al., 2018). Scoping reviews are often adopted to explore broad research questions and locate and holistically understand existing publications. The global adoption of remote work as a result of the COVID-19 pandemic is an evolving topic; hence, this approach was considered proper compared with the analysis of scarce and likely unrepresentative scholarly literature and narrow study purpose.

Data Collection

Considering the real urgency to better understand how remote work is affecting organizations and their employees, the academic and gray literature were searched and analyzed in this review.

Academic Literature

Web of Science (WoS) international interdisciplinary literature database was used to locate relevant scholarly literature. Several rounds of pilot studies were conducted to identify the most sensitive keywords in October–November 2020 including "Covid" and "remote work," "tele-work" or "tele-work," "distance work," or "home work." These keywords are also in line with the remote work-related categories proposed by ILO (2020a). The references of articles included in the final set were "snow-balled" to check for additional relevant studies that may have not been indexed in the WoS.

Gray Literature

LinkedIn, the world's major professional network with more than 700 million international users (LinkedIn, 2020), was selected to locate relevant gray literature. It allows its users to publish Pulse articles in real time. These can also be found via the Google search engine. LinkedIn Pulse is often used by professionals to share their expert knowledge and expertise (LinkedIn Help, 2020). As an increasing number of professionals are embracing this established platform rather than setting up (or maintaining) their own independent online presence (e.g., blog) (Samuel, 2015), LinkedIn Pulse was selected for finding the latest practitioners' contributions on COVID-19 and remote work.

Meanwhile, Google Advanced Search engine was used to interrogate LinkedIn Pulse (by using site: "www.linkedin.com/pulse") in October–November 2020 with the help of the same keywords used to locate the relevant scholarly articles (i.e., "Covid" and "remote work," "tele-work" or "tele-work," "distance work" or "homework"). The search was conducted with a signed-out Google account to attain the most relevant results and not those personalized and customized by Google (Google Search Help, 2020). The results were restricted to the first 20 organic results in English, thus excluding paid content. Further results were not considered, as only 0.8% of users searching Google click on something from the second page (Dean, 2019).

Data Analysis

The data were extracted into a pre-developed Excel spreadsheet containing the following fields: publication year, country, publication type, use of a theoretical framework, journal discipline, industry sector, benefits for employees and organizations, challenges for employees and organizations, and recommendations.

The journals' discipline was verified in the Scimago Journal Ranking Portal (2020). As aforementioned, the categories of benefits and challenges from remote work are spread in interdisciplinary literature, and no single common framework can classify these categories, considering also that benefits and challenges can vary for employees and organizations. Therefore, the data analysis in this research started with an "open" data coding approach (Glaser & Strauss, 1967), reflecting as faithfully as possible the terminology used in the qualifying studies (Tursunbayeva, 2018). This approach helped elicit the categories and themes of benefits and challenges from remote work present in the literature, as well as relevant suggestions and recommendations.

Results

Academic Literature: Publication Characteristics

In all, 41 results were generated by the search strategy. Of these results, 27 were qualified for the analysis together with five additional "snowballed" articles (see Appendix 1). 21 of these studies were published as research articles (e.g., case studies or reviews). The remaining publications were commentaries ($n = 3$), editorials ($n = 3$), and other types of publications (e.g., special communication, best practice, brief report, or letter). Almost all included studies (except one) were published as open access papers. The topics were mostly published in *Work—A Journal of Prevention Assessment & Rehabilitation* and *Sustainability* journals (both with $n = 3$ articles).

Less than half of the papers ($n = 15$) specified the theoretical perspective or scientific approach to the analysis they employed. Six articles were published in mono-discipline health journals; four articles in business, management, and accounting; and three in social science journals, whereas 18 articles were published in interdisciplinary journals on business, management, and accounting; computer science; economics, econometrics, and finance; energy; environmental science; social science;

psychology; decision sciences; and medicine. One article from a journal not covered by Scimago Journal Ranking Portal was manually assigned to the engineering category.

A total of 18 articles were specific to a particular country: four to Italy, three to the U.S., two to Australia, two to the U.K., and one each to Ireland, Indonesia, Canada, Japan, Lithuania, Mexico, and Portugal. The remaining 14 publications were not specific to a particular country.

The majority ($n = 26$) of the publications were not specific to a particular sector or mentioned several sectors together. Two studies focused on the educational sector (i.e., on universities), whereas the remaining studies focused on architecture, health, social work, and library sectors.

Gray Literature: Publication Characteristics

All 20 Gy literature publications obtained from the search strategy (see Appendix 2) were published between March and August 2020, although most of them ($n = 6$) were published in May. The first result in Google organic search, with 1913 likes and 176 comments, is the most "influential" qualifying article (Dean, 2019). It was published by Spaven, LinkedIn News Editor in the U.K. Overall, all the gray literature publications were posted by LinkedIn's recognized and informal influencers (e.g., chief executive officers, managing directors, founders, and LinkedIn news editors); their authors have approximately 64,000 followers. Some of these articles are also part of LinkedIn newsletters including "UK Workforce Confidence Index," "Get Hired," "Reimagine Work," "The Rise of Remote Work," and "Digital Workplace Newsletter." The latter two newsletters focus exclusively on remote working.

Analysis and Discussion

The analysis revealed an important number of benefits/opportunities and challenges associated with remote work during the COVID-19 pandemic. These were classified according to the categories that emerged from the analysis, separately for organizations and employees. Figure 6.1 presents the benefits common for both stakeholders in separate categories.

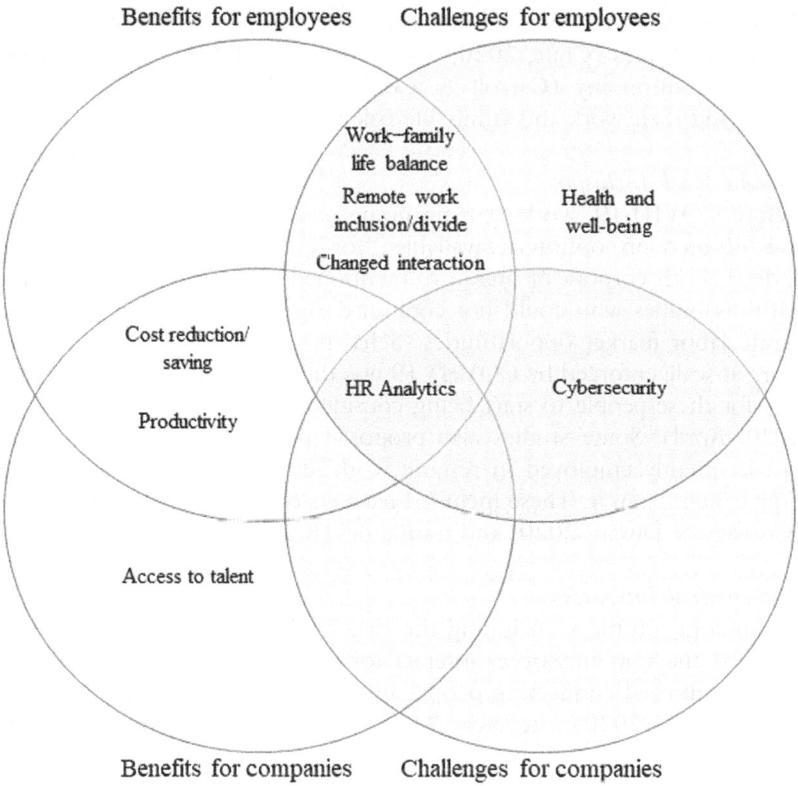

Fig. 6.1 Benefits and challenges for organizations and employees

Benefits for Employees

Work–Family Life Balance

Overall, gray literature on remote work claims that employees are allowed to live and work where and how they want (Schenker, 2020) and operate when they are the most productive (Herd, 2020; Schawbel, 2020, April) in the remote work setting. Besides, spending less time in offices and more time with families was associated with reduced office stress (Fransz, 2020, July) and was reported to make employees happier (Fransz, 2020, July; Schawbel, 2020a, May). In scholarly literature, the flexibility associated with remote work was considered helpful for motivating employees (Craft, 2020; Rapuano et al., 2020), enhancing their perceived autonomy (Carroll & Conboy, 2020), and, more broadly, improving their work and family life balance.

Remote Work Inclusion

Before COVID-19, working from home or elsewhere outside the office was deemed an option unavailable "for everyone" (Seaman, 2020). Indeed, both corpora of literature mentioned that, for example, people with disabilities who could not commute were often excluded from the onsite labor market opportunities (Schawbel, 2020, May). The remote work at scale enforced by COVID-19 was thus mentioned as an opportunity for these people to start being considered for these jobs (Schawbel, 2020, April). Some studies also proposed professional roles that were not frequently employed in remote work settings previously but could now benefit from it. These included teachers or educational professionals (Crowley & Doran, 2020) and translators (Kramer & Kramer, 2020).

Orchestrated Interaction

Technology advances, including the cloud and collaboration tools, have changed the way employees interact for work (Schawbel, 2020, April). Thus, it allowed connecting people anywhere and at any time. As stated by Schawbel (2020), the New York Times bestselling author, "people are better connected than ever whether they are separated by 10 desks or 10,000 miles," thanks to the use of technology. During COVID-19, many employees lost their reliance on environmental affordances such as office spaces, meeting rooms, and common areas (Waizenegger et al., 2020). Thus, to continue working on their projects and socializing with other colleagues, they had to rely even more on technologies. Interestingly, this technology empowered remote-work-orchestrated collaboration by reducing the frequency of some spontaneous interactions such as ad hoc meetings and improved the quality of data sharing and communication (Molino et al., 2020). Finally, the enforced remote work for regular onsite teams was reported to increase the integration of employees who are used to working remotely and usually have not participated in social gatherings of their onsite teams (Waizenegger et al., 2020).

Benefits for Companies

Access to Talent

The gray literature frequently mentioned obtaining access to any talent worldwide without the restriction of physical location as an important benefit gained by organizations during COVID-19. For example, according to the founder and CEO of Firstbase, a platform that helps companies supply, finance, and manage the physical equipment needed for remote workers, "A physical office means you can hire the best person you can afford in a 30-mile radius, disqualifying you from 99.9% of the world's talent" (Herd, 2020). However, companies are said to have already been frequently using flexible work policies (including remote work) for attracting talents (Li et al., 2020) even before the pandemic.

Benefits for Employees and Companies

Productivity

Diverse gray and academic literature publications (e.g., Lee et al., 2020; Shapiro, 2020) claim that remote work can increase the productivity of employees as a result of orchestrated interactions. This aspect was also frequently mentioned as a benefit for their employers. For example, the global workplace analytics costs and benefits survey reported that "teleworkers in some large companies are 35–40% more productive than office workers doing the same job" (Schenker, 2020). Meanwhile, the workers who denied this flexibility were found to be less productive and overall uninterested in taking on additional projects (Germano, 2010, as cited in Craft, 2020). Simultaneously, some scholars, such as Moretti et al. (2020), found that the productivity of some employees working remotely in Italy decreased during the pandemic. The productivity was also reported to vary depending on gender, as female employees working remotely in the U.S. seemed to be less productive than their male counterparts after the outbreak (Feng & Savani, 2020).

Interestingly, the higher productivity of employees working remotely is predicted to result in the growth of the average labor income for these professionals (Bonacini et al., 2021). Moreover, having employees located remotely in diverse geographical locations and time zones allowed companies to extend their work time to 24 hours per day, thereby increasing their international competitiveness (Raišienė et al., 2020).

Cost Reduction/Saving

Some organizations using remote work reported a reduction of their overhead costs (Schenker, 2020), which is associated with the rethinking of their physical workspaces and potential different use of these spaces. For example, in the case in which institutional spaces were unoccupied or occupied less during COVID-19, companies were able to save on utility or real estate costs (Hickey & Tang, 2015, as cited in Craft, 2020). However, companies had to consider some extra expenses for computers or internet access for employees who needed to work outside the office space (Dey et al., 2020).

The remote work permitted time and cost savings for employees; these were primarily associated with commute-related expenses (Fransz, 2020a, August; Schawbel, 2020, May) and were deemed one of the primary reasons why remote working is becoming increasingly popular among employees (Raišienė et al., 2020).

Human Resource (HR) Analytics

The use of technology in remote work creates a digital exhaust (Leonardi, 2020), which is the information generated when employees interact with websites and services. Analyzing these data by applying HR analytics techniques is becoming popular among organizations. In particular, HR analytics approaches are applied to remote work data to monitor employees, assess their performance, and identify approaches for strengthening organizational remote working practices. Some studies also mentioned that several companies have started combining these remote work data with the data from other data sets (e.g., employee performance data). However, most qualifying studies have not specified what kind of HR analytics methodologies or tools were adopted. An exception to this is a gray literature publication of Green (2020), who states that the use of organizational network approach during the pandemic promised the companies to fast-track the development of new guidelines and policies, track employee exhaustion, improve remote employee onboarding, avoid employee isolation, and explore and forecast the COVID-19 diffusion within the company.

Challenges for Employees

Work–Family Life Balance
According to some LinkedIn authors, remote work can disrupt employees' work–family life balance and reduce their happiness (Fransz, 2020b, August; Schenker, 2020). For example, some employees worked frequently during the weekend to make up for productivity losses associated with family responsibilities during the week (Tavares et al., 2020). Analyzing social work teams in the U.K., Cook et al. (2020) also identified the difficulty for many workers to compartmentalize and separate work from home life, feeling particularly disoriented during the first few days of lockdown.

Health and Well-Being
According to Fransz (2020, July), employees can find working from home uncomfortable compared with working from the office with ergonomic furniture. Thus, some academic studies associated the use of non-ergonomic equipment at home (e.g., not adjustable in height monitor or kitchen chair) with the increase in musculoskeletal disorders (e.g., low back and neck pain) of permanent remote workers. Both literature sources also mentioned that the enforced remote work during COVID-19 could increase the mental health issues of the affected employees (Moretti et al., 2020). These mental health issues are due to their feeling of anxiety, stress, anger, annoyance, tolerance, frustration (Madero Gómez et al., 2020; Seaman, 2020), or uncertainty caused by changes in the business practices, work protocols, and market conditions (Lee et al., 2020). Moreover, during the COVID-19 pandemic, employees often felt lonely and isolated (Fransz, 2020a, August) from their coworkers and clients due to changes in socialization. The psychological risks associated with remote working were particularly frequently mentioned for working parents, who had to manage overlapping responsibilities and unstructured working time (Bouziri et al., 2020).

Remote Work Divide
Digital skill shortage was recognized as a potential barrier for effective remote work and overall positive employee experience. For example, non-digital natives are found to have difficulty adapting to technologies and being constantly connected in remote work (Li et al., 2020). Similarly, the lack of proper support infrastructure resources at homes, such as a suitable place to work, good internet speed, or printer (Baskin, 2020;

Fransz, 2020b, August), was also stated as a potential challenge that could contribute to the so-called remote work divide.

Scholarly literature mentioned that the perception about remote work could vary depending on employees' gender, age, level of education, or geographical location. Thus, for example, qualifying studies described a profile of employees for whom the remote work is less possible and those who found it the most challenging. According to Gallacher and Hossain (2020), who conducted their study in Canada, the former included poorer employees, men, employees without a college degree, single, younger, and nonimmigrant employees; those who are from the private sector and small firm; and either seasonal, contractual, or part-time employees. Meanwhile, Couch et al. (2020) who collected personal stories of working from home during the pandemic from various employees concluded that working women and mothers (including those who work in academia) are those who found remote work the most challenging because it created tension between the business, household, and social dimensions of their lives. This challenge was frequently associated with the unequal domestic rearrangements of parenting duties for women in some countries (e.g., Italy) during lockdown (Manzo & Minello, 2020). However, these findings disagree with those of Raišienė et al. (2020), who reported that for Lithuania, younger and middle-aged employees who are mostly female with a higher educational degree and sufficient professional and remote work experience are the most satisfied with this way of working, whereas men with a university degree and over 20 years of industry experience and who started working remotely only due to COVID-19 are the most dissatisfied with remote work. However, these findings are slightly misaligned with those of Bonacini et al. (2021), who concluded that remote work in Italy benefits, among others, mostly older men.

Changed Interaction

Withdrawal of workplace environmental spaces (Waizenegger et al., 2020) due to COVID-19 is claimed to impede the trust-based relationship between some categories of employees (e.g., older men) (Raišienė et al., 2020) and, more broadly, their knowledge sharing and co-ordination (Molino et al., 2020). The latter was found to be particularly damaging for knowledgeable workers, who no longer had space for formal meetings and conversations, and for new employees, who could no longer easily interact with their colleagues physically, which negatively affected their learning journey.

Challenges for Employees and Companies

Cybersecurity

Cybersecurity is an important challenge associated with remote work for both organizations and employees (Schenker, 2020). The increase in cyberattacks, such as spyware and malware phishing (Weil & Murugesan, 2020), was associated with the remote access given by the organizations to employees for mission-critical operational programs (Byme, 2020). Moreover, it is associated with the augmented number of human errors made by employees distracted by greater financial and personal stress at home. Furthermore, it is related to the changing cyberattack surfaces (Schenker, 2020) and some vulnerabilities in existing remote work technologies.

Trust, Surveillance, and HR Analytics

Trust issues were often mentioned as one of the biggest challenges associated with remote work for organizations and employees (Fransz, 2020b, August). In particular, employers were reported to have less visibility over employees' behavior in remote work, and some of them were apprehensive that employees may take advantage of their newfound freedom and flexibility. Hence, organizations' use of surveillance software to monitor employees working remotely is showing an increasing trend (Dey et al., 2020). However, the remote employee monitoring and tracking or the application of the so-called HR analytics techniques to the remote work data, which promised many benefits to organizations and employees, have also raised some employees' trust issues and ethical concerns around, for example, potential inappropriate collection or use of employee data or opening a window into their homes and private lives (Laas, 2020). Thus, potentially exposing the companies to ethical or even to reputational risks.

Solutions and Recommendations

The analysis also revealed several recommendations to address the challenges caused by remote work to employees, managers, and organizations (see Table 6.1) and maximize its benefits for these stakeholders. To assist the contextualization and interpretation of the findings, the recommendations are grouped according to remote work's benefits and challenges that emerged from the literature, alongside other relevant literature and real-world examples.

Table 6.1 Recommendations that emerged from the literature

	Organizations	Managers	Employees
Work–family life balance			⊕
Health and well-being	⊕		
Remote work inclusion/divide	⊕		
Orchestrated interaction	⊕		
Productivity	⊕	⊕	⊕
Trust, surveillance, and HR analytics	⊕	⊕	
Cybersecurity	⊕		
Access to talent	⊕		

Work–Family Life Balance
It has already been demonstrated that perceived job flexibility can positively influence work and family life balance (Hill et al., 2001). To achieve this balance, employees were advised to draw a clear line between their private and professional spaces by, for example, adopting a compartmentalization psychological defense mechanism. This mechanism allows them to temporarily "compartmentalize" something stressful and move to another duty (Cook et al., 2020). Moreover, employees were also advised not to lose their routine due to the flexibility associated with remote work, as this aspect could keep them organized and productive (Lopez-Leon et al., 2020).

Health and Well-Being
The analysis presented in this paper demonstrated that remote work can have unintended consequences on employees' physical and psychological health, and as such, it has never been more crucial for organizations to invest in corporate wellness (Green, 2020).

In particular, to address physical risks, organizations should provide employees with ergonomic equipment (Tavares et al., 2020). Meanwhile, to ensure their psychological well-being, continuous communication must be facilitated, and employee corporate wellness programs must be extended with online psychological support or online fitness platforms or applications (e.g., providing yoga exercises) (Sharma et al., 2020). More broadly, companies were also advised to approach the organization of remote work creatively and entrepreneurially.

Remote Work Divide

The analysis revealed that remote work is not universally beneficial for all employee types and the perception of employees about remote work can vary depending on their characteristics. However, the studies almost unanimously agreed that employees prefer to have remote work as a working option (e.g., Feng, 2020).

Overall, organizations must create remote work policies that consider the differential effects of remote work on different categories of employees and contain practical help that some employee categories such as working parents (particularly, when the schools are closed) (Feng, 2020) might need. The latter is claimed to be the area where employers have been failing the most during the COVID-19 pandemic (Plans, 2020).

Orchestrated Interaction

The analysis reveals that technology is the main facilitator for communication and collaboration in remote working (Lopez-Leon et al., 2020; Razif et al., 2020). Thus, to ensure effective remote work, the European Framework Agreement, for example, recommends companies provide employees with the necessary technological material, including hardware and software. This measure was even introduced in several collective agreements created during the expansion of remote work about a decade ago (Belzuneg-Eraso & Erro-Garcés, 2020). The companies were also advised to establish comprehensive supporting organizational systems, such as good IT support that can help employees with their technical queries (Haworth, 2020).

Moreover, managers and employees should establish a network (Lopez-Leon et al., 2020) and facilitate clarity by over communicating (Lee et al., 2020).

Productivity

The academic research on remote work and productivity produced mixed results. Indeed, the success of remote work was largely associated with how organizations and employees "did it" (Green, 2020). The remote work is projected to become the "new normal" way of working for, at least, the nearest future. Hence, organizations are suggested to create remote work policies that can keep employees safe, while keeping them in the business (Sutton, 2020). Herd (2020) even stated that "not developing a remote work strategy is strategic suicide." The companies were also recommended to offer employee training on enhancing the competencies needed for successful remote work and offer manager training on identifying the signs of employee burnout (Plans, 2020). Consequently, this aspect would increase employees' productivity and overall employee experience (Wrycza & Maślankowski, 2020).

For employees to maintain productivity, a suitable place at home must be chosen for remote work, and proactive communication with peers, managers, and employees must be maintained (Sutton, 2020).

Trust, Surveillance, and HR Analytics

Managers' high control needs were mentioned as a frequent barrier to remote work programs in organizations (Das, 2021b; Schawbel, 2020, March). Thus, to preserve the climate of confidence between organizations and employees crucial for remote work (Belzunegui-Eraso & Erro-Garcés, 2020), organizations should balance the desire for efficiency with allowing employees to work with a necessary degree of autonomy (Millerd, 2020). This is claimed to be achieved by, for example, applying the principles of project management or implementing effective communication strategies (Schenker, 2020).

Consequently, managers must resist micromanagement and develop the qualities needed to lead a remote workforce including trust, respect, shared values, and culture (Phillips, 2020).

Finally, more employees seem to adopt remote working during COVID-19 and beyond; thus, we should expect to see more automated or artificial intelligence solutions that are designed to help remote workers become more efficient and productive (Schenker, 2020). Thus, the success of remote work might also lie in the employers' legal and ethical compliance with their use of technology and HR analytics approaches (Tursunbayeva et al., 2018). Indeed, some contexts have comprehensive protocols overseeing this aspect, such as the European General Data Protection Directive. Others, including many developing countries waiting for their relevant laws to be strengthened, should fill this space with ethical policies drawing on the increasing recently relevant evidence (Tursunbayeva et al., 2018).

Cybersecurity

The remote work at scale requires a degree of technology security across industries than ever before. Consequently, the whole IT industry is currently re-evaluating its planning and offerings, as well as business/IT risk management posed by the new operational environment (Weil & Murugesan, 2020). Some of these technology champions have quickly mobilized to provide free remote software licenses for various remote monitoring and operations software to their customers (Byme, 2020). Overall, diverse guidelines have been offered to address top remote work-related security concerns during COVID-19 at the disposal of those interested (Weil & Murugesan, 2020).

Access to Talent

The companies that champion flexible working opportunities, among which also remote work, such as Dell Technologies, reported that their flexible working programs positively impacted their businesses, their approaches to talent recruitment, and even environmental footprint. These programs also improved organizational retention programs and encouraged a change in how they think about work (Earle, 2003). Finally, these programs shifted the focus of organizations from the physical location of employees or time they spent working to their outcome (Schawbel, 2020, May). The adaptors of flexible working also reported that their programs are improving in line with the advancements of accessible technology.

Conclusion and Future Research Directions

The interest in remote work research and practice has risen at an exponential rate during the COVID-19 pandemic (Wrycza & Maślankowski, 2020), which triggered remote work globally. This working approach has meaningfully affected not only companies, many of which were unprepared to face these challenges, but also employees who needed to cope with new remote work policies, software, and working style (Li et al., 2020). Thus, this study aimed to locate, map, and synthesize the existing published scholarly and practitioner literature concerning the benefits and challenges of remote work during COVID-19.

The analyzed publications provide fair geographical coverage with the highest number of studies originating in Italy. This is reasonable, as Italy was the first European country to face the COVID-19 lockdown. Moreover, it is an interesting case to study because before COVID-19, Italy had one of the lowest percentages of remote workers across Europe (Eurofound & ILO, 2017). Interestingly, none of the qualifying studies came from China, where the outbreak had initiated.

The analysis also reveals that the qualifying studies are interdisciplinary, mostly atheoretical, and non-sector-specific. This aspect implies that so far, there is still little formal research on this topic, including investigations adapting multilevel, multi-stakeholder, multi-method, and sector- and culture-sensitive approaches (Caligiuri et al., 2020).

The analysis indicates that the qualifying studies provide a balanced overview of the benefits/opportunities and challenges caused by remote work during COVID-19 for employees and employers. According to the analysis, the benefits for employees included improved work–family life balance due to the flexibility associated with remote work; the inclusion of some categories of employees (e.g., people with disabilities) previously excluded from the labor market; and orchestrated interaction, owing to the reduced spontaneous contacts. Interestingly, the challenges from remote work for employees were aligned with these three categories. However, here the analysis revealed that employees' work–family life balance can be affected by conflicting professional and family responsibilities, especially for some specific categories of employees, such as working parents. The changed way of interacting was observed to be uncomfortable for some with potentially unintended consequences, while more broadly the perception of employees about remote was found to vary depending on employees' characteristics. Finally, the literature also revealed that some psychological and physical health and well-being consequences exist for employees who were enforced to work from home during COVID-19. However, scholarly research acknowledged that more scientific evidence is needed to examine the impact of remote work on employees' health and well-being (Moretti et al., 2020), paying specific attention to, for example, the employees' cognitive and psychosomatic conditions (Charalampous et al., 2019).

One benefit from remote work specific to organizations was access to the worldwide market of talents. However, potentially, this aspect can also benefit talented candidates living far from the main labor market opportunities, who now get a chance to apply and compete for jobs from any part of the world. The remaining benefits were reported for both organizations and employees, including cost savings and productivity gains. Cost saving was related to the real estate or commute expenses, whereas productivity was reported to increase as a result of, for example, orchestrated virtual interactions. However, the findings on the productivity gains were mixed and varied depending on diverse factors, including employees' geographical location or characteristics, thereby opening opportunities for future research.

HR analytics emerged as a common benefit and challenge for both organizations and employees. The HR analytics benefits identified in this study echo the latest definition of HR analytics, which refers to it as an "area of HRM practice, research, and innovation concerned with the use of information technologies, descriptive, and predictive data analytics and visualization tools for generating actionable insights about workforce dynamics, human capital, and individual and team performance that can be used strategically to optimize organizational effectiveness, efficiency and outcomes, and improve employee experience" (Tursunbayeva et al., 2018). Meanwhile, the challenges were associated with important ethical and trust concerns related to the use of these innovations for the employees' rights to privacy and autonomy, as well as with broader ethical questions about the future of human work and employment in a digitized, algorithm-driven society. Thus, more research analyzing ethical risks and challenges of HR analytics is needed to guide organizations and inform and encourage the equilibrated ethical and responsible use of these innovations. This research can also potentially investigate specific approaches with respect to the ways in which remote work data can be collected, analyzed, or used, as the studies analyzed in this review have mostly neglected these important aspects.

The remaining challenge shared by employees and organizations was cybersecurity associated with an increased number of cyberattacks.

In synthesis, many benefits and challenges that emerged from the analysis are in line with those discovered in previous research on the implications of remote work (e.g., Cooper et al., 2020; Crawford et al., 2011; Whiting, 2020). However, some unique categories also emerged, such as remote work inclusion/divide or HR analytics. Moreover, compared with previous generic remote work research separately presenting benefits and challenges for employees and organizations, this study reveals some common benefits and challenges for these stakeholders. It also presents suggestions on the ways in which the challenges from remote work at scale could be addressed (The Case for Remote Work in Health Care - SPONSOR CONTENT FROM SIEMENS HEALTHINEERS, 2020). These recommendations (Table 6.1) are often dedicated to organizations and less frequently to employees or managers. This aspect confirms the important role organizations play in creating and engaging productive working structures through remote work strategies and policies (Sutton, 2020) while implying the passive role of employees in these processes.

Notably, some authors highlighted that many of the remote work challenges are actually not the direct result of the remote work but that of the remote work during lockdown (Baskin, 2020). Moreover, many challenges faced by the companies and employees root into deeper societal challenges. For example, the use of flexible work measures still mirrors classical gender roles and gender-segregated employment market dynamics (Hofacker & Konig, 2013).

Overall, this largest remote work experiment demonstrated that flexible work is needed for organizations and some employees. Moreover, it produced a footprint that will form the base for managerial decisions and policies for decades to come. Therefore, remote work should be properly studied and understood. In addition to all of the aforementioned suggested areas for research, these investigations could address broader HR management-related literature gaps related to the large-scale remote work such as employee engagement; commitment or identification in remote work; managerial/leadership styles; and competencies needed to co-ordinate, lead, or motivate remote teams identified as crucial components to make lasting changes (Plans, 2020). All of these, together with the findings of this review, can guide existing and future adaptors, scholars with interest in this topic, and policymakers who are crucial to support and promote solid and responsible remote working practices (Nomura et al., 2020).

Appendix 1: Included Academic Literature

No	*Reference*	*Publication type*	*Theoretical framework*	*Industry sector*	*Country*
1	Belzunegui-Eraso, A., & Erro-Garcés, A. (2020). Teleworking in the context of the Covid-19 crisis. *Sustainability*, 12, 3662	Article	Yes	Non-sector specific	Non country specific
2	Bonacini, L., Gallo, G., & Scicchitano, S. (2021). Working from home and income inequality: risks of a "new normal" with COVID-19. *Journal of Population Economics*, 34(1), 303–360	Article	Yes	Non-sector specific	Italy
3	Bouziri, H., Smith, D. R. M., Descatha, A., Dab, W., & Jean, K. (2020). Working from home in the time of COVID-19: how to best preserve occupational health? *Occupational and Environmental Medicine*, 77(7), 509	Letter	N/A	Non-sector specific	Non country specific
4	Carroll, N., & Conboy, K. (2020). Normalising the "new normal": Changing tech-driven work practices under pandemic time pressure. *International Journal of Information Management*, 55, 102186	Article	Yes	Non-sector specific	Non country specific

(continued)

(continued)

No	*Reference*	*Publication type*	*Theoretical framework*	*Industry sector*	*Country*
5	Cook, L., Zschomler, D., Biggart, L., & Carder, S. (2020). The team as a secure base revisited: remote working and resilience among child and family social workers during COVID-19. *Journal of Children's Services*	Article	Yes	Social work	U.K
6	Couch, D. L., O'Sullivan, B., & Malatzky, C. (2020). What COVID-19 could mean for the future of "work from home": The provocations of three women in the academy. Gender, Work & Organization	Article	Yes	Educational	Australia
7	Craft, A. R. (2020). Remote work in library technical services: Connecting historical perspectives to realities of the developing COVID-19 Pandemic. Serials Review, 46(3), 227–231	Column	N/A	Library technical services	U.S
8	Crowley, F., & Doran, J. (2020). COVID-19, occupational social distancing and remote working potential: An occupation, sector and regional perspective. *Regional Science Policy & Practice*	Article	N/A	Non-sector specific	Ireland

(continued)

(continued)

No	*Reference*	*Publication type*	*Theoretical framework*	*Industry sector*	*Country*
9	Dey, M., Frazis, H., Loewenstein, M., & Sun, H. (2020). Ability to work from home: evidence from two surveys and implications for the labor market in the COVID-19 pandemic. *Monthly Labor Review*	Article	N/A	Non-sector specific	U.S
10	Feng, Z., & Savani, K. (2020), Covid-19 created a gender gap in perceived work productivity and job satisfaction: implications for dual-career parents working from home. *Gender in Management*, Vol. ahead-of-print No. ahead-of-print	Article	Yes	Non-sector specific	U.S
11	Gallacher, G., & Hossain, I. (2020). Remote work and employment dynamics under COVID-19: Evidence from Canada. *Canadian Public Policy*, 46(S1), S44–S54	Article	Yes	Non-sector specific	Canada
12	Haworth, A. (2020). View from Portsmouth during the COVID-19 pandemic: Remote dermatology work. *Clinical and Experimental Dermatology*, 45(7), 813–814	Editorial	N/A	Health (Dermatology)	U.K

(continued)

(continued)

No	*Reference*	*Publication type*	*Theoretical framework*	*Industry sector*	*Country*
13	Jesus, T., Landry, M., & Jacobs, K. (2020). A "new normal" following COVID-19 and the economic crisis: Using systems thinking to identify challenges and opportunities in disability, telework, and rehabilitation. *Work*	Article	Yes	Non-sector specific	Non country specific
14	Kramer, A., & Kramer, K. (2020). The potential impact of the Covid-19 pandemic on occupational status, work from home, and occupational mobility. *Journal of Vocational Behavior*, 119, 103442	Editorial	N/A	Non-sector specific	Non country specific
15	Lee, E., Chastain J., & Lau, W. (2020). Guide to remote work and team management during—and after—COVID-19. *Architect*	Best practice	N/A	Architecture	Non country specific
16	Leonardi, P. M. (2020). COVID-19 and the new technologies of organizing: Digital exhaust, digital footprints, and artificial intelligence in the wake of remote work. *Journal of Management Studies*	Commentary	N/A	Non-sector specific	Non country specific

(continued)

(continued)

No	*Reference*	*Publication type*	*Theoretical framework*	*Industry sector*	*Country*
17	Lewis, P., Wild, U., & Erren, T. C. (2020). Working from home during and after COVID-19: Watch out for *erythema ab igne* when using laptops. *British Journal of General Practice*, 70(697), 404	Article	N/A	Non-sector specific	Non country specific
18	Li, J., Ghosh, R., & Nachmias, S. (2020). In a time of COVID-19 pandemic, stay healthy, connected, productive, and learning: words from the editorial team of HRDI. *Human Resource Development International*, 23(3), 199–207	Editorial	N/A	Non-sector specific	Non country specific
19	Lopez-Leon, S., Forero, D. A., & Ruiz-Díaz, P. (2020). Recommendations for working from home during the COVID-19 pandemic (and beyond). *Work* (Reading, Mass.), 66(2), 371–375	Article	N/A	Non-sector specific	Non country specific
20	Madero Gómez Sergio, Ortiz Mendoza Oscar Eliud, Ramírez Jacobo, & Olivas-Luján Miguel R. (2020). Stress and myths related to the COVID-19 pandemic's effects on remote work. *Management Research: Journal of the Iberoamerican Academy of Management*, 18(4), 401–420	Article	Yes	Non-sector specific	Mexico

(continued)

(continued)

No	Reference	Publication type	Theoretical framework	Industry sector	Country
21	Manzo, L. K. C., & Minello, A. (2020). Mothers, childcare duties, and remote working under COVID-19 lockdown in Italy: Cultivating communities of care. *Dialogues in Human Geography*, 10(2), 120–123	Commentary	N/A	Non-sector specific	Italy
22	Molino, M., Ingusci, E., Signore, F., Manuti, A., Giancaspro, M.L., Russo, V., Zito, M., & Cortese, C.G. (2020). Wellbeing costs of technology use during Covid-19 remote working: An investigation using the Italian translation of the technostress creators scale. *Sustainability*, 12, 5911	Article	Yes	Non-sector specific	Italy
23	Moretti, A., Menna, F., Aulicino, M., Paoletta, M., Liguori, S., & Iolascon, G. (2020). Characterization of home working population during COVID-19 emergency: A cross-sectional analysis. *International Journal of Environmental Research and Public Health*, 17(17), 6284. PubMed	Article	Yes	Non-sector specific	Italy

(continued)

(continued)

No	*Reference*	*Publication type*	*Theoretical framework*	*Industry sector*	*Country*
24	Nash, M., & Churchill, B. (2020). Caring during COVID-19: A gendered analysis of Australian university responses to managing remote working and caring responsibilities. *Gender, Work & Organization*, 27(5), 833–846	Article	Yes	Educational	Australia
25	Nomura, S., Yoneoka, D., Tanoue, Y., Kawashima, T., Shi, S., Eguchi, A., & Miyata, H. (2020). Time to reconsider diverse ways of working in Japan to promote social distancing measures against the COVID-19. *Journal of Urban Health*, 97(4), 457–460	Brief report	N/A	Non-sector specific	Japan
26	Phillips, S. (2020). Working through the pandemic: Accelerating the transition to remote working. *Business Information Review*, 37(3), 129–134	Article	N/A	Non-sector specific	Non country specific
27	Raišienė, A. G., Rapuano, V., Varkulevičiūtė, K., & Stachová, K. (2020). Working from home—Who is happy? A survey of Lithuania's employees during the COVID-19 quarantine period. *Sustainability*, 12(13)	Article	Yes	Non-sector specific	Lithuania

(continued)

(continued)

No	Reference	Publication type	Theoretical framework	Industry sector	Country
28	Razif, M., Miraja, B.A., Persada, S.F., Nadlifatin, R., Belgiawan, P.F., Redi, A.A.N.P. & Lin, S.C., (2020). Investigating the role of environmental concern and the unified theory of acceptance and use of technology on working from home technologies adoption during COVID-19. *Entrepreneurship and Sustainability Issues. VsI Entrepreneurship and Sustainability Center*, 8(1), 795–808	Article	Yes	Non-sector specific	Indonesia
29	Sharma, K., Anand, A., & Kumar, R. (2020). The role of Yoga in working from home during the COVID-19 global lockdown. *Work*, 66(4), 731–737	Commentary	N/A	Non-sector specific	Non country specific
30	Tavares, F., Santos, E., Diogo, A. & Ratten, V. (2020). Teleworking in Portuguese communities during the COVID-19 pandemic, *Journal of Enterprising Communities: People and Places in the Global Economy*, Vol. ahead-of-print No. ahead-of-print	Article	N/A	Non-sector specific	Portugal

(continued)

(continued)

No	Reference	Publication type	Theoretical framework	Industry sector	Country
31	Waizenegger, L., McKenna, B., Cai, W., & Bendz, T. (2020). An affordance perspective of team collaboration and enforced working from home during COVID-19. *European Journal of Information Systems*, 29(4), 429–442	Special communications	N/A	Non-sector specific	Non country specific
32	Wrycza, S., & Maślankowski, J. (2020). Social media users' opinions on remote work during the COVID-19 pandemic. Thematic and sentiment analysis. *Information Systems Management*, 37(4), 288–297	Article	Yes	Non-sector specific	Non country specific

Appendix 2: Included Gray Literature

Google Search Engine results pages	Author	Job title (LinkedIn headline)	Followers	Article title
#1	Emily Spaven-	UK editor at LinkedIn News	22.246	How effective is remote work?
#2	Jason Schenker	Futurist | Economist | Speaker | 30 × Author | 12 × Bestseller | 10 × LinkedIn Learning Instructor | Board Member	144.162	The outlook for remote work in 2020—Before and after COVID-19

(continued)

(continued)

Google Search Engine results pages	*Author*	*Job title (LinkedIn headline)*	*Followers*	*Article title*
#3	Chris Herd	Founder & CEO @ Firstbase	34.526	COVID accelerated remote work by 10 years
#4	Sara Sutton	Founder & CEO of FlexJobs	6.497	How remote work can help organizations survive COVID-19, and be more resilient in the future
#5	Mandy Fransz, 2020, July	Transforming purpose-driven solopreneurs into client-magnetizing thought leaders on LinkedIn | ex-LinkedIn | Remote Work Advocate | Top 1% SSI | Let's connect?	11.542	The future of remote work: How will COVID-19 change the way we work?
#6	Andrew Seaman	Senior Editor for Job Search & Careers at LinkedIn News	91.627	Landing a job that lets you work from home during the pandemic
#7	David Green	People Analytics leader | Director, Insight222 & myH Rfuture.com | Conference speaker | Host, Digital HR Leaders Podcast	74.625	COVID-19: Resources for HR and People Analytics
#8	Dan Schawbel	New York Times Bestselling Author & Managing Partner of Workplace Intelligence	155.223	The leaders championing the remote work movement
#9	Jason F	Co-founder & CEO of Basecamp	69.179	Remote work is its own thing, it's not in-person work done at a distance

(continued)

(continued)

Google Search Engine results pages	*Author*	*Job title (LinkedIn headline)*	*Followers*	*Article title*
#10	Dan Schawbel	New York Times Bestselling Author & Managing Partner of Workplace Intelligence	155.223	How coronavirus is accelerating the relocation of workers from cities into suburbs
#11	Kelly Watt	Digital twins for Facility Operations, Compliance, Security & Public Safety. Quick and painless. Increase efficiency, safety, reduce risk	10.987	Remote work through digital twins—staying safe during COVID-19
#12	Dan Schawbel	New York Times Bestselling Author & Managing Partner of Workplace Intelligence	155.223	How coronavirus is accelerating the remote workplace
#13	Paul Millerd	Curious Human & Solopreneur | Reimagine Work Podcast | Teach Strategy Consulting Skills | Not An Influencer	5.248	Many companies are "going remote" without a plan, here are five tips & resources to help you navigate the shift
#14	Gary Shapiro	President and CEO at Consumer Technology Association	311.661 (LinkedIn influencer)	How COVID-19 is speeding the transition to remote work—and how tech can help
#15	Patrick Byrne	CEO–GE Digital	8.352	How digital innovation is enabling remote work at an industrial scale
#16	Nick Deligiannis	Managing Director, Australia & New Zealand at Hays	5.270	Remote work after COVID-19: 6 considerations for managers

(continued)

(continued)

Google Search Engine results pages	*Author*	*Job title (LinkedIn headline)*	*Followers*	*Article title*
#17	James Dellow	Digital strategist, collaboration consultant and human-centred designer	2.495	Why remote work is so hard—and how it can be fixed; return of the intranet; & Coronavirus fast-forwarding the office into 'Enterprise 4.0.'
#18	Mandy Fransz, 2020a, August	Transforming purpose-driven solopreneurs into client-magnetizing thought leaders on LinkedIn | ex-LinkedIn | Remote Work Advocate | Top 1% SSI | Let's connect?	11.542	Building an all-remote company—An interview with Iwo Szapar, CEO @ Remote-How
#19	Elizabeth Baskin	CEO at Tribe, Inc. | Member at Forbes Agency Council | she/her/hers	8.968	Will remote work be the new normal?
#20	Mandy Fransz, 2020b, August	Transforming purpose-driven solopreneurs into client-magnetizing thought leaders on LinkedIn | ex-LinkedIn | Remote Work Advocate | Top 1% SSI | Let's connect?	11.542	Remote work stories from advocates around the world—An interview with Josephine Tse

References

Arksey, H., & O'Malley, L. (2005). Scoping studies: Towards a methodological framework. *International Journal of Social Research Methodology, 8*(1), 19–32. https://doi.org/10.1080/1364557032000119616

Baruch, Y., & Nicholson, N. (1997). Home, sweet work: Requirements for effective home working. *Journal of General Management, 23*(2), 15–30. https://doi.org/10.1177/030630709702300202

Baskin, E. (2020, June). Will remote work be the new normal? *LinkedIn*. https://www.linkedin.com/pulse/remote-work-new-normal-elizabeth-baskin?articleId=6681919247821762560

Behera, M., Dash, M., Ayasa Kanta Mohanty, A. K. & Das, S. (2019). Entrepreneurial ecosystem: A geographical upliftment. *Revista Espacios, 40*, 26–36. Retrieved from http://www.revistaespacios.com/a19v40n01/19400126.html

Beheshti, N. (2020). Is remote work good or bad for employee engagement? Your leadership holds the answer. *Forbes*. https://www.forbes.com/sites/nazbeheshti/2020/08/27/is-remote-work-good-or-bad-for-employee-engagement-your-leadership-holds-the-answer/?sh=165889d976f9

Belzunegui-Eraso, A., & Erro-Garcés, A. (2020). Teleworking in the context of the Covid-19 crisis. *Sustainability, 12*, 3662.

Bonacini, L., Gallo, G., & Scicchitano, S. (2021). Working from home and income inequality: Risks of a "new normal" with COVID-19. *Journal of Population Economics, 34*(1), 303–360. https://doi.org/10.1007/s00148-020-00800-7

Bouziri, H., Smith, D. R. M., Descatha, A., Dab, W., & Jean, K. (2020). Working from home in the time of COVID-19: How to best preserve occupational health? *Occupational and Environmental Medicine, 77*(7), 509. https://doi.org/10.1136/oemed-2020-106599

Byrne, P. (2020, April). How digital innovation is enabling remote work at an industrial scale. *LinkedIn*. https://www.linkedin.com/pulse/how-digital-innovation-enabling-remote-work-industrial-pat-byrne

Caligiuri, P., De Cieri, H., Minbaeva, D., & Verbeke, & Zimmermann, A. (2020). International HRM insights for navigating the Covid-19 pandemic: Implications for future research and practice. *Journal of International Business Studies, 51*, 697–713. https://doi.org/10.1057/s41267-020-00335-9

Carroll, N., & Conboy, K. (2020). Normalising the "new normal": Changing tech-driven work practices under pandemic time pressure. *International Journal of Information Management*, *55*, 102186. https://doi.org/10.1016/j.ijinfomgt.2020.102186

Charalampous, M., Grant, C. A., Tramontano, C., & Michailidis, E. (2019). Systematically reviewing remote e-workers' well-being at work: A multidimensional approach. *European Journal of Work and Organizational Psychology, 28*(1), 51–73. https://doi.org/10.1080/1359432X.2018.1541886

Cook, L., Zschomler, D., Biggart, L., & Carder, S. (2020). The team as a secure base revisited: Remote working and resilience among child and family social workers during COVID-19. *Journal of Children's Services*. https://doi.org/10.1108/JCS-07-2020-0031/full/html

Cooper, C., Kurland, N., & Gephart, R. P. (2020). Telecommuting, professional isolation, and employee development in public and private organizations. *Journal of Organizational Behavior, 23*(4), 511–532.

Couch, D. L., O'Sullivan, B., & Malatzky, C. (2020). What COVID-19 could mean for the future of "work from home": The provocations of three women in the academy. *Gender, Work & Organization, n/a*(n/a). https://doi.org/10.1111/gwao.12548

Craft, A. R. (2020). Remote work in library technical services: Connecting historical perspectives to realities of the developing COVID-19 pandemic. *Serials Review, 46*(3), 227–231. https://doi.org/10.1080/00987913.2020.1806658

Crawford, J., Maccalman, L., & Jackson, C. (2011). The health and well-being of remote and mobile workers. *Occupational Medicine (Oxford, England), 61*, 385–394. https://doi.org/10.1093/occmed/kqr071

Crowley, F., & Doran, J. (2020). COVID-19, occupational social distancing and remote working potential: An occupation, sector and regional perspective. *Regional Science Policy & Practice, n/a*(n/a). https://doi.org/10.1111/rsp3.12347

Das, S. (2020). Innovations in digital banking service brand equity and millennial consumerism. In *Digital transformation and innovative services for business and learning* (pp. 62–79). IGI Global. https://doi.org/10.4018/978-1-7998-5175-2.ch004

Das, S. (2021a). A systematic study of integrated marketing communication and content management system for millennial consumers. In *Innovations in digital branding and content marketing* (pp. 91–112). IGI Global. https://doi.org/10.4018/978-1-7998-4420-4.ch005

Das, S. (2021b). Search engine optimization and marketing: A recipe for success in digital marketing (1st ed.). CRC Press. https://doi.org/10.1201/9780429298509

Dean. (2019). Here's what we learned about organic click through rate. *Blacklinko*. https://backlinko.com/google-ctr-stats

De Vries, H., Tummers, L., & Bekkers, V. (2019). The Benefits of teleworking in the public sector: Reality or rhetoric? *Review of Public Personnel Administration, 39*(4), 570–593.

Dey, M., Frazis, H., Loewenstein, M., & Sun, H. (2020). Ability to work from home: Evidence from two surveys and implications for the labor market in the COVID-19 pandemic. *Monthly Labor Review*. https://doi.org/10.21916/mlr.2020.14

Dua, S., Singh, I., & Das, S. (2021). Banking innovative service with digital brand equity for new age consumers: Internet banking and millennial consumerism. In *Innovations in digital branding and content marketing* (pp. 134–159). IGI Global. https://doi.org/10.4018/978-1-7998-4420-4.ch007

Duy, N. T., Mondal, S. R., Van, N. T. T., Dzung, P. T., Minh, D. X. H., & Das, S. (2020). A study on the role of Web 4.0 and 5.0 in the sustainable tourism ecosystem of Ho Chi Minh City, Vietnam. *Sustainability*, *12*(17), 7140. https://doi.org/10.3390/su12177140

Earle, H. A. (2003). Building a workplace of choice: Using the work environment to attract and retain top talent. *Journal of Facilities Management*, *2*(3), 224–257(14).

Eurofound, & ILO (International Labour Office). (2017). *Working anytime, anywhere: The effects on the world of work*. Publications Office of the European Union, Luxembourg, and *the* International Labour Office, Geneva. http://www.ilo.org/wcmsp5/groups/public/---dgreports/---dcomm/---publ/documents/publication/wcms_544138.pdf.

Farrer, L. (2020). 5 proven benefits of remote work for companies. *Forbes*. https://www.forbes.com/sites/laurelfarrer/2020/02/12/top-5-benefits-of-remote-work-for-companies/?sh=3ad12d0216c8

Feng, Z., & Savani, K. (2020). Covid-19 created a gender gap in perceived work productivity and job satisfaction: Implications for dual-career parents working from home. *Gender in Management*, Vol. ahead-of-print No. ahead-of-print. https://doi.org/10.1108/GM-07-2020-0202

Fransz, M. (2020, July). The future of remote work: How will COVID-19 change the way we work? *LinkedIn*. https://www.linkedin.com/pulse/future-remote-work-how-covid-19-change-way-we-mandy-fransz

Fransz, M. (2020a, August). Building an all-remote company—An interview with Iwo Szapar, CEO @ Remote-How. *LinkedIn*. https://www.linkedin.com/pulse/building-all-remote-company-interview-iwo-szapar-ceo-mandy-fransz

Fransz, M. (2020b, August). Remote work stories from advocates around the world—An interview with Josephine Tse. *LinkedIn*. https://www.linkedin.com/pulse/remote-work-stories-from-advocates-around-world-interview-fransz?trk=read_related_article-card_title

Gallacher, G., & Hossain, I. (2020). Remote work and employment dynamics under COVID-19: Evidence from Canada. *Canadian Public Policy, 46*(S1), S44–S54. https://doi.org/10.3138/cpp.2020-026

Glaser, B. G., & Strauss, A. L. (1967). *The discovery of Grounded Theory: Strategies for qualitative research*. Aldine Publishing Company

Google Search Help. (2020). https://support.google.com/websearch/answer/54068?co=GENIE.Platform%3DAndroid&hl=en

Green, D. (2020, March). COVID-19: Resources for HR and people analytics. *LinkedIn*. https://www.linkedin.com/pulse/covid-19-resources-hr-people-analytics-david-green

Gupta, D. K., Jena, D., Samantaray, A. K., & Das, S. (2019). HRD climate in selected public sector banks in India. *Revista ESPACIOS*, *40*(11).
Haworth, A. (2020). View from Portsmouth during the COVID-19 pandemic: Remote dermatology work. *Clinical and Experimental Dermatology, 45*(7), 813–814. https://doi.org/10.1111/ced.14285
Herd, C. (2020, May). COVID accelerated remote work by 10 years. *LinkedIn*. https://www.linkedin.com/pulse/covid-accelerated-remote-work-10-years-chris-herd
Hill, E. J., Hawkins, A. J., Ferris, M., & Weitzman, M. (2001). Finding an extra day a week: The positive influence of perceived job flexibility on work and family life balance. *Family Relations, 50*(1), 49–58. https://doi.org/10.1111/j.1741-3729.2001.00049.x
Hofacker, D., & Konig, S. (2013). Flexibility and work-life conflict in times of crisis: A gender perspective. *International Journal of Sociology and Social Policy, 33*(9–10), 613–635. https://doi.org/10.1108/IJSSP-04-2013-0042
Hopwood, S. P. (2019). Why remote working is the future for startups. *E27*. https://e27.co/why-remote-working-is-the-future-for-startups-20190530/
International Labour Organization. (2020a). *Defining and measuring remote work, telework, work at home and home-based work*. https://www.ilo.org/wcmsp5/groups/public/---dgreports/---stat/documents/publication/wcms_747075.pdf
International Labour Organization. (2020b). *An employers' guide on working from home in response to the outbreak of COVID-19*. https://www.ilo.org/wcmsp5/groups/public/---ed_dialogue/---act_emp/documents/publication/wcms_745024.pdf
Iqbal, S., Suh, J., Czerwinski, M., Mark, G., & Teevan, J. (2020). *Remote work and well-being*. https://www.microsoft.com/en-us/research/publication/remote-work-and-well-being/
Kramer, A., & Kramer, K. (2020). The potential impact of the Covid-19 pandemic on occupational status, work from home, and occupational mobility. *Journal of Vocational Behavior*, *119*, 103442. https://doi.org/10.1016/j.jvb.2020.103442
Laas, M. (2020). Working from home during Covid. *Data & Society*. https://datasociety.net/library/hr-tip-sheet-for-cautions-on-workplace-surveillance/
Lee, E., Chastain J., & Lau, W. (2020). Guide to remote work and team management during—and after—COVID-19. *Architect*.
Leonardi, P. M. (2020). COVID-19 and the new technologies of organizing: Digital exhaust, digital footprints, and artificial intelligence in the wake of remote work. *Journal of Management Studies*, *n/a*(n/a). https://doi.org/10.1111/joms.12648
Li, J., Ghosh, R., & Nachmias, S. (2020). In a time of COVID-19 pandemic, stay healthy, connected, productive, and learning: Words from the editorial

team of HRDI. *Human Resource Development International, 23*(3), 199–207. https://doi.org/10.1080/13678868.2020.1752493

LinkedIn. (2020). https://about.linkedin.com

LinkedIn. https://www.linkedin.com/pulse/landing-job-lets-you-work-from-home-during-pandemic-andrew-seaman

LinkedIn Help. (2020). https://www.linkedin.com/help/linkedin/answer/47545/publishing-platform-guidelines?lang=en

Lopez-Leon, S., Forero, D. A., & Ruiz-Díaz, P. (2020). Recommendations for working from home during the COVID-19 pandemic (and beyond). *Work (Reading, Mass.)*, 66(2), 371–375. https://doi.org/10.3233/WOR-203187

Madero Gómez, S., Ortiz Mendoza, O. E., Ramírez, J., & Olivas-Luján, M. R. (2020). Stress and myths related to the COVID-19 pandemic's effects on remote work. *Management Research: Journal of the Iberoamerican Academy of Management, 18*(4), 401–420. https://doi.org/10.1108/MRJIAM-06-2020-1065

Manzo, L. K. C., & Minello, A. (2020). Mothers, childcare duties, and remote working under COVID-19 lockdown in Italy: Cultivating communities of care. *Dialogues in Human Geography, 10*(2), 120–123. https://doi.org/10.1177/2043820620934268

McGowan, H. E. (2020). How the coronavirus pandemic is accelerating the future of work. *Forbes*. https://www.forbes.com/sites/heathermcgowan/2020/03/23/the-coronavirus-pandemic-accelerates-the-future-of-work-and-provides-opportunity/?sh=201efc5f317f

Millerd, P. (2020, March). Many companies are "going remote" without a plan, here are five tips & resources to help you navigate the shift. *LinkedIn*. https://www.linkedin.com/pulse/many-companies-going-remote-without-plan-here-five-tips-paul-millerd

Mohanty, P. C., Dash, M., Dash, M., & Das, S. (2019). A study on factors influencing training effectiveness. *Revista Espacios, 40*, 7–15. Retrieved from http://www.revistaespacios.com/a19v40n02/19400207.html

Molino, M., Ingusci, E., Signore, F., Manuti, A., Giancaspro, M. L., Russo, V., Zito, M., & Cortese, C. G. (2020). Wellbeing costs of technology use during Covid-19 remote working: An investigation using the Italian translation of the technostress creators scale. *Sustainability, 12*, 5911.

Mondal, S. (2021). A systematic study of new age consumer engagement and exploration for digital entertainment for over-the-top platforms in various digital media. In *Innovations in digital branding and content marketing* (pp. 113–133). IGI Global. https://doi.org/10.4018/978-1-7998-4420-4.ch006

Mondal, S. R. (2020). A systematic study for digital innovation in management education: An integrated approach towards problem-based learning in Vietnam. In *Digital innovations for customer engagement, management, and organizational improvement* (pp. 104–120). IGI Global. https://doi.org/10.4018/978-1-7998-5171-4.ch006

Mondal, S., & Sahoo, K. K. (2020). A study of green building prospects on sustainable management decision making. In *Green building management and smart automation* (pp. 220–234). IGI Global. https://doi.org/10.4018/978-1-5225-9754-4.ch011

Moretti, A., Menna, F., Aulicino, M., Paoletta, M., Liguori, S., & Iolascon, G. (2020). Characterization of home working population during COVID-19 emergency: A cross-sectional analysis. *International Journal of Environmental Research and Public Health, 17*(17), 6284. PubMed. https://doi.org/10.3390/ijerph17176284

Nadanyiova, M., & Das, S. (2020). Millennials as a target segment of socially responsible communication within the business strategy. *Littera Scripta, 13*(1), 119–134. https://doi.org/10.36708/Littera_Scripta2020/1/8

Nomura, S., Yoneoka, D., Tanoue, Y., Kawashima, T., Shi, S., Eguchi, A., & Miyata, H. (2020). Time to reconsider diverse ways of working in Japan to promote social distancing measures against the COVID-19. *Journal of Urban Health, 97*(4), 457–460. https://doi.org/10.1007/s11524-020-00464-4

Office for National Statistics. (2020). Coronavirus and homeworking in the UK: April 2020. https://www.ons.gov.uk/employmentandlabourmarket/peopleinwork/employmentandemployeetypes/bulletins/coronavirusandhomeworkingintheuk/april2020

Parent-Thirion, A., Biletta, I., Cabrita, J., Vargas, O., Vermeylen, G., Wilczynska, A., & Wilkens, M. (2017). *Eurofound, sixth European working conditions survey–overview report (update)*. Publications Office of the European Union.

Phillips, S. (2020). Working through the pandemic: Accelerating the transition to remote working. *Business Information Review, 37*(3), 129–134. https://doi.org/10.1177/0266382120953087

Plans, D. (2020). Workplace culture: Let's take this opportunity to make lasting changes. *Forbes*. https://www.forbes.com/sites/davidplans/2020/10/28/workplace-culture-lets-take-this-opportunity-to-make-lasting-changes/?sh=690df3546403

Raišienė, A. G., Rapuano, V., Varkulevičiūtė, K., & Stachová, K. (2020). Working from home—Who is happy? A survey of Lithuania's employees during the COVID-19 quarantine period. *Sustainability, 12*(13). https://doi.org/10.3390/su12135332

Razif, M., Miraja, B. A., Persada, S. F., Nadlifatin, R., Belgiawan, P. F., Redi, A. A. N. P., & Lin, S. C. (2020). Investigating the role of environmental concern and the unified theory of acceptance and use of technology on working from home technologies adoption during COVID-19. *Entrepreneurship and Sustainability Issues*. VsI Entrepreneurship and Sustainability Center, 8(1), 795–808.

Samuel, A. (2015). Have LinkedIn and medium killed the old-fashioned blog? *Harvard Business Review*.

Saplakoglu, Y., & Writer, S. (2020). COVID-19 has the potential to be as deadly as the 1918 flu. *Live Science*. https://www.livescience.com/1918-flu-covid-19-comparison.html

Schawbel, D. (2020, March). How coronavirus is accelerating the remote workplace. *LinkedIn*. https://www.linkedin.com/pulse/how-coronavirus-accelerating-remote-workplace-dan-schawbel

Schawbel, D. (2020, April). The leaders championing the remote work movement. *LinkedIn*. https://www.linkedin.com/pulse/leaders-championing-remote-work-movement-dan-schawbel

Schawbel, D. (2020, May). How coronavirus is accelerating the relocation of workers from cities into suburbs. *LinkedIn*. https://www.linkedin.com/pulse/how-coronavirus-accelerating-relocation-workers-from-cities-schawbel

Schenker, J. (2020, May). The outlook for remote work in 2020—Before and after COVID-19. *LinkedIn*. Retrieved from https://www.linkedin.com/pulse/outlook-remote-work-2020-before-after-covid-19-jason-schenker?articleId=6665459660264402944

Scimago Journal Ranking Portal. (2020). Scimago Journal & Country Rank

Seaman, A. (2020, April). Landing a job that lets you work from home during the pandemic.

Shapiro, G. (2020, April). How COVID-19 is speeding the transition to remote work—And how tech can help. *LinkedIn*. https://www.linkedin.com/pulse/how-covid-19-speeding-transition-remote-work-tech-can-gary-shapiro

Sharma, E., & Das, S. (2020). Measuring impact of Indian ports on environment and effectiveness of remedial measures towards environmental pollution. *International Journal of Environment and Waste Management, 25*(3), 356–380. https://doi.org/10.1504/IJEWM.2019.10021787

Sharma, K., Anand, A., & Kumar, R. (2020). The role of Yoga in working from home during the COVID-19 global lockdown. *Work, 66*(4), 731–737. https://doi.org/10.3233/WOR-203219

Singh, L. B., Mondal, S. R., & Das, S. (2020). Human resource practices & their observed significance for Indian SMEs. *Revista ESPACIOS, 41*(07). Retrieved from http://www.revistaespacios.com/a20v41n07/20410715.html

Singh, S., Mondal, S., Singh, L. B., Sahoo, K. K., & Das, S. (2020). An empirical evidence study of consumer perception and socioeconomic profiles for digital stores in Vietnam. *Sustainability, 12*(5), 1716. https://doi.org/10.3390/su12051716

Siri, R., Mondal, S. R., & Das S. (2020) Hydropower: A renewable energy resource for sustainability in terms of climate change and environmental protection. In *The handbook of environmental chemistry*. Springer. https://doi.org/10.1007/698_2020_635

Sutton, S. (2020, March). How remote work can help organizations survive COVID-19, and be more resilient in the future. *LinkedIn*. https://www.linkedin.com/pulse/how-remote-work-can-help-organizations-survive-covid-19-sara-sutton

Taskin, L., & Edwards, P. (2007). The possibilities and limits of telework in a bureaucratic environment: Lessons from the public sector. *New Technology, Work, and Employment, 22*(3), 195–207.

Tavares, F., Santos, E., Diogo, A. & Ratten, V. (2020). Teleworking in Portuguese communities during the COVID-19 pandemic. *Journal of Enterprising Communities: People and Places in the Global Economy*, Vol. ahead-of-print No. ahead-of-print. https://doi.org/10.1108/JEC-06-2020-0113

The Case for Remote Work in Health Care - SPONSOR CONTENT FROM SIEMENS HEALTHINEERS. (2020, September 9). *Harvard Business Review*. https://hbr.org/sponsored/2020/09/the-case-for-remote-work-in-health-care

Tursunbayeva, A. (2018). *Human resource management information systems in healthcare: Processes of development, implementation and benefits realization in complex organizations*. FrancoAngeli.

Tursunbayeva, A., Di Lauro, S., & Pagliari, C. (2018). People analytics—A scoping review of conceptual boundaries and value propositions. *International Journal of Information Management, 43*, 224–247. https://doi.org/10.1016/j.ijinfomgt.2018.08.002

United Nations, Covid-19 response. (2020). *COVID and the rule of law: A dangerous balancing act*. https://www.un.org/en/coronavirus/covid-and-rule-law-dangerous-balancing-act

Van, N. T. T., Vrana, V., Duy, N. T., Minh, D. X. H., Dzung, P. T., Mondal, S. R., & Das, S. (2020). The role of human–machine interactive devices for post-COVID-19 innovative sustainable tourism in Ho Chi Minh City, Vietnam. *Sustainability, 12*(22), 9523. https://doi.org/10.3390/su12229523

Vega, R. P., Anderson, A. J., & Kaplan, S. A. (2015). A within-person examination of the effects of telework. *Journal of Business and Psychology, 30*(2), 313–323.

Waizenegger, L., McKenna, B., Cai, W., & Bendz, T. (2020). An affordance perspective of team collaboration and enforced working from home during COVID-19. *European Journal of Information Systems, 29*(4), 429–442. https://doi.org/10.1080/0960085X.2020.1800417

Weil, T., & Murugesan, S. (2020). IT risk and resilience—Cybersecurity response to COVID-19. *IT Professional, 22*, 4–10. https://doi.org/10.1109/MITP.2020.2988330

Whiting, K. (2020). Most leaders think remote working will hit productivity—this is why. *World Economic Forum*. https://www.weforum.org/agenda/2020/10/remote-working-productivity-future-of-jobs/

WHO. (2020). Rolling updates on coronavirus disease. (Covid-19).

Wrycza, S., & Maślankowski, J. (2020). Social media users' opinions on remote work during the COVID-19 pandemic. Thematic and sentiment analysis. *Information Systems Management*, *37*(4), 288–297. https://doi.org/10.1080/10580530.2020.1820631

Yuhan, C., Dongqi, C., & Zixuan, L. (2020). COVID-19 virus pneumonia's economic effect in different industries: A case study XE "Case study/Case studies" in China. *Journal of Applied Finance and Banking*, *10*(5), 129–147.

CHAPTER 7

Dynamic Role of Technology in Managing Workforce in Service Delivery During COVID-19 Pandemic

Dora Almeida, Maria José Sousa, and Antonio Miguel Pesqueira

Introduction

The COVID-19 pandemic that took all organizations by surprise brought immense changes in methods and work equipment, in the sense that mobilization was limited, services were on standby or stopped, and new ways of providing services had to be considered in this new context (Das, 2021a; Mondal & Das, 2021; Sharma & Das, 2021). This chapter

D. Almeida (✉)
Universidade Europeia, Lisbon, Portugal

M. J. Sousa
Instituto Universitário de Lisboa, Lisbon, Portugal
e-mail: maria.jose.sousa@iscte-iul.pt

A. M. Pesqueira
Bavarian Nordic, Zug, Switzerland

S. R. Mondal et al. (eds.), *HR Analytics and Digital HR Practices*,
https://doi.org/10.1007/978-981-16-7099-2_7

analyzes the role of technology in the organizational world, particularly in the workforce, and the provision of services during and after the COVID-19 pandemic. The explosion in digital connectivity on a global scale is not new (Ravi & Mondal, 2021; Siri & Das, 2021). This has expanded rapidly over the past two decades, thanks to digital technology, and has revolutionized changes in corporate performance and competition on a global level (Bwalya & Mutula, 2014; Gauld et al., 2010). The authors intend to use this chapter to clarify the current view after several changes in the organizational context. Changes in some companies to the state of the art and its follow-up areas. With human resource management, we also have a pandemic that will affect the workforce and the way they manage their productivity, and even human resources will have to adjust to new circumstances and behaviors. Therefore, this chapter also addresses the potential shortage of internal talent and the resulting disruption to processes, including difficulties in managing human resources and approaching business processes. All the variants that the authors mentioned above will be related to service delivery during the pandemic.

Technology

Technology has become a daily presence in our lives and work with no exception (Duman and Das, 2021; Mondal, 2020a; Yegen & Mondal, 2021). Recent developments for human resource analytics propel the employees and organizations to be more techno-savvy (Lengnick-Hall & Lengnick-Hall, 2018). Digitalized effective workforce management stands out as the main effective result of these new dynamic innovations of technology in human resources (Berber et al., 2018; Sharma et al., 2020). Technology affects all possible stages of human resource management starting from recruitment to career planning for the employees (Tooranloo et al., 2017). Technology could be ambiguous as it has its pros and cons for organizations (Das, 2020a). Across countries, the effect on the workforce and functions has a wide variation by technology (Das, 2021b). For rich countries, it is forecasted that around 9% of jobs will be automated by 2023 (Das, 2021c; Mondal, 2021). In relatively low-income countries technology penetration is in a nascent stage and expected to be incremental in near future (Arntz et al., 2016; Drum, 2013). As per Michaels et al. (2014), better technological skills will get earnings for individuals as well.

Technology affects different workers in its indomitable way diversely, those from educational industry may find technology very much not attractive than those of IT professionals who are very much techno-savvy (Dua et al., 2021; Duy et al., 2020). Technology is likely to bring clear advantages to a workforce that will mainly, but not completely, adapt to change (Singh et al., 2020a; Siri et al., 2020; Van et al., 2020). Technology-driven skills are in demand in science, engineering, project management, and nanotechnology fields (World Bank, World Development Indicators, 2016). So, high-skilled data-driven technology-oriented professionals will be in demand in near future (Katz & Krueger, 1998). These professionals are likely to affect the entire organization's working culture collectively (Michaels et al., 2014). It has been registered in this pandemic phase that digital use has been increasing strongly and technology has increasingly assumed a fundamental role on the part of the workforce (Das, 2020b; Mondal, 2020b; Sharma & Das, 2020). However, it is essential to verify the degree to which this change was significant since technology has long been part of the daily lives of companies and employees (Mondal & Sahoo, 2020; Nadanyiova & Das, 2020).

It is always interesting to explore the amount of technology used in organizations and how the collective role has changed significantly before and after COVID-19 (Mohanty et al., 2019). Even though governments around the world are proposing (and making many mandatory) to work from home, the truth is that many have only changed their job and not the technology used (Behera et al., 2019). It is therefore important to review what are the key changes in this new context of how organizations work and, consequently, the technology that goes with them (Gupta et al., 2019).

Digital Information

The digital environment has revolutionized the production and circulation of information (Quaglietta & Alvord, 2020). We highlighted how the information-support and bio dimensionality was replaced by information-support-technology three-dimensionality, which means that man is no longer able to directly access digital information, and the mediation of a technological platform is necessary (Vennam, 2020). Contrary to what one might think, this passage does not cause the support to disappear, since information always lacks a physical dimension to exist. That support becomes the digital environment (Pacheco, 2015).

Pinto (2009) therefore proposes a new preservation model that covers the entire cycle of information life and is necessary to implement measures that move the whole digital information life cycle from initiation to use. Sustainable long-term benefits will come after implementation of a reliable approach and authenticate digital stability, adding to the complexity of the problems experienced by those skilled in the art of sustaining producers of digital information, including computer programs, those who should consider their future preservation in the design of their products, and it is clear that at times the responsibility for preservation rested solely with the organizations that were responsible for the safekeeping of the collections (Pinto, 2009). The retrieval of digital information can be prepared by computer software which will be more than basic information. Everything you see and hear can be effectively digitized (Bailey, 1993). Thus, the database can contain music films, music, or images of works of art. Some databases can only contain images or multimedia works that collect data in audio/visual or textual form. We can then highlight some aspects of digital information, as follows:

- **Reproducibility**. A digital information object can be copied endlessly without any loss of quality. Unlike, for example, a physical book, a photo, or an audio recording (Ware & Grantham, 2003).
- **Ease of sharing**. Digital information can be easily copied and circulated rapidly at minimal cost than analog data in the past. Communicating information to groups is costly and therefore requires some resources and dedication (Youssef, 2012). In this way, technologies such as email and websites enable the same sharing/transmission for many people with just one touch.
- **Flexibility**. Various information can be produced digitally in very different ways: text, films, sound, images, etc. Others. It can even be used to control physical movement through a digital controller (Taylor, 1913).
- **Easily modified**. Digital representations can easily be changed. It's easy and already normal to change an image, be it color, size, or even props, as well as simply adding text to images and other kinds of features. All these changes can, in some cases and if desired, be made from scratch without noticing their tampering (Zhu et al., 2020).
- **Difficulty of interception**. As each physical existence of data cannot be linked with its digital counterpart, researchers find there is always a connection between these two information sources to have synchronization.

Digital information became a daily ally of organizations during the COVID-19 in the sense that any information received, even though it was already digital, became even more relevant when another form of disclosure became complicated and, in many cases, impossible in this pandemic digital information has become more than ever a general means of communication in all areas. The COVID-19 pandemic information can be attributed to both digital and viral simultaneously through social and traditional media, for example, by circulating data by government or health authorities, it has reached every corner of the world very rapidly. The death toll is being closely followed by all the government authorities as it is increasing everywhere. Pictures along with quarantine stories are everywhere to feel and document. So, as a result, everyone can feel the fearful frightening consequences of this pandemic all over the world. Also many pieces of information are circulated which are not true and they create more chaos and confusion among the mass.

Virtual Working

All the logistic and inter-communication channels are differently placed among various organizations which affect the employees a lot in this unprecedented times (Gigerenzer, 2015). Globally employees are communicating virtually through various digital platforms in order to stay well communicated and achieve their common objectives (Sukumadas & Sawhney, 2004). Face-to-face direct physical interaction cannot be possible due to lockdown restrictions and social distancing. So, the employees after repeated exposure to these virtual platforms of communication sharing become experts and very much technology-driven for their convenience. So, here the importance of secure, powerful, suitable, and easy to operate virtual platform is the need of the hour. The most critical of all technological interventions is to get a balance for all types of interventions possible for employees and organizations (Oshri et al., 2008). As per Jackson, Paul J. (1999), in virtual working the intention is to build on this former work by focusing on the issues and dynamics which can establish the new ways of working. Virtual working brought to organizations new challenges in structuring, managing, and generally dealing with work. Relating new social and organizational dynamics and considerate of which may be a substantial point to the effective operation and management of the innovation involved.

The ability of the work team to keep all updated about technological developments is the most critical for organizations. Virtual teams consist of geographically separated people who work with modern computer technologies across the boundaries of space and time. Its members rarely or never contact physically (Johnson et al., 2001). While some new companies of twenty-first century use technology and virtual working to their success, still some traditional organizations averse to it and depend on the physical way of communication for their operation. The executive team is increasingly determined to be more productive by taking advantage of some of the technologies and properties of the virtual team. Because of the invasiveness of technology in most modern businesses, it may not be more practical to distinguish between traditional face-to-face and virtual teams. Owing to this pandemic, many organizations are working virtually with physically dispersed workforce for the first time. As the number of infections has risen, governments everywhere have imposed restrictions geographically and forced organizations to work remotely. Employees depend on the digital mode of communication for their operation (Raghuram et al., 2019).

Smart Working

"Smart working is known as a new model of work that uses the new technologies and the development of existing technologies to improve both the performance and the satisfaction that is obtained from the job. It should not be confused with the term co-working, which refers to a shared workspace, usually by self-employed professionals" (Ehorus, 2017). It is based on two fundamental premises: having a more profitable and efficient way of working, using technology as a great ally (Ehorus, 2017).

The most innovative potential of the workforce is kept unknown due to unsuitable models of operation (Oksanen & Sthle, 2013), consequently many companies are restructuring their models to include smart working (Plantronics, 2014). Smart Work is an alternative organizational model focused on flexibility and autonomy. The dynamic developments in internet and mobile technologies have increasingly enabled companies to support the ongoing implementation of smart work models (Ahuja et al., 2007).

Methodology

This chapter aims to analyze the dynamic role technology plays in service delivery by the workforce. The authors decided on a quantitative method, taking into account the object of investigation and the current situation. Quantitative data are independent and authors tried to be unbiased (Freixo, 2011; Malhotra, 2004).

According to the object of study and the field of application-defined, it was decided to use the quantitative method, to be able to compare the data of the survey. The investigation method considered most suitable was the inquiry by questionnaire. Also taking into account the current measures that eventually limit the possibility of inquiries and/or face-to-face interviews that could have been taken into account for the study in question.

The questionnaire helps in collecting measurable information or data and measures the hypothesis (Fortin, 2009; Freixo, 2011). Demographic quantifiable data gives an insight of socioeconomics factors (McIntyre, 1999). According to Pinsonneault and Kraemer (1993), surveys also point for historical data among the focus groups. As per McIntyre (1999) survey, although is very challenging, it brings attitudinal attributes. The questionnaire used by the authors contained closed and opened-ended questions. Most of the parts of those last were to complement closed questions, especially in case of none of the answers above-mentioned fit on the respondents.

Data Analysis and Discussions

The information produced by this chapter questionnaire can be used to better understand the technology, processes, and work habits resulted from the COVID-19 pandemic crisis. The results from the questionnaire are presented below and with a key objective to provide a consistent overview of all relevant topics and data analysis highlights. This section of the article deals with the analytical part of the research, where the design of the research is developed, the approach of statistical analysis, and the development of hypotheses, which are derived from the research question: RQ1: What dynamic role does technology play in the management of workers in the provision of services during and after the COVID-19 pandemic crisis?

Table 7.1 Data sheet

Fieldwork	From 20 March to 20 November
Number of samples	90
Type of sample	Convenience and Quota sampling
Type of survey	Online Structured Questionnaire
Geographical information	Not accumulated

Source Authors' own data analysis

a. **Data collection overview**

The information was collected using a structured questionnaire that was created after a literature search. A convenience sample was used (non-probabilistic sampling method). The fieldwork was carried out between March and November 2020 with the participation of 90 people. In order to ensure that the data is more representative, we have selected people from companies all over the world and sent the invitation to participate in the questionnaire by email. Table 7.1 (5) shows a summary of the information on data collection and the technical issues of the sample.

b. **Data analysis and observations**

To examine what is the dynamic role of technology in managing workforces in service delivery during and after the COVID-19 pandemic crisis, it was executing a descriptive analysis of what is approximately the percentage that is further processed for value generation. The initial descriptive analysis performed was related with the age group from the questionnaire respondents, where 43% of all the respondents were part of the 40s age group, 17% between 30 and 35 years, 14% from 35 to 40 years age group, 13% from 25 to 30 years group, and lastly 12% from 18 to 25 years age group (Fig. 7.1).

In terms of the respondents' gender, the majority was feminine with a clear percentage of 66% from the total group of answers. Only 1% from all the questionnaire population didn't want to reply to the presented gender question (Fig. 7.2).

Below we can find the descriptive analysis and understanding of the main professional area from the questionnaire respondent that allow us

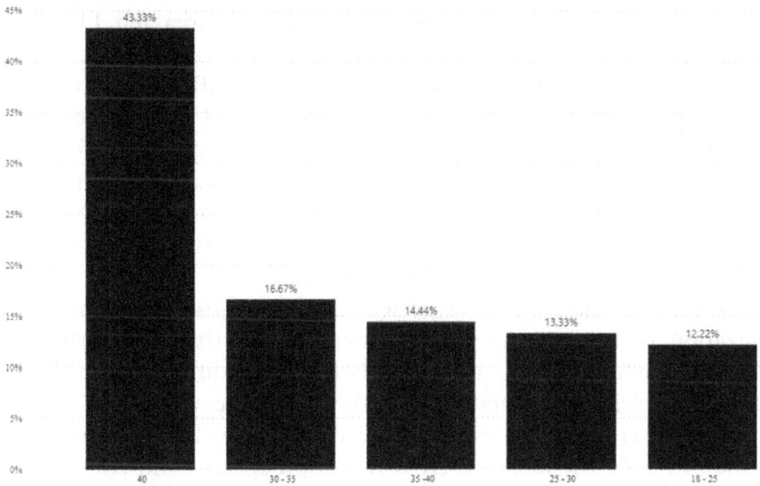

Fig. 7.1 Descriptive analysis of the age groups from the questionnaire respondents (*Source* Authors' own data analysis)

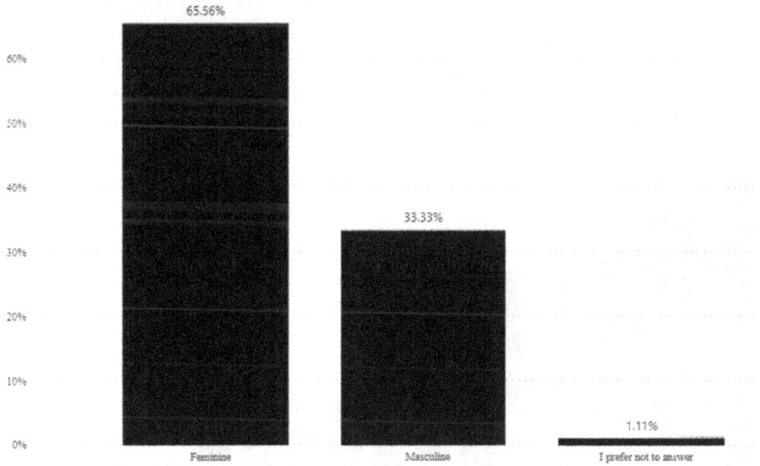

Fig. 7.2 Descriptive analysis of the gender from the questionnaire respondents (*Source* Authors' own data analysis)

to understand that 13% were from the management area and 11% from the education and marketing/publicity areas (Fig. 7.3).

It was also executed an analysis of the major differences from the selected questionnaire variables that were in total 53 with as described previously 90 observations and without any duplicated records for analysis. Of the analyzed variables, 44 were categorical and nine were numerical. In terms of the descriptive analysis summary, the below table helps us to understand all relevant statistical indicators and before we start presenting the comparative data observations (Table 7.2).

The following charts will now present the major observations and data visualization in terms of the comparative analysis that was performed in this study and to better understand the major differences from the selected variables before and during the pandemic crisis of COVID-19. For a better comprehension of the data that will be presented we describe in the below table for cross-validation analysis and comparative understanding of the data inputs for the necessary graphical interpretation. Below we can find the selected block of questions used to better understand the variation and key differences from the assessed parameters before and during COVID-19 (as the answerers were collected still during the COVID-19 pandemic crisis).

To proceed with a consistent and meaningful data analysis, we proceeded with a selection of the most relevant questions that presented

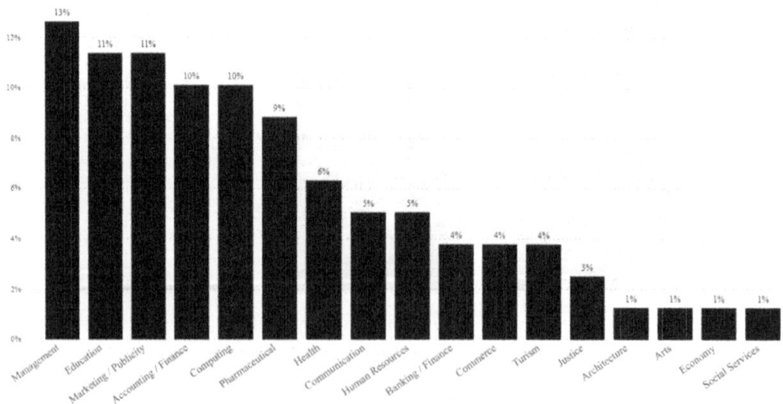

Fig. 7.3 Descriptive analysis of the main professional area from the questionnaire respondents (*Source* Authors' own data analysis)

Table 7.2 Descriptive key indicators for statistics and quantile statistics key indicators selection

Standard deviation from all variables	26.12470096
Coefficient of variation (CV)	0.5741692518
Kurtosis	−1.2
Mean	45.5
Variance	682.5
Fifth percentile	5.45
Range	89

Source Authors' own data analysis

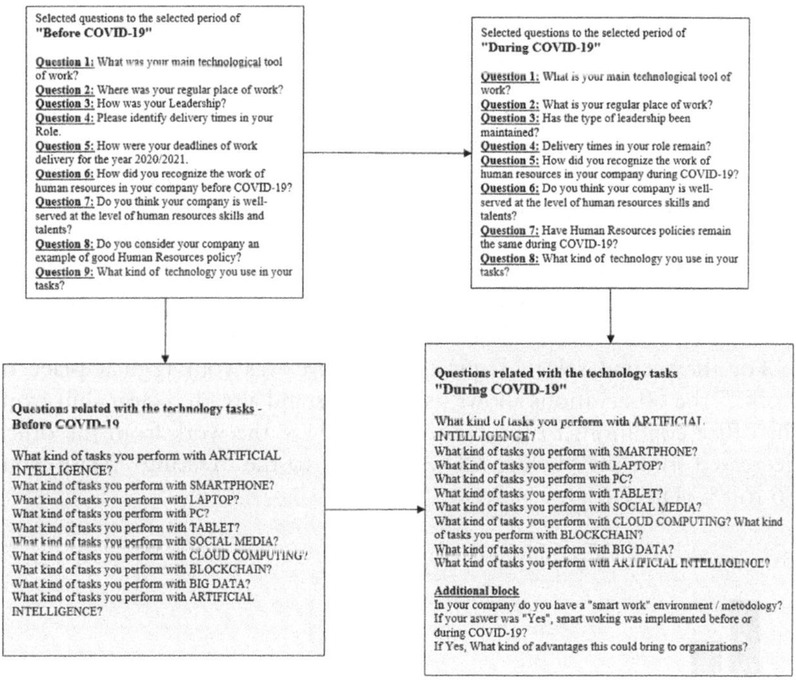

Fig. 7.4 Selected block of questions from the questionnaire to perform comparative analysis (*Source* Authors' own data analysis)

valid conclusions in terms of data analysis and support to the conclusions and discussions. For the questions part of the assessment of the task and as we can see from the Fig. 7.4, those questions and related answers were condensed in terms of collected inputs and we produced several textual

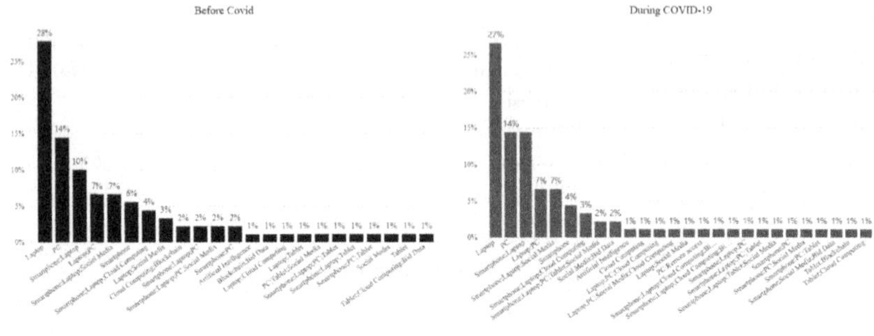

Fig. 7.5 First selected question (*Source* Authors' own data analysis)

and semantic analyses using simple natural language processing analysis through word clouds and words frequency to understand the answers and provided feedback in terms of the variation of tasks before COVID and during. Those analyses and conclusions will be later presented in the final part of this section. To the first comparative variable, the selected question was: What was your main technological tool of work? The provided answers allow us to understand a growing indication of the usage of smartphones and a residual decrease in terms of laptop usage (Fig. 7.5).

For the second selected question "Where was your regular place of work?," the observations allows us to understand already a clear shift from the office conditions to the home office where the work from the office decreased from the "before COVID" time to the "During" phase from 36 to 8% (Fig. 7.6).

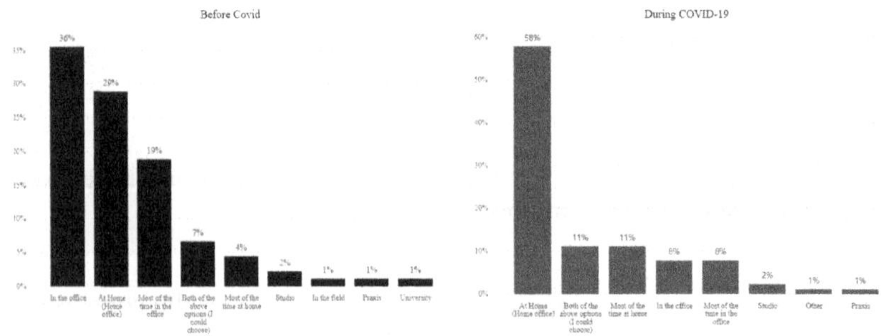

Fig. 7.6 Second selected question (*Source* Authors' own data analysis)

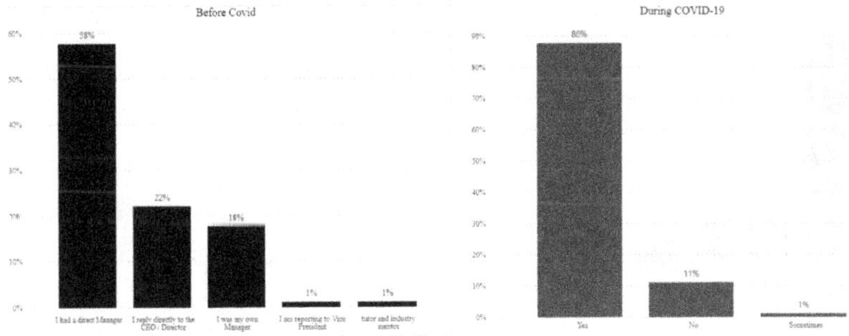

Fig. 7.7 Third selected question (*Source* Authors' own data analysis)

Answering the third question, the answers provide clear indications that during the pandemic the type of leadership was maintained where only 11% replied as the leadership style have been changed from the previous answers (Fig. 7.7).

Answering the fourth question, the major conclusion is that no major differences were registered in terms of changes to the delivery times from the work before and during the pandemic.

- **Question 4**: Please identify delivery times in your Role.
- **Question 4**: Delivery times in your role remain?

Of all respondents, 52% replied that all deadlines were stipulated by the organization and during COVID, the overall deliverables were maintained (Fig. 7.8).

Proceeding to the analysis from question 6 to question 7 from during the period we can understand that all the involved work from the human resources during the pandemic increased in terms of the delivery quality and overall perception of all the involved efforts (Fig. 7.9).

- **Question 6**: How did you recognize the work of human resources in your company before COVID?
- **Question 5**: How did you recognize the work of human resources in your company during COVID?

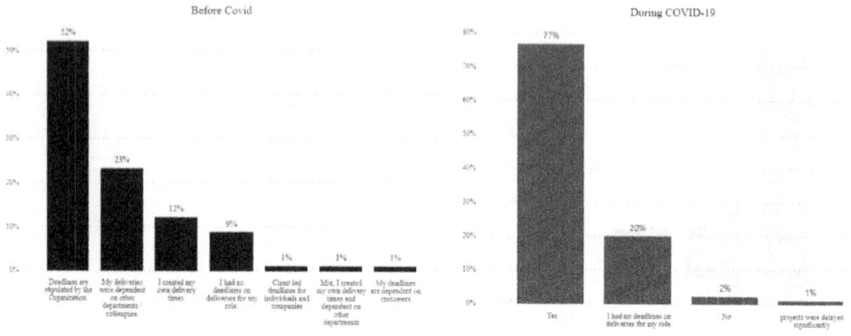

Fig. 7.8 Fourth selected question (*Source* Authors' own data analysis)

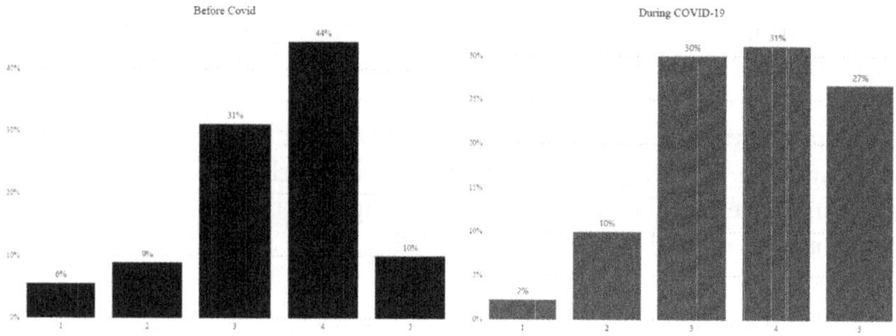

Fig. 7.9 Question 6 from the before COVID and question 5 from the during phase (*Source* Authors' own data analysis)

Regarding the questions that aim to better understand the level of the human resources skills and talents, we were able to understand an increase in the positive perception and a clear increase in terms of agreement and confirmation that during COVID the skills and talents were perceived from a more positive manner (Fig. 7.10).

One of the most relevant questionnaire questions was related to the technology usage from both periods "What kind of technology you use in your tasks?" The main analysis conducted from this graph allows us to understand that before COVID, the usage of smartphones and laptops were predominant, where without major differences we were able also to understand that even during COVID the laptops and smartphones continue to have a consistent usage. The laptop continued to be the main technology without major surprise as from the analyzed data the main

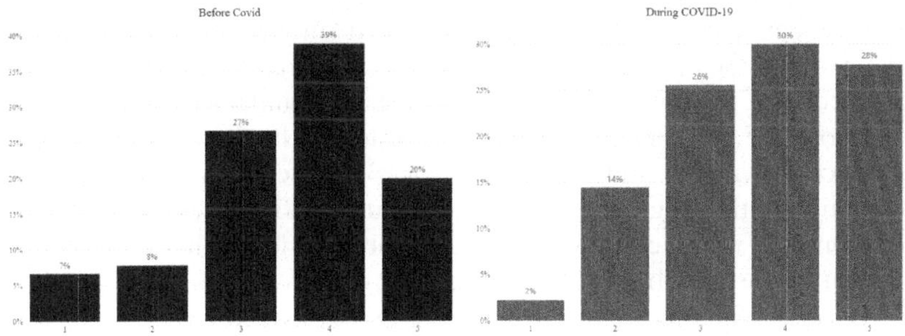

Fig. 7.10 Question 7 from the before COVID and question 6 from the during phase (*Source* Authors' own data analysis)

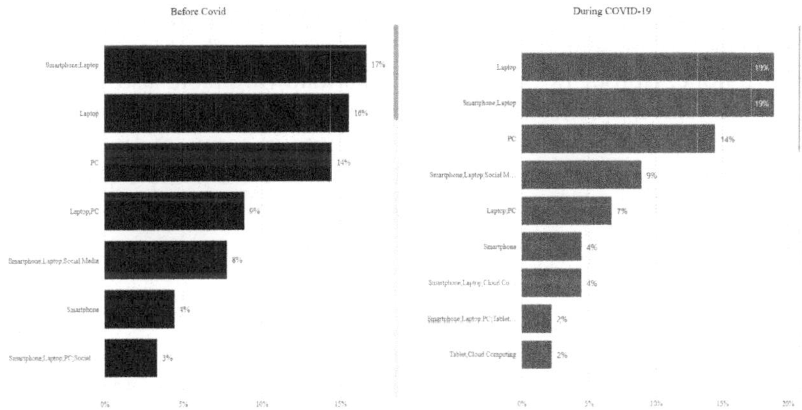

Fig. 7.11 Question 9 from the before COVID and question 8 from the during phase (*Source* Authors' own data analysis)

differences are in terms of the work location and methods and not so much in terms of the used technology (Fig. 7.11).

Proceeding to the second group of questions (tasks), and according to Fig. 7.4, we condensed and aggregated the main conclusions from the collected text. The questions related to the tasks had open answers and allowed to collect more details in terms of the different tasks and procedures in using the different technologies. To present an effective way to understand the collected data, we proceeded with an aggregated view of all the free-text notes and answers from the questionnaire questions. Initially, we conducted some text analysis like the count of words and frequency of terms, then we conducted simple visualization graphs like world clouds to better understand the most relevant terms and then proceed with the context mapping and meaning understanding.

Below we can find an example of one of the many word clouds produced to better understand the words' frequency and initial understanding of the aggregated answers. Figure 7.11 presented the word frequency in all the collected answers to the question: What kind of tasks do you perform with LAPTOP? (Fig. 7.12).

To have a full picture of the keywords and described terms, we present below the aggregation and summary of all collected answers to the second part of the questionnaire that aimed to understand the relevant tasks in connection with the described technologies. In terms of the collected comments, we didn't have clear observations and valuable notes from the questions related to big data, block chain, cloud computing, and tablets. Therefore, we presented conclusions and our data analysis in terms of the smartphone, laptop, PC, and tablets. The following table also shows the keywords and frequency of the most mentioned notes from the collected answers in which we observed some changes in terms of laptop usage (more virtual and remote tasks) and an increase from the PC usage in terms of videoconferences and virtual meetings (Table 7.3).

Fig. 7.12 Question 9 from the before COVID and question 8 from the during phase (*Source* Authors' own data analysis)

Table 7.3 Collected open text from questionnaire questions analysis

Questionnaire question	*Most relevant presented tasks "Before COVID-19"*	*Key words and frequency—"Before COVID-19"*	*Most relevant presented tasks—"During COVID-19*	*Key words and frequency—"During COVID-19"*
What kind of tasks do you perform with SMARTPHONE?	• Calls, chats, and emails • Proceed with business appointments and scheduling calls • Text messages, social media management, and information sharing • Check websites for competitive analysis and connecting with people and coordinating projects • Conferences and reply to emails	Calls ($n = 7$) meetings ($n = 6$) conferences ($n = 4$) emails ($n = 3$)	• Several comments sharing that all tasks continue as before • Appointments and meetings scheduling • Sending emails, working with excel and company software • Finance and project management, presentations • Social media, video chat for coaching, delivery workshops, and live video broadcast	Same ($n = 5$) appointments ($n = 3$) social media ($n = 2$) no changes ($n = 2$)

(continued)

Table 7.3 (continued)

Questionnaire question	*Most relevant presented tasks "Before COVID-19"*	*Key words and frequency—"Before COVID-19"*	*Most relevant presented tasks—"During COVID-19*	*Key words and frequency—"During COVID-19"*
What kind of tasks do you perform with LAPTOP?	• client deliverables like decks, excels, and internal software • analytics and reports creation and data analysis • Tasks made with Microsoft office, emails, and sending emails • Power points usage, intranet, and access to company software and platforms	Excel ($n = 4$) PowerPoints ($n = 2$) reports ($n = 2$)	• Virtual classes, interactivity by email, and recording of classes • Spreadsheets, and communication via email using Zoom • Sending emails, working with excel and company software • Finance and project management, presentations • Social media, video chat for coaching, delivery workshops, and live video broadcast	Email ($n = 7$) media ($n = 6$) excel ($n = 4$)
What kind of tasks do you perform with a PC?	• Presentations and analysis • Data management and programming • reports creation, emails, and Microsoft office usage	Presentations ($n = 8$) Programming ($n = 5$) Analysis ($n = 4$)	• virtual classes, interactivity by email, and recording of classes • emails and data management • Same as above, data management and presentations but an increase for videoconferences	Data ($n = 5$) Videoconferences ($n = 4$) Virtual ($n = 3$)

Questionnaire question	*Most relevant presented tasks "Before COVID-19"*	*Key words and frequency—"Before COVID-19"*	*Most relevant presented tasks—"During COVID-19*	*Key words and frequency—"During COVID-19"*
What kind of tasks do you perform with TABLET?	• Remote meetings and quick sales analysis • Emails and meetings management • Conferences	Email (n = 6) Remote meetings (n = 4)	• Remote meetings and conferences	Remote (n = 4) Conferences (n = 2)

Source Authors' own data analysis

Discussion

According to Ahuja et al. (2007), mentioned in the literature review, the evolution and diffusion of technologies, namely devices with numerous functionality and easy to use, allows companies to gradually implement smart work models. In a natural way, this pandemic has brought some dynamism to the technology used, namely in task changes with new devices with the same purpose and delivery (Candeais & Morhard, 2018). If before, virtual work was implemented to experiment and be able to verify the results of various ways of working, as new challenges in managing and structuring (Jackson, 1999), currently is an imposed reality but well-received considering the evolution that until now was noted. The digital environment has revolutionized the production and circulation of information (Pacheco, 2015), and it is increasingly noted that this revolution will not end or stagnate as long as we have factors such as the pandemic that make digital dynamics transform in various ways and find new ways to act (Mamaghani, 2006).

In general, we have come to see the importance of technology in the organizational world and how it can be dynamic and easily change according to various factors (Munsterberger, 1913). All the literature turned to the field of technology, already mentioned here, is found in one way or another with what the various authors mentioned, namely in terms of management, platforms used, and even perception of the activity of human resources.

Specifically the quality of workers' performance during the pandemic is based on the quality of interactions, communication, and coordination between the team member and the managers, most of the time through technologies (Gimenez-Nadal et al., 2018). Although it is difficult to assess the nature and impact of digital communication, it is consensual that has enormous potential that can be exploited by companies, thus optimizing their information and communication systems (Eurofound, 2015). This is the case of software tools for collaborative group work that enable teamwork, through cloud-computing technologies, exploring the capabilities of communication through digital technologies (Song et al., 2019). Thus, it allows the development of a set of tasks, including (a) conduct, in real-time, interactive work sessions between several users, regardless of the physical distance between them; (b) the creation of a central point of access to all available information resources, necessary for the group's activity, simplifying the access, circulation, and use of critical and complementary information; (c) the use of email, chat, audio, and video conferencing tools as priority means of communication between team members; (d) support for project management features, which are indispensable for integrating the contribution of each member of the team; (e) allow the use of shared documents (texts, spreadsheets, etc), vital for teleworking situations (Eurofound and the International Labour Office, 2017).

In this context, it is these cooperation tools, such as email, online discussions, or conferences, information sharing via the Internet (making information available for everyone to access quickly and at low costs), videoconferences, and sharing of applications in online meetings (where data can be manipulated using applications such as spreadsheets, databases or graphical applications) that allow the creation of an effective information and communication system. During the pandemic crises, it was possible to verify that digital collaboration methods allowed cost savings and also allowed the development of better organizational relationships and the maximization of the advantages of communication between workers.

Limitations and Future Scope of Research

The main limitation of this study is the little literature existing about COVID-19 and technology. It is noticed that more and more data are emerging about this pandemic and COVID-19, but they are all still very volatile and with regular changes, due to the novelty of this whole world state. Analysis of this impact could be much more profound if we could carry out the same study, but we can already say that the pandemic was no longer installed. After analyzing the data, it was understood that it would be interesting in the future to be able to investigate how labor relations have/had an impact in terms of the pandemic and also in the service delivery. Also, it may still be pertinent to understand the changes in leadership when going through a pandemic, and where all aspects of the company can be called into question. Also it is relevant to analyze which work methods supported by technologies need to be adapted to a new context of work. And investigate the work segmentation possibilities that can be supported by technology. Another important research will be regarding the skills needed, and the analyses of future work scenarios that may emerge from the pandemic situation. We would also recommend a larger number of respondents in order to have an even more global perspective on this technological dynamism in organizations.

Conclusion

The purpose of this research chapter was to demonstrate and communicate the key differences and variations in terms of technology usage and adoption before and during the pandemic crisis of COVID-19. The use of technologies was essential to implement remote work that was mandatory during the pandemic situation. However, the use of new technologies alone does not eliminate the existing organizational deficiencies that underlie operational rigidity and dysfunctions. Nevertheless, the communication processes and the work were digital-based as a necessary need to keep the world moving. In this context, the value of the produced analysis via an online questionnaire allowed us to conclude that several changes occurred in terms of working locations, tasks, procedures, and levels of skills.

COVID-19 has been increasing the way that virtual and remote technologies have been used and enhancing the digital transformation and information sharing across several different industries and companies. A disruptive innovation has occurred as a consequence of the pandemic situation, and the need to rethink the way the jobs were delivered, to prevent the spread of a deadly virus unknown and without a cure being known or a vaccine to prevent the spread on large scale. The organizations had to transform their selves very rapidly to face the challenges of the digital—that was the solution to continue their activity—and the workers needed to learn new ways of work, communicate, and share information and knowledge.

The primary data collected with the questionnaire was validated and analyzed through several analysis procedures like validation of all responses. The statistical analysis performed allowed us to understand the phenomenon also from a comparative perspective where the time dimension was before and during COVID-19.

The main conclusion derived from this research—there is a need in the academic and practitioner community to have more knowledge on the involved variables that causes organizational changes and future perspectives for innovation models that allows the organizations to increase the employees' productivity and performance levels, even when the workplace and working conditions changes abruptly. It is interesting to note that the technology used, remained significantly the same, before and during COVID. Where there were changes was in the tasks practiced with each of the most used technologies, as there was a need to rethink the organizations goals to match the needs of a population confined to their homes.

Regarding the workplace, there was a change to work from home, during COVID-19, however, it is important to mention that there are no significant changes in terms of deadlines and delivery of work, besides all the constraints regarding a balance in work and family/personal life, as all the family was at home with different duties and schedules. We also concluded that the organizational structure was maintained and that there was a significant increase in satisfaction with human resources. In addition, and important to note is the verification of increased competence by human resources after COVID-19. We can understand that there were efforts made by the HR team to keep the teams motivated so that there are no major changes in their communication and way of working, regardless of the situation experienced.

References

Ahuja, M. K., Chudoba, K. M., Kacmar, C. J., McKnight, D. H., & George, J. F. (2007). IT road warriors: Balancing work-family conflict, job autonomy, and work overload to mitigate turnover intentions. *MIS Quarterly, 31*(1), 1–17.

Arntz, M., Gregory, T., & Zierahn, U. (2016, May). *The risk of automation for jobs in OECD countries: A comparative analysis*. Organisation for economic co-operation and development (Employment and Migration Working Chapters, No. 189). OECD Publishing.

Bailey, T. (1993). *Discretionary effort and the organization of work: Employee participation and work reform since Hawthorne*. Columbia University.

Behera, M., Dash, M., Mohanty, A. K., & Das, S. (2019). Entrepreneurial ecosystem: A geographical upliftment. *Revista Espacios, 40*, 26–36. http://www.revistaespacios.com/a19v40n01/19400126.html

Berber, N., Đorđević, B., & Milanović, S. (2018). Electronic human resource management (e-HRM): A new concept for digital age. *Strategic Management, 23*(2), 22–32.

Bwalya, K. J., & Mutula, S. M. (Eds.). (2014). *E-Government: Implementation, adoption and synthesis in developing countries*. de Gruyter Saur.

Candeais, V., & Morhard, R. (2018). *The human costs of epidemics are going down but the economic costs are going up: Here's why*. World Economic Forum 2018. https://www.weforum.org/agenda/2018/05/how-epidemics-infect-the-global-economy-and-what-to-do-about-it/

Das, S. (2020a). Innovations in digital banking service brand equity and millennial consumerism. In *Digital transformation and innovative services for business and learning* (pp. 62–79). IGI Global. https://doi.org/10.4018/978-1-7998-5175-2.ch004

Das, S. (2020b, February). *Media impact of advertising on consumer buying behaviour a comparative study of different media*. Shiksha o Anusandhan University. http://hdl.handle.net/10603/273691

Das, S. (2021a). A systematic study of integrated marketing communication and content management system for millennial consumers. In *Innovations in digital branding and content marketing* (pp. 91–112). IGI Global. https://doi.org/10.4018/978-1-7998-4420-4.ch005

Das, S. (2021b). *Digital entertainment: The next evolution in service sector*. Springer Nature. https://doi.org/10.1007/978-981-15-9724-4. Print ISBN 978-981-15-9723-7. Online ISBN 978-981-15-9724-4

Das, S. (2021c). *Search engine optimization and marketing: A recipe for success in digital marketing* (1st ed.). CRC Press. https://doi.org/10.1201/9780429298509

Drum, K. (2013). Welcome, robot overloads; Please don't fire us? Smart machines probably won't kill us all, but they'll definitely take our jobs and sooner than you think. *Mother Jones*.

Dua, S., Singh, I., & Das, S. (2021). Banking innovative service with digital brand equity for new age consumers: Internet banking and millennial consumerism. In *Innovations in digital branding and content marketing* (pp. 134–159). IGI Global. https://doi.org/10.4018/978-1-7998-4420-4.ch007

Duman, Ü. O., & Das, S. (2021). The dynamic rise of digital brands' market Mavens in digital entertainment: A complete know how for curious customers. In *Digital entertainment* (pp. 147–172). Palgrave Macmillan. https://doi.org/10.1007/978-981-15-9724-4_8

Duy, N. T., Mondal, S. R., Van, N. T. T., Dzung, P. T., Minh, D. X. H., & Das, S. (2020). A study on the role of web 4.0 and 5.0 in the sustainable tourism ecosystem of Ho Chi Minh City, Vietnam. *Sustainability*, *12*(17), 7140. https://doi.org/10.3390/su12177140

Ehorus. (2017). *Do you know what smart working is?* https://ehorus.com/smartworking/

Eurofound. (2015). *Third European company survey—Overview report*. Publications Office of the European Union.

Eurofound and the International Labour Office. (2017). *Working anytime, anywhere: The effects on the world of work*. Publications Office of the European Union, Luxembourg, and the International Labour Office, Geneva.

Fortin, M. (2009). *O Processo de investigação – da concepção à realização*. Lusociencia.

Freixo, M. V. (2011). *Metodologia da pesquisa: fundamentos, métodos e técnicas*. Instituto Piaget.

Gauld, R., Goldfinch, S., & Horsburgh, S. (2010). Do they want it? Do they use it? The "demandside" of e-government in Australia and New Zealand. *Government Information Quarterly, 27*(2), 177–186.

Gigerenzer, G. (2015). *Risk savvy: How to make good decisions*. Penguin.

Gimenez-Nadal, J. I., Molina, J. A., & Velilla, J. (2018). The commuting behavior of workers in the United States: Differences between the employed and the selfemployed. *Journal of Transport Geography, 66*, 19–29.

Gupta, D. K., Jena, D., Samantaray, A. K., & Das, S. (2019). HRD climate in selected public sector banks in India. *Revista ESPACIOS, 40*(11), 14–20.

Jackson, P. J. (Ed.). (1999). *Virtual working: Social and organizational dynamics (Management of Technology and Innovation)*. Routledge.

Johnson, P., Heimann, V., & O'Neill, K. (2001). The wonderland of virtual teams. *Journal of Workplace Learning, 13*(1), 24–29.

Katz, L., & Krueger, A. (1998). QJE computing inequality: Have computers changed the labor market? *Quarterly Journal of Economics, 113*(4), 1169–1214.

Lengnick-Hall, M. L., & Lengnick-Hall, C. A. (2018). e-HRM: Digital approaches, directions & applications. In M. Thite (Ed.), *Strategic management approach to technology-enabled HRM* (pp. 45–61). Routledge.

Malhotra, N. K. (2004). *Marketing research*. Prentice Hall.

Mamaghani, F. (2006). Impact of information technology on the workforce of the future: An analysis. *International Journal of Management, 23*(4), 845–850.

McIntyre, L. J. (1999). *The practical skeptic: Core concepts in sociology*. Mayfield Publishing.

Michaels, G., Natraj, A., & Reenen, V. J. (2014). Has ICT polarized skill demand? Evidence from eleven countries over twenty-five years. *Review of Economics and Statistics, 96*(1), 60–77.

Mohanty, P. C., Dash, M., Dash, M., & Das, S. (2019). A study on factors influencing training effectiveness. *Revista Espacios, 40*, 7–15. http://www.revistaespacios.com/a19v40n02/19400207.html

Mondal, S. R. (2020a). A systematic study for digital innovation in management education: An integrated approach towards problem-based learning in Vietnam. In *Digital innovations for customer engagement, management, and organizational improvement* (pp. 104–120). IGI Global. https://doi.org/10.4018/978-1-7998-5171-4.ch006

Mondal, S. R. (2020b, February). *Factors influencing store image loyalty and satisfaction from customer perspective an empirical study in retail sector*. Shiksha O Anusandhan University. http://hdl.handle.net/10603/273688

Mondal, S. (2021). A systematic study of new age consumer engagement and exploration for digital entertainment for over-the-top platforms in various digital media. In *Innovations in digital branding and content marketing* (pp. 113–133). IGI Global. https://doi.org/10.4018/978-1-7998-4420-4.ch006

Mondal, S. R., & Das, S. (2021). Examining diabetic subjects on their correlation with TTH and CAD: A statistical approach on exploratory results. In *Machine learning and the internet of medical things in healthcare* (pp. 153–177). Academic Press. https://doi.org/10.1016/B978-0-12-821229-5.00007-0

Mondal, S., & Sahoo, K. K. (2020). A study of green building prospects on sustainable management decision making. In *Green building management and smart automation* (pp. 220–234). IGI Global. https://doi.org/10.4018/978-1-5225-9754-4.ch011

Munsterberger, H. (1913). *Psychology and industrial efficiency*. The University of Michigan.

Nadanyiova, M., & Das, S. (2020). Millennials as a target segment of socially responsible communication within the business strategy. *Littera Scripta, 13*(1), 119–134. https://doi.org/10.36708/Littera_Scripta2020/1/8

Oksanen, K., & Ståhle, P. (2013). Physical environment as a source for innovation: Investigating the attributes of innovative space. *Journal of Knowledge Management, 17*(6), 815–827.

Oshri, I., Van Fenema, P., & Kotlarsky, J. (2008). Knowledge transfer in globally distributed teams: The role of transactive memory. *Information Systems Journal, 8*(6), 593–596.

Pacheco, A. (2015). *Informação digital: o vértice comum entre a Diplomática e a Ciência da Informação*. Master's thesis, Universidade de Lisboa, Faculdade de Letras. https://core.ac.uk/download/pdf/78464281.pdf

Pinsonneault, A., & Kraemer, K. L. (1993). Survey research methodology in management information systems: An assessment. *Journal of Management Information Systems, 10*, 75–105.

Pinto, M. (2009). *Preservmap: Um roteiro da preservação na era digital*. Edições Afrontamento.

Plantronics. (2014). *Smarter working*. www.plantronics.com/us/solutions/smarterworking

Quaglietta, J., & Alvord, D. (2020). *Coronavirus impact on service delivery continuity, employees and customers*. Gartner Information Technology Research.

Raghuram, S., Hill, N. S., Gibbs, J. L., & Maruping, L. M. (2019). Virtual work: Bridging research clusters. *Academy of Management Annals, 13*(1), 308–341. https://journals-aom-org.ezp-prod1.hul.harvard.edu/doi/10.5465/annals.2017.0020

Ravi, S., & Mondal, S. R. (2021). Digital entertainment based do it yourself content & advertisement as a factor of driving force for trust & customer patronage. In *Digital entertainment* (pp. 127–146). Palgrave Macmillan. https://doi.org/10.1007/978-981-15-9724-4_7

Sharma, E., & Das, S. (2020). Measuring impact of Indian ports on environment and effectiveness of remedial measures towards environmental pollution. *International Journal of Environment and Waste Management, 25*(3), 356–380. https://doi.org/10.1504/IJEWM.2019.10021787

Sharma, E., & Das, S. (2021). Integrated model for women empowerment in rural India. *Journal of International Development*, 1–18. https://doi.org/10.1002/jid.3539

Sharma, E., Nigam, N., & Das, S. (2020). Measuring gap in expected and perceived quality of ICT enabled customer services: A systematic study of top ten retailers of India. *International Journal of Applied Systemic Studies, 9*(2), 159–184. https://doi.org/10.1504/ijass.2020.113260

Singh, L. B., Mondal, S. R., & Das, S. (2020a). Human resource practices & their observed significance for Indian SMEs. *Revista ESPACIOS*, *41*(7). http://www.revistaespacios.com/a20v41n07/20410715.html

Singh, S., Mondal, S., Singh, L. B., Sahoo, K. K., & Das, S. (2020b). An empirical evidence study of consumer perception and socioeconomic profiles for digital stores in Vietnam. *Sustainability, 12*(5), 1716. https://doi.org/10.3390/su12051716

Siri, R., Mondal, S. R., & Das, S. (2020). Hydropower: A renewable energy resource for sustainability in terms of climate change and environmental protection. In *The handbook of environmental chemistry*. Springer. https://doi.org/10.1007/698_2020_635

Siri, R., & Das, S. (2021). A study on processing of information storage & use of new age consumers in digital wellness sector through story telling & creating interest. In *Digital Entertainment* (pp. 45–63). Palgrave Macmillan. https://doi.org/10.1007/978-981-15-9724-4_3

Song, Y., Wang, H., Wei, X., & Wu, L. (2019). Efficient attribute-based encryption with privacy preserving key generation and its application in industrial cloud. *Security and Communication Networks, 8*, 1–9.

Sukumadas, N., & Sawhney, R. (2004). Workforce agility through employee Involvement. *IIE Transactions, 36*, 1011–1021.

Taylor, F. (1913). *Principles of scientific management*. Harper.

Tooranloo, H. S., Azadi, M. H., & Sayyahpoor, A. (2017). Analyzing factors affecting implementation success of sustainable human resource management (SHRM) using a hybrid approach of FAHP and type-2 fuzzy DEMATEL. *Journal of Cleaner Production, 162*, 1252–1265.

Van, N. T. T., Vrana, V., Duy, N. T., Minh, D. X. H., Dzung, P. T., Mondal, S. R., & Das, S. (2020). The role of human-machine interactive devices for post-COVID-19 innovative sustainable tourism in Ho Chi Minh City Vietnam. *Sustainability, 12*(22), 9523. https://doi.org/10.3390/su12229523

Vennam, S. (2020). *Cloud computing*. https://www.ibm.com/cloud/learn/cloud-computing#toc-what-isclo-mt3Y0Fsu

Ware, J., & Grantham, C. (2003). The future of work: Changing patterns of workforce management and their impact on the workplace. *Journal of facility Management, 2*(2), 142–159.

World Bank, World Development Indicators. (2016). *Firms using banks to finance working capital (% of firms).* http://data.worldbank.org/indicator/IC.FRM.BKWC.ZS?view=chart

Yegen, C., & Mondal, S. R. (2021). Sharenting: A new paradigm of digital entertainment of new age parenting and social media. In *Digital entertainment* (pp. 213–231). Palgrave Macmillan. https://doi.org/10.1007/978-981-15-9724-4_11

Youssef, A. E. (2012). Exploring cloud computing services and applications. *Journal of Emerging Trends in Computing and Information Sciences, 3*(6), 838–847.

Zhu, H., Wei, L., & Niu, P. (2020). The novel coronavirus outbreak in Wuhan, China. *Global Health Research and Policy, 5*, 6.

CHAPTER 8

Technological Dynamism of Workforce Management for Effective Education Service Delivery During and After Covid-19

Mansi Tiwari and Subhra R. Mondal

Introduction

The global pandemic has caused the most unprecedented disruption in the service industries specially in tourism and education (Das, 2021a; Mondal & Das, 2021; Sharma & Das, 2021). While tourism is an augmented service industry, education is always a fundamental service sector for all the countries (Ravi & Mondal, 2021; Siri & Das, 2021). Due to COVID-19 around the world, 1.6 billion students are affected.

M. Tiwari
United World School of Business (UWSB), Karnavati University, Gandhinagar, India
e-mail: mansitiwari@unitedworld.in

S. R. Mondal (✉)
The Honors Programme, Duy Tan University, Da Nang, Vietnam
e-mail: subhraranimondal@duytan.edu.vn

S. R. Mondal et al. (eds.), *HR Analytics and Digital HR Practices*,
https://doi.org/10.1007/978-981-16-7099-2_8

Closure of educational institutes has affected students of mainly low- and middle-income countries around the world (Duman & Das, 2021; Mondal, 2020; Yegen & Mondal, 2021). So, to bring around some parity and help the students, innovative approaches like online teaching, training, and mobile application-based teaching is coming up. Distance education programs backed by UNESCO are also gaining momentum around world. Somehow the main objective is to find way of excellence for students to excel in these difficult times (Das, 2020; Sharma et al., 2020). Resources are always scarce. Students find it difficult to operate through an online portal and sometimes they find it very hard to get internet connectivity. According to Mondal (2020, February); technological updating is also a challenge to students. Similarly, the new normal online education service is also giving its own headache to the teachers too. From the study of Das (2020, February); suddenly the students found themselves in choppy waters of new technological disruption. But with constant pushing and development, now somehow the teachers and students are coming on the same page in these online portals. This online teaching has its own social and economic repercussions on the total society (Das, 2021b). But in any case, this will be the new normal way of operation in the education industry, and it will be staying like this for the next decade too (Das, 2021c; Mondal, 2021).

In this chapter, we investigate various applied issues which appear to be significant in moving forward to in imparting online digital mode of education and related services (Dua et al., 2021). These issues pivot around three critical factors: between "creation frameworks" and "information frameworks" associated with the education industry; in between "information utilizing" and "information evolving/ making" components inside information frameworks; what's more, among "open" and "shut" information frameworks (Bell & Albu, 1999). Education is what is popularly understood as the process of delivering or sharing knowledge among people to facilitate learning (Duy et al., 2020). Various changes have been encountered even witnessed where one could see the drastic change in especially the ways adopted by the academicians to provide effective learning atmosphere (Van et al., 2020).

In ancient India, the GURUKUL system existed for many years where students get the education far away from their families with their Gurus (Teachers). But gradually it shifted from the Gurukul system to classroom culture where the modernized infrastructure is made available to

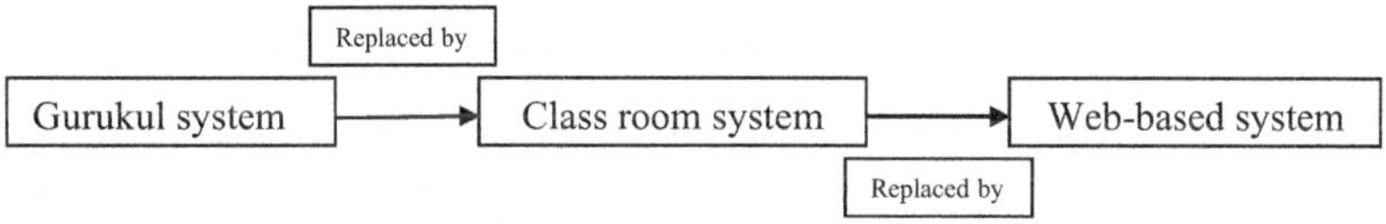

Fig. 8.1 Depiction of transformation of education system

impart the skills & knowledge among the students as shown in Fig. 8.1. The major & prominent change took place when technology enters the field of education. The Interactive Communication Technologies (ICT) facilities, modern classrooms with projectors, internet for virtual classes, books replaced by the PowerPoint presentations, the e-learning content preparations, m-learning & what not (Siri et al., 2020). This change was adopted by many students as well as by the teachers but in limited set of circumstances (Singh et al., 2020). But, after the spread of deadly virus all over the world especially in developing countries, things have become very difficult to manage with when it is asked to adopt web-based teaching & learning system (Singh, Mondal, & Das, 2020). This led to the numerous issues & problems encountered by the teachers specially in the case of primary education in public schools of remote areas, where neither the teachers are comfortable nor the students with the new modes of e-learning (Sharma & Das, 2020). The situation was not so good especially for higher education where college students and faculties need to be online all the time for making the intellectual exchange fruitful (Das, 2020; Mondal, 2020).

The objective of this chapter is to raise & highlight the issues that took place during the transition from physical classroom teaching to virtual classroom or web-based teaching & learning system due to COVID-19. The agenda is to discuss the workforce management diabolical raising the hindrances among academicians due to the COVID-19. What pressure they are dealing with? What is demanded from them on the name of making novel profession effective & efficient? How it's affecting the quality in performance & last but not the least what strategies one should follow as an organization in education sector for making their workforce management effective in COVID-19.

Background

Technological Dynamism is the process of technological change (Harris & Al-Bataineh, 2015). This concept was also defined by Albu in 2009, understood as the rate of exchange in prediction of new technologies. In simple words understood as technological advancement. With the growth of innovation & technology the global competition has increased (Schubert et al., 2016).

To improve the productivity or performance when companies integrate the function with the effective use of human capital. According to *CIO Whitepapers Review*, workforce management is defined as, "a synchronized set of procedures that an organization uses to enhance the profitability of its representatives on the individual, departmental, and entity-wide levels" (Hanks, 2021). There are various studies which have been conducted to highlight the benefits of online or web-based teaching & learning system (Mohanty et al., 2019; Mondal & Sahoo, 2020). Such studies have been done at different locations & in different colleges & universities almost all over the world to portray the effectiveness of the e-learning system especially before the pandemic COVID-19 (Behera et al., 2019; Gupta et al., 2019). Few glimpse of all those researchers are mentioned in Table 8.1

The above summary is disclosing the fact that before COVID-19, be it adoption or acceptance in different countries among the students or academicians was either gradually increasing or it was applicable in certain category of subjects or situations. But, due to this pandemic, it becomes a very much known fact that everyone must adopt the e-learning or work from home culture very exhaustively in every sector & academic or education is one of that.

Every sector faces the repercussions of work from home or doing it online differently. The other segment of information will highlight the scenario which took place in academics due to the COVID-19 among academicians & students (Nadanyiova & Das, 2020). Pandemic challenged the educators to shift from traditional to online mode of teaching & learning & many were reluctant too but at the end no option, they were left with the adoption & acceptance toward e-learning (Dhawan, 2020). She also stated that institutions were judged on the criteria of their adaptation for the changed conditions along with the quality maintenance in teaching–learning.

More in connection for COVID-19, e-learning researchers mentioned about the issues where increase usage of ICT along with its transformation in education are prominently discussed. Academician's knowledge doesn't

Table 8.1 Glimpse of adoption for e-learning before COVID-19 in different countries

Author name	*Outcome*
Allan and Lawless (2003)	Emphasized on different types of stress such as cyber stress and techno-stress due to online team working and pressure
Tuparova et al. (2006)	Postulated that academicians have very positive attitude for online internet teaching. But senior teachers with more than 10 years of experience are less interested in online use of tools
Aggarwal (2009)	Showed that Indian E-learning system has lot of potential but have very slow progress due to lack of marketing and awareness
Ishaq et al. (2009)	Found that Students use various interactive communication technologies on their personal computers for E-learning and they have a greater involvement for the same
Harris et al. (2016)	Emphasized on faster technological adoption in academics for bringing revolution to learning 2.0
Kisanga (2016)	Found that with computer exposure academicians' attitude towards E-learning will be very much enhanced
Almaiah et al. (2019)	Studied Mobile learning. They studied for using mobile as a tool for E-learning activities which students are very keen to use due to its comfortable use
Flavell et al. (2019)	Postulated that with confidence level and perceptual comfortability in use will help in further development of learning 2.0
Suprato and Sidupa (2019)	Showed that online learning is having positive perception among students, and they are happy to use them

limit up to the subjective one but extended as they improvised with the challenge of using the ICT for teaching and learning which means educators engaged in mastering their IT knowledge for making the education easy for their students (König et al., 2020).

There was one more study identified during the review of literature where authors mentioned about the era of pandemic "COVID-19" and student's acceptance for e-learning. This study outbreaks the challenges for the conduct of online studies and classes. Two major factors where accessibility is first & second was that students were not prepared for the online experience of teaching as they were more connected with the conventional approach of teaching & learning (Aboagye et al., 2020).

Objective of the Chapter

Issues, Controversies, Problems

The major focus of this chapter is based on how academicians/teachers as a workforce & their institutions as management are dealing together in COVID-19 where the competitive spirit is high in making teaching more effective so that institutions could also excel in terms of growth & advancement. Here are some major issues which come across due to technological dynamisms for managing workforce in education system during COVID-19.

1. ***ICT Modification Issues***

   Transformation in ICT facilities has dominated the entire education system. The only problem is such alteration has been reached in colleges & universities but still gap could be sensed in implementation as it also demands fostering for digitalization in colleges & schools.

   Not only the students but also the staff should be given such platforms where they could also enhance their technical skills as both are more connected with the conventional way of teaching & learning as per the literature. Digital literacy is important. It is to be put into deeper consideration on how teachers could be trained for the technology-based pedagogy.
2. ***Teacher's/Faculty's Knowledge***

   Early adoption of digitalization due to COVID-19, teacher's competence used to be judged by their knowledge. The knowledge was classified into Content Knowledge (CK), Pedagogical Content Knowledge (PCK) & General Pedagogical Knowledge (GPK) (Guerriero, 2019).

   But due to the COVID-19, teacher's knowledge has been extended up to master the challenges due to the association of increased ICT which results in terms of expectation where the teacher should be competent enough in applying technology in their teaching practices more than the subjects they teach.
3. ***Teacher's Self Efficacy***

   Self-belief on own capacity in execution of expected behavior is also a major concern when it comes to perform under specific circumstances. The same resulted in teaching–learning system also due to COVID-19 that teacher's confidence in regard to their successful online teaching turned as more important than their subjective knowledge & skills. If they perceive more such efficacy they will be motivated more to perform better (lMeganTschannen-Moran & Hoy, 2001).

4. ***Networking Errors***

   Availability of internet will only be supportive measure to make teaching effective during COVID-19. It invites inevitable issues like downloading errors, login problems, installation issues, audio & video problems & many more. Teachers could not control these issues all the time & if one wants to see student's perspective then it will end up in disengagement on student's part (Song et al., 2004).

Even More Issues, Controversies, and Problems

There are some more issues & problems which teachers are facing due to the behavioral treatment by their institutions especially during COVID-19. The relationship among employers & staff also has been changed which resulted in different workforce management during COVID-19. The issues which educators are facing are lined up to highlight the problems of workforce in education services.

1. **Economic Issues**

This economic crisis due to COVID-19 put a lot of pressure on schools, colleges, & universities across the world as such institutions closed their premises. At times to admissions & the start of new academic session fee recovery for the mentioned service becomes toughest to collect at most. Fee for hostel facility, fee for transportation were totally non-recoverable. This non-recovery of fee led to deductions in payments of workforce.

2. **Growth and Advancement**

Every employee dreams for growth & advancement be it financial or non-financial in nature. COVID-19 not only impacted the current but future aspirations of employees. Withholding of promotions, increments blocked on the name of COVID-19 even when employees in academia devoted their 24 × 7 time to cope with changes in learning management systems.

3. **Work for Unlimited Working Hours**

Initially, there was a concern about how academia people will manage up the challenging e-learning methods of teaching. But surprisingly, gradually they learned & became comfortable with the usage & adaptability of e-learning & teaching system. Later it was identified that there are no fixed working hours for them. They worked double time as employer tendency identified as "work from home" means no work for employees in academia.

4. **Introspection During Online Classes**

It has been also identified in education services that management never trusted on workforce when it comes to taking online sessions with students. High level of vigilance & introspection followed by top management people during the sessions through joining classes as presenters on different online platforms like MS Teams, ZOOM, etc. which took mental pressure up to another higher level of stress among academicians.

5. **Publication Pressure**

During COVID-19 in academics, another stressful angel turned for publication. It was assumed already that working from home academics is one of the simplest tasks to perform. Academicians have enough time to focus on research publication in lockdown period. This could be true if no classes or working hours were limited but as per the issues discussed above, this pie was also difficult to cook.

On witnessing the above issues & problems one could say that yes it was very challenging for manpower in academia to survive & sustain during COVID-19. But yes, we can see the other side of the coin that is the scenario after COVID-19 in academia or education system.

Based on mentioned controversies there are some studies where strength, weakness, opportunities and challenges are discussed. This analysis has been done to ensure e-learning as good & effective practices during crises. Such a crisis disrupts the educational process in many ways. This not only results in closure of schools & universities but made difficult for teachers & other employees in education services as they faced lot of psychological issues like fears, anxiety, depression, & stress which resulted in lack of focus & concentration.

Over the latest couple of years, e-learning has started getting noticeable quality in developing countries. Massive Open Online Courses (MOOC) also are introduced to aid these online learning processes. Still there is a sense of hesitancy among the educational set up in these countries. Due to challenges of pandemic now these online learning portals are in demand. Teachers went along with them in far off educating by methods for relatively few stages, for instance, Google Meet, Microsoft Teams, ZOOM, Skype, etc. So, there must be mutual understanding of the available tools among the platform and teachers primarily and secondarily students must find it convenient. (Dhawan, 2020).

Strength

The concept of e-learning has its own strength in implementation which are the reasons due to which today it has been able to reach to household in these turbulent times of COVI-19. It is flexible and student-friendly in terms of time of use along with place of learning. There is no hindrance to strict use for a particular time and place. Also, the modules of courses are having the power of customization which provide a greater core strength to the execution in all over the world. The tools of Google, Microsoft, and Zoom help the online education to reach everywhere due to better internet connectivity. Faculties take help of these platforms to have both audio-visual reach to the students which is equivalent to effective direct teaching. In this way, online teaching becomes more fun and interactive for the curious students. The flexibility of education is the real high point which enables students to avoid any unprecedented times which can affect their study. This way they can save time and act effectively for completing their education. This way the physical and mental health of students can be protected in any kind of environment. New technologically innovative approaches help in getting the students out of woods and place them with an advantage of acquiring all the knowledge even in these unprecedented turbulent times of COVID-19.

Weakness

Communication distortion and breakage are the important loopholes of e-learning. As there is no physical human interaction, communication overrides technology and if faculties and students are not adopting the changes soon, then there will always be a communication distortion.

Sometimes casual and freakish behavior of students makes it very difficult for all to provide qualitative service result in mostly dissatisfaction and disturbance. Technology and psychology are two different complementary elements. If the technology fails to consider the psychology of students, then it is very difficult to make a peace between them. The byproduct of this feud between technology and psychology results in more pertinent disturbance among the students and e-learning deemed to be failed.

Opportunities

If one looks for the futuristic positive side of only e-learning in COVID-19, then we will find a lot of relevant relatable opportunities. Like remote working, online method of learning is the only solution of the relevant sector to run during COVID-19. The after effect of COVID-19 will also be there for some time as the fear psychosis will not go quickly. So, to stay in the game of business online portals for learning will be continuing for some time. The curiosity around this smart way of operation will attract higher education institutes to keep the learning to go uninterrupted. Technology always inspires the new generation and when it combines with new innovations and flexibility it attracts a huge interest. Also, with help of online learning, the critical thinking ability of students will be developed as they also understand the effects of pandemic.

Challenges

There will always be challenges for online learning which are confined to issues related to faculties, students and content or method of study. Student engagement for the time of class is a measure issue as psychologically they may show disinterest. Faculties will find it hard to move from physical direct offline mode of education to intangible online mode. So, a perfect mix of intangibility and tangibility will make the faculties ease into the mode of online teaching. Also, it will attract students to explore tools for teaching. Content and its quality control are a pertinent issue in all service rendering. The faster rate of solving the queries regarding usage will keep students and faculties interested. Internet connectivity and availability of devices for online learning can also be an issue for developing countries. Effective government support for infrastructural growth can solve this. Economical financial technological support to the education industry not only increase the chances of success for online mode but also help them to reach all households. Mobile devices and computers can be provided to students and faculties for the efficient results of web-based teaching. Audio-visual tools should be used to create awareness and interest among the students.

Suggestions

It should be a fundamental concern of world techno and educational leaders to find a way to deal with COVID-19 induced deadlock of direct educational activities. Due to this pandemic educational sector has suffered like any other service industry. If leaders are not going to take proactive steps, then the whole educational sector will be crippled, and it will not be possible to revive it sooner. Till now UNESCO guidelines are helping the organizations and government subsidiaries to run and get the best out of these online learning programs. Indisputably the most tremendous development that countries can take to hustle the returning of schools and government systems must find some way to control the transmission and COVID-19 effects. Some of those guidelines can be as follows.

- **Guarantee the safety of all**

  Government authorities should form the standard operating procedures for reopening of schools and keep a backup plan for online education. A key condition to returning is having the option to guarantee a safe re-visitation of actual premises, while keeping up physical distance and executing general wellbeing measures, for example, the utilization of masks and incessant hand washing.
- **Inclusive reopening**

  Proper hygienic and safety should be maintained for small children in pre-school and primary standards. Before reopening the school, premises must be sanitized inclusively. Proper medical backup must be ensured so that children can be given a sense of security until the vaccines have not been administered.
- **Provide good financial support and coordinated efforts for educational institutes**

  Pandemic has affected the global economic health and public finances by aiding in recession. This pandemic-induced recession also affects the global educational institutes. So first, they need to be strengthened. Domestic and international funding for education must be more. This must be the top priority. The official development assistance for all levels of education around the world must be increased.

- **Aim to build resilient ecosystem for sustainable education after pandemic**
  The core development must be done in sustainable development which can bring resilience for education at different levels. Schools can safely reopen by focusing on financial social inclusion, taking appropriate reinforcement at all possible levels, ensuring strong coordination and effective leadership which can bring new faith in all stakeholders.
- **Reposition of education learning ecosystem**
  The disruptive change of e-learning also points toward the dynamic adoption of education sector for web-based learning in these turbulent times. The quick adoption of e-learning activities also shows that education sector can work on repositioning of its total operation to some extent. It presents a unique opportunity for the stakeholders to work out plans for effective restricting and repositing of education system in post-pandemic times. The touch points for this digitalized revolution of education sector should be based on methods of prevention for absenteeism, profitable model of education, faculties wellbeing and monetary benefits, good internet connectivity, data maintenance, and flexible monitoring of students.
- **Holistic education policy**
  There can be a holistic approach toward the overall education sector which will be focused on developmental learning, social, and emotional upbringing of students in post-pandemic times. In developing countries, a lot of students have lost either both or single parent due to COVID-19. So, the government and corporate houses can help financially to support the wholesome educational needs of these students.
- **Cooperative educational ecosystem**
  As teachers are the frontline employees of education sector, they are the key for any type of interaction between students, parents, and governments across the world. Their proximity toward students attracts the policymakers attention toward them. So, in a better positive correlated cooperative atmosphere between policymakers and educational stakeholders is a must to implement any kind of changes.

It is always positive to have experienced teachers at helm of things to be more pronounced and useful.

- **Cooperation between Policymakers and civil society**

  As COVID-19 has affected the society from grassroot to the higher echelon, it is prudent to have a cooperative atmosphere for all possible civic bodies and policymakers. Civil society is the main stakeholder for any kind of service and education sector is not averse to it (Harris et al., 2016). So, for safe and hygiene smooth reopening of schools or continuous support of e-learning is concerned, we need to have a cooperative atmosphere otherwise it is very difficult to operate in post-COVID-19.

- **Effective training of teachers for their readiness to use technology**

  Every level of teacher must have the training and exposure to Interactive computerized technologies (ICT) and other important tools for their effective use in upcoming e-learning implementation (Kirby, 2020). So, teachers must get a prioritized training for their benefit in implementing ICT to its full usage. ICT will certainly help the teachers to engage users and amplify the students' knowledge.

Conclusion

The educational impact of the COVID-19 emergency has been unprecedented. It has set the clock back in meeting global educational goals, unilaterally influencing the developing countries. But then again, the school network has proven hard and laid a foundation for recovery (Policy Brief: Education During Covid-19 and beyond, 2020). There remains the danger of not accepting the e-learning by all the stakeholders to some extent. Any negative effect also has a positive side which speaks about all the possible ways and effects of adopting these changes and developing the students' skills which can satisfy post-COVID-19 learning outcomes. There is limitless drive and undiscovered values that we can rely on in rebuilding not only the school's basic administrations, but also its central sustainable goals. It is the duty of governments and the global authorities to remain consistent with standards and to drive changes forward so that not only do young students regain their secure future, but all the faculties discover their role in implementing this e-learning in future.

References

Aboagye, E., Yawson, J. A., & Appiah, K. N. (2020). COVID-19 and E-learning: The challenges of students in tertiary. *Social Education Research*, 109–115.

Aggarwal, D. (2009, February). Role of E-learning in a developing country like India. In *3rd National Conference, Computing For Nation Development, February* (pp. 26–27).

Allan, J., & Lawless, N. (2003). Stress caused by on-line collaboration in e-learning: A developing model. *Education + Training*, *4*(8/9), 564–572. https://doi.org/10.1108/00400910310508955

Almaiah, M. A., Alamri, M. M., & Al-Rahmi, W. (2019). Applying the UTAUT model to explain the students' acceptance of Mobile learning system in higher education. *IEEE Access, 7*, 174673–174686.

Behera, M., Dash, M., Ayasa Kanta Mohanty, A. K. & Das, S. (2019). Entrepreneurial ecosystem: A geographical upliftment. *Revista Espacios, 40*, 26–36. Retrieved from http://www.revistaespacios.com/a19v40n01/19400126.html

Bell, M., & Albu, M. (1999). Knowledge Systems and technological dynamism in industrial clusters in developing countries. *World Development, 27*(9), 1715–1734.

Das, S. (2020). Innovations in digital banking service brand equity and millennial consumerism. In *Digital transformation and innovative services for business and learning* (pp. 62–79). IGI Global. https://doi.org/10.4018/978-1-7998-5175-2.ch004

Das, S. (2020, February). *Media impact of advertising on consumer buying behaviour a comparative study of different media*. Shiksha o Anusandhan University. http://hdl.handle.net/10603/273691

Das, S. (2021a). A systematic study of integrated marketing communication and content management system for millennial consumers. In *Innovations in digital branding and content marketing* (pp. 91–112). IGI Global. https://doi.org/10.4018/978-1-7998-4420-4.ch005

Das, S. (2021b). *Digital entertainment: The next evolution in service sector*. Springer Nature. https://doi.org/10.1007/978-981-15-9724-4. Print ISBN978-981-15-9723-7. Online ISBN978-981-15-9724-4

Das, S. (2021c). *Search engine optimization and marketing: A recipe for success in digital marketing* (1st ed.). CRC Press. https://doi.org/10.1201/9780429298509

Dhawan, S. (2020). Online learning: A panacea in the time of COVID-19 crisis. *Journal of Educational Technology Systems, 49*(1), 5–22.

Dua, S., Singh, I., & Das, S. (2021). Banking innovative service with digital brand equity for new age consumers: Internet banking and millennial consumerism. In *Innovations in digital branding and content marketing* (pp. 134–159). IGI Global. https://doi.org/10.4018/978-1-7998-4420-4.ch007

Duman, Ü. O., & Das, S. (2021). The dynamic rise of digital brands' market mavens in digital entertainment: A complete know how for curious customers. In *Digital entertainment* (pp. 147–172). Palgrave Macmillan. https://doi.org/10.1007/978-981-15-9724-4_8

Duy, N. T., Mondal, S. R., Van, N. T. T., Dzung, P. T., Minh, D. X. H., & Das, S. (2020). A study on the role of Web 4.0 and 5.0 in the sustainable tourism ecosystem of Ho Chi Minh City, Vietnam. *Sustainability*, *12*(17), 7140. https://doi.org/10.3390/su12177140

Flavell, H., Harris, C., Price, C., Logan, E., & Peterson, S. (2019). Empowering academics to be adaptive with eLearning technologies: An exploratory case study. *Australasian Journal of Educational Technology*, *35*(1).

Guerriero, S. (2019). *Teachers' pedagogical knowledge and the teaching profession educational research and innovation.* OECD Publishing, Paris. doi.org/https://doi.org/10.1787/9789264270695-en

Gupta, D. K., Jena, D., Samantaray, A. K., & Das, S. (2019). HRD climate in selected public sector banks in India. *Revista ESPACIOS*, *40*(11).

Hanks, C. (2021, October 20). *In-demand staffing solutions for businesses.* Wonolo. https://www.wonolo.com/

Harris, J., & Al-Bataineh, A. (2015, April). One to one technology and its effect on student academic achievement and motivation. In *Global learn* (pp. 579–584). Association for the Advancement of Computing in Education (AACE).

Harris, J. L., Al-Bataineh, M. T., & Al-Bataineh, A. (2016). One to one technology and its effect on student academic achievement and motivation. *Contemporary Educational Technology*, *7*(4), 368–381.

Ishaq, K., Zin, N. A. M., Rosdi, F., Abid, A., & Ijaz, M. (2009). The impact of ICT on students' academic performance in public private sector universities of Pakistan.

Kirby, S. (2020, June 2). *World economic forum.* 5 ways COVID-19 has changed workforce management. Retrieved from https://www.weforum.org/agenda/2020/06/COVID-19-homeworking-symptom-of-changing-face-of-workforce-management/

Kisanga, D. (2016). Determinants of teachers' attitudes towards e-learning in Tanzanian higher learning institutions. *International Review of Research in Open and Distributed Learning: IRRODL*, *17*(5), 109–125.

König, J., Jäger Biela, D. J., & Glutsch, N. (2020). Adapting to online teaching during COVID-19 school closure:teacher education and teacher competence effects among early career teachers in Germany. *European Journal of Teacher Education*, *43*, 608–622.

lMeganTschannen-Moran, & Hoy, A. W. (2001). Teacher efficacy: Capturing an elusive construct. *Teaching and Teacher Education, 17*(7), 783–805. https://doi.org/10.1016/S0742-051X(01)00036-1

Mohanty, P. C., Dash, M., Dash, M., & Das, S. (2019). A study on factors influencing training effectiveness. *Revista Espacios, 40*, 7–15. Retrieved from http://www.revistaespacios.com/a19v40n02/19400207.html

Mondal, S. (2021). A systematic study of new age consumer engagement and exploration for digital entertainment for over-the-top platforms in various digital media. In *Innovations in digital branding and content marketing* (pp. 113–133). IGI Global. https://doi.org/10.4018/978-1-7998-4420-4.ch006

Mondal, S. R. (2020). A systematic study for digital innovation in management education: An integrated approach towards problem-based learning in Vietnam. In *Digital innovations for customer engagement, management, and organizational improvement* (pp. 104–120). IGI Global. https://doi.org/10.4018/978-1-7998-5171-4.ch006

Mondal, S. R. (2020, February). *Factors influencing store image loyalty and satisfaction from customer perspective an empirical study in retail sector*. Shiksha o Anusandhan University. http://hdl.handle.net/10603/273688

Mondal, S., & Sahoo, K. K. (2020). A study of green building prospects on sustainable management decision making. In *Green building management and smart automation* (pp. 220–234). IGI Global. https://doi.org/10.4018/978-1-5225-9754-4.ch011

Mondal, S. R., & Das, S. (2021). Examining diabetic subjects on their correlation with TTH and CAD: A statistical approach on exploratory results. In *Machine learning and the internet of medical things in healthcare* (pp. 153–177). Academic Press. https://doi.org/10.1016/B978-0-12-821229-5.00007-0

Nadanyiova, M., & Das, S. (2020). Millennials as a target segment of socially responsible communication within the business strategy. *Littera Scripta, 13*(1), 119–134. https://doi.org/10.36708/Littera_Scripta2020/1/8

Ravi, S., & Mondal, S. R. (2021). Digital entertainment based do it yourself content & advertisement as a factor of driving force for trust & customer patronage. In *Digital entertainment* (pp. 127–146). Palgrave Macmillan. https://doi.org/10.1007/978-981-15-9724-4_7

Schubert, T., Baier, E., & Rammer, C. (2016). Technological capabilities,technological dynamism and innovation offshoring. *ZEW*, 1–28. Retrieved from http://ftp.zew.de/pub/zew-docs/dp/dp16044.pdf

Sharma, E., & Das, S. (2020). Measuring impact of Indian ports on environment and effectiveness of remedial measures towards environmental pollution. *International Journal of Environment and Waste Management, 25*(3), 356–380. https://doi.org/10.1504/IJEWM.2019.10021787

Sharma, E., & Das, S. (2021). Integrated model for women empowerment in rural India. *Journal of International Development,* 1–18. https://doi.org/10.1002/jid.3539

Sharma, E., Nigam, N., & Das, S. (2020). Measuring gap in expected and perceived quality of ICT enabled customer services: A systematic study of top ten retailers of India. *International Journal of Applied Systemic Studies, 9*(2), 159–184. https://doi.org/10.1504/ijass.2020.113260

Singh, L. B., Mondal, S. R., & Das, S. (2020). Human resource practices & their observed significance for Indian SMEs. *Revista ESPACIOS, 41*(07). Retrieved from http://www.revistaespacios.com/a20v41n07/20410715.html

Singh, S., Mondal, S., Singh, L. B., Sahoo, K. K., & Das, S. (2020). An empirical evidence study of consumer perception and socioeconomic profiles for digital stores in Vietnam. *Sustainability, 12*(5), 1716. https://doi.org/10.3390/su12051716

Siri, R., & Das, S. (2021). A study on processing of information storage & use of new age consumers in digital wellness sector through story telling & creating interest. In *Digital entertainment* (pp. 45–63). Palgrave Macmillan. https://doi.org/10.1007/978-981-15-9724-4_3

Siri, R., Mondal S. R., Das S. (2020). Hydropower: A renewable energy resource for sustainability in terms of climate change and environmental protection. In *The handbook of environmental chemistry*. Springer. https://doi.org/10.1007/698_2020_635

Song, L., Singleton, E. S., Hill, J. R., & Koh, M. H. (2004). Improving online learning: Student perceptions of useful and challenging characteristics. *The Internet and Higher Education, 7*, 59–70.

Suprato, D., & Sidupa, C. (2019, December). University students' perceptions of implementation of English online learning system. In *Prosiding International conference on Information Technology and Business (ICITB)* (pp. 31–37).

Tuparova, D., Tuparov, G., Ivanov, S., Karastranova, E., & Peneva, J. (2006). Teachers' attitude towards e-learning courses in Bulgarian universities. *Current Developments in Technology-Assisted Education, 3*, 1755–1759.

Van, N. T. T., Vrana, V., Duy, N. T., Minh, D. X. H., Dzung, P. T., Mondal, S. R., & Das, S. (2020). The role of human-machine interactive devices for post-COVID-19 innovative sustainable tourism in Ho Chi Minh City Vietnam. *Sustainability, 12*(22), 9523. https://doi.org/10.3390/su12229523

Yegen, C., & Mondal, S. R. (2021). Sharenting: A new paradigm of digital entertainment of new age parenting and social media. In *Digital entertainment* (pp. 213–231). Palgrave Macmillan. https://doi.org/10.1007/978-981-15-9724-4_11

CHAPTER 9

Human Governance Analytics for Public Organizations

Maria José Sousa, David Ferraz, António Sacavém, and João Salis Gomes

Introduction

In this current data-driven working culture, those organizations that operate with qualitative and reliable data are having a high probability of success (Ferraz, 2020). Integration and implementation of new information-driven governance is always an imperative solution for new normal organizational management in post-pandemic times (Mondal &

M. J. Sousa (✉) · D. Ferraz · A. Sacavém · J. S. Gomes
ISCTE—Instituto Universitário de Lisboa, Lisbon, Portugal
e-mail: maria.jose.sousa@iscte-iul.pt

D. Ferraz
e-mail: david.ferraz@iscte-iul.pt

A. Sacavém
e-mail: antonio.sacavem@universidadeeuropeia.pt

J. S. Gomes
e-mail: joao.gomes@iscte-iul.pt

S. R. Mondal et al. (eds.), *HR Analytics and Digital HR Practices*,
https://doi.org/10.1007/978-981-16-7099-2_9

Das, 2021; Sharma & Das, 2021). Proper data-driven governance propels the management group to develop strategies and frameworks which can bring quality, accuracy, and most importantly insights to marvel the digital governance (Duman & Das, 2021; Ravi & Mondal, 2021). Data privacy, transparency, and information security are some of the prominent issues in bringing out the effective governance (Das, 2021a; Siri & Das, 2021). Information clarity is very much necessary for implementation as ambiguity brings risks in management (Mondal, 2020a; Yegen & Mondal, 2021). Data governance is also quite cost-effective in longer run and provides better human resource analytics (Das, 2020a; Sharma et al., 2020; L. B. Singh et al., 2020).

The aim of this exploratory study was to systematize the main concepts about Human Governance in the Digital Economy (Bersin, 2017). Organizations have been continuously evolving in reaction to globalization, demographic, technological change, unpredictable, competitive, and sophisticated markets, attempting to adopt management strategies and efficiency principles (Mondal, 2021). In this context to help Public organizations to respond to changes, the Human Governance analytics are the basilar for better decision-making processes (Dua et al., 2021; Duy et al., 2020; Van et al., 2020). Accurate information regarding the people management help to define more adequate strategies, and better goals to achieve the mission of the organization.

Analytics can also be a base to look at the future of the organization with the definition of future scenarios regarding new organizational practices, and new public services to respond to the challenges of the society and the needs of the citizens, focusing on digital services (Das, 2020b; Mondal, 2020b). The focal goal is to create a more efficient Public Administration considering principles of the digital government and adjusting the Public Servants' competencies to the needs of a digital transformation that is occurring all over the world and specifically in the Public Administrations (Sharma & Das, 2020).

The need for a reorientation in strategic planning and resource management, including employee skills, is the base of the focus of this chapter, being the aspects of human governance (Davis et al., 1997) in the digital transformation phase of organizations essential to change

A. Sacavém
Universidade Europeia, Lisbon, Portugal

the traditional administrative perspective of organizations, bringing a new perspective of effectiveness and productivity to a strategic role (Hanapiyah et al., 2016).

The first section of the chapter presents a conceptual approach to Human Governance. The following section offers the empirical study regarding the HG Analytics proposed, and finally, the discussion and conclusions.

Background

Human Governance Conceptualization

The concept of human resource governance provides necessary impetus in terms of reducing communication channels, greater autonomy, and better peer cooperation which ultimately helps the organization to have competitive, committed, and experienced workforce at their disposal (Das, 2021b; Behera et al., 2019; Gupta et al., 2019). It is a healthy mix of good execution of ethics and decision-making which supports good corporate social responsibility and sustainable development for all types of stakeholders (Mohanty et al., 2019; Mondal & Sahoo, 2020; Nadanyiova & Das, 2020).

It stands for effective decision-making in an overall process where standards must be maintained for utmost importance, while safeguarding the ideals of openness, fairness, freedom, and accountability (S. Singh et al., 2020; Siri et al., 2020). The principles of honesty, fairness, freedom, and accountability all frame the foundations. Transparency of the disclosure of precise details on all matters relating to the management and performance of human resources in an organization (Gould-Williams, 2003). Justice to protect workers' rights and deal fairly and fairly with all internal stakeholders, including minorities. Accountability: managers are responsible for their decisions. Workers are accountable for their performance and their representations of the organization.

In a digital era, clouded by surmounts of information inherent to a world which is evolving towards high levels of complexity, governance structures are pressured to adapt and to develop new models for decision-making. With IoT and 5G emergence, a new framework for relationships is facing organizations (Van Weyenbergh, 2019). Governance structures, both in private and public realm, have been pressured to provide increased information for future strategies and activities (Abeysekera, 2013), which leads to the development of meaningful models of human governance that will help the organization to deal more effectively with an ethical challenge for decisive process and provide guaranteed compliances at all levels. The concept of governance for human resources at an organization is a value-added holistic thought which helps the workforce to behave properly in different types of organizations (Hanapiyahak et al., 2016) and integrates the actions and processes that lead to a prosperous society (Sarawati, 2018). Moreover, is a driving force for subjective well-being (Arfah & Aziuddin, 2009) and "good" governance may include ingredients such as participation, inclusiveness, integrity, fairness, effectiveness, and accountability (Graham et al., 2003).

According to Falk (1995), two forms of governance can be highlighted: "inhuman governance" and "human governance". The former refers to the unequal distribution of wealth and the exploitation of the individual and the environment (Falk, 1995), and the latter, on the other hand, highlights people-centered principles of success and an increasing adherence to human rights, treating each human being with dignity and integrity (Falk, 1995). Furthermore, integrity is a key concept in human governance since it is related with employee wellness (i.e., Schabracq, 2003), job performance (i.e., Ones et al., 1993), productive work relationships (i.e., Cameron et al., 2004), and organizational trust (i.e., Becker, 1998).

In a world of enormous complexity, uncertainty, characterized by a web of pervasive and tangled relationships, increasingly based on digital processes and tools, a distributed human governance model has been proposed (Van Weyenbergh, 2019). According to this model, hierarchies, processes, and tools should be reinvented, from static to dynamic, from rigidity to agility, and from centralization to participation (Van Weyenbergh, 2019), in order to adjust governance, to a human–machine interaction (HMI) that helps in effectively helping in decision-making with mutual cooperation of human and computers (Licklider, 1990), which may coexist along with algorithmic-assisted governance, where social media may be a tool of influence and freedom of speech.

Human Governance Analytics

Human governance is framed by the values of transparency, justice, independence, and accountability. Transparency to the disclosure of accurate information on all human capital management issues in organization.

Justice to protect workers' rights and deal fairly and fairly with all internal stakeholders, including minorities. Accountability, Managers are responsible for their decisions. Workers are accountable for their performance and their representations of the organization.

The economic and social development impacts the private companies, public institutions, foundations, and other organizations and it is necessary to measure their performance that allows organizations to grow in a more reasonable way by reducing weaknesses, potentializing modern practices, and allowing for a sustained financial development which puts people in the center. New theories of public management encourage organizations to strategically manage workers (OECD, 2019) to allow public organizations' objectives to be in sync with workforce. It brings the concept of right person at right place with right set of skills into practical execution. The introduction of more objective process management allows governments to improve productivity, social growth, responsiveness, and consistency in the delivery of services. A brand-new working culture is evolving, focused on communication and embodied by both long-term objectives of public organizations that rely primarily on good practices for economic and social growth.

Human governance and the way organizations respond to certain political stimuli are affected by political context. Indeed, policy should allow public organization leaders to stabilize jobs, avoid profit-generating policies, and use funds appropriately (Roe, 2003). Labor politics, market conditions, and the transformational acceleration intrinsic to the digital era influence the human governance in organizations and the way interactions are developed with the stakeholders.

Work-life balance (WLB) signifies a healthy relationship between work and employee's personal life, which is significant to have good productivity for organization (Kelliher et al., 2019). It indicates a healthy working environment (e.g., Kalliath & Brough, 2008), but digital information technologies sometimes create problems that affect work-life balance and have a negative impact on employee and organization (ILO, 2017). Human governance in the field of the digital age will be invited to reconsider how to reframe work-life balance policies. New practices are recommended for WLB-like teamwork and flexi timing to improve mental health of employee.

Knowledge systems such as exchanging, maintaining, and generating knowledge are influenced by the implementation of governance processes (Foss, 2007). In order to find the specific tools and technologies from which organizations exert their impact on information systems in the digital age, human governance needs to create foundations based on individual action and interaction. The emergence of the digital age has increased the prevalence of human resource organizations that have significant consequences for the advancement of governance structures, such as authority relationships and incentive systems architecture.

Competencies are essential to making public agencies proactive without hurting efficiency in coping with any possible eventuality. Several critical aspects like process automation, workforce engagement, internal service delivery, external quality of service, customer satisfaction, organizational culture, new technology requirement, and techno-leadership require ensuring future new normal sustainable developmental goals in this digital era (Hooda & Singla, 2020). To encourage sustainable employability, attitudes and transparency are very important, since it is important for all workers to sharpen their skills and achieve sustainable employability. Employees aim to anchor positive attitudes and to add more dynamism and proactivity to their work to provide greater employability and ability to continuously adjust to changing markets.

In organizations, vitality and well-being are evolving in human governance to establish successful strategies for health and safety. Organizations must develop own health and security protocols to ensure safety that encourages the participation and engagement of workers at all levels. Job variables directly affect the health of workers, individual performance, and risk management.

Tasks must keep ergonomics in mind to develop human performance. Another critical aspect is personal factors that include physicality and mental health into consideration for getting the desired behavior from them. Internal strong points of employee can be developed by training and acquiring experience from time to time. This will also help in reducing human error.

Work relations and content of work are facing increased levels of complexity since competition raised, budgetary limitations are expanding and major changes in technology are taking place. To address the abovementioned challenges, new policies, systems, and habits are in need to be implemented. The main drive is to leverage client's value, mainly, by working collaboratively in the realm of fruitful networks, which will promote organizational transformation and a new mindset among people. To achieve these strategic goals, leaders need to rely on accurate data which will be helpful for the decision-making process. Therefore, analytics are a key component of the process. Currently, public organizations need to respond quickly as the global world is continuously evolving, influencing their organizational structures, policies, and processes. Analytics are instruments in this sense that can assist us to solve the problems of a more digitalized environment. The public organisms that decided to implement the right analytics strategies will be making more accurate decisions. Public organizations will support their decisions in key performance indicators (KPIs) which will allow them to check whether the key objectives are being achieved or not. In the age of big data and high complexity processes, decision-making procedures need to be focused on analytics, which are becoming an important method for consolidating corporate strategies, not only helping to increase efficiency of the processes but also to forecast future results.

Empirical Research

Bibliometric Analysis

This research is characterized as bibliometric research of exploratory nature and qualitative approach. To achieve the objective of identifying and analyzing the analytics in studies previously published. The methodological procedures of this research are outlined through the three steps.

Step 1: Identify the Articles with HG Analytics

To identify HRM Analytics and definitions, a bibliometric analysis was set and developed through the following research protocol as represented in Fig. 9.1.

Following is shown in Table 9.1 with the summary of the number of the articles based on the type of publications.

Step 2: Identify the Analytics in the Articles Selected

In the bibliometric research, it was possible to identify the main analytics associated with Human Governance Analytics, to answer the Research Question (RQ): Which analytics are more important in Human Governance for Public Administration? One of the dimensions of Human governance that is global to the organizations is Talent Management, and the literature showed that the main analytics identified can be split into the categories: Talent Management, Talent Development, and Talent Assessment (Table 9.2).

Step 3: HG Analytics definitions (Table 9.3).

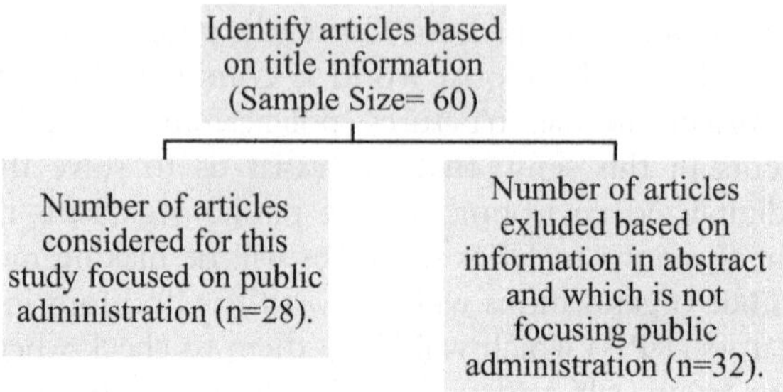

Fig. 9.1 Flowchart outlining the literature review (*Source* Authors' own conception)

Table 9.1 Number of articles ($N = 28$)

	Number(s)
Article in A periodical	1
Book section	3
Conference proceedings	6
Journal article	17
Misc	1

Source Authors' data analysis

Talent search and acquisition is motivated by the reorganizations of current activities in the workforce, cultural shifts both positive and negative, generational perspectives, social change/awareness leading to increases in publicity and/or reporting, industry expectation, and economic factors. Talent development focuses on how it is possible to improve employee skills and competencies. Organizations offer learning opportunities and resources to workers for their progress. This is a technique adopted by organizations to attract their highly skilled employees. Talent performance appraisal signifies periodical assessment of job performance of employee, namely, skills, accomplishments, and contribution to the organization.

A framework of factors can indicate towards performance monitoring of the organization continuously. The outcomes are used to monitor, further evaluate, and act to enhance results.

Table 9.2 Human governance analytics in public administration studies

Talent search and acquisition	*Talent development*	*Talent assessment*
Candidate success profiles	Employee engagement	Medical insurance
Recruitment analysis	Succession plans	
Workforce planning (head counting)	Employment sustainability	Employee performance
Employee retention	ROE (Return on emotion)	Leadership gap
Hiring metrics	Induction	ROI (Return on investment
Turnover	Organizational climate	Accident levels
Number of qualified candidates per position	Team performance	Overtime pay
	Employee training	Employee absenteeism
	Compensation and rewards	Time management
	Payroll budget	Compensation and rewards
	Organizational structure levels	Payroll budget
	Employee mobility	
	Employee satisfaction	

Source Authors' data analysis

Case Studies in Public Administration

A case study's main objective is to provide the most reliable interpretation possible for a case (Creswell, 1998). It involves evidence-based qualitative analysis (Leonard-Barton, 1990), and analyzing the characteristics of phenomena (Campbell & Stanley, 1963). The main data collection methods are open or closed interviews, focus groups, ethnography, participative and non-participative observations (Flick, 2009), and content analysis (Bardin, 1977).

Moreover, the main types of qualitative studies are according to Creswell (1998): case studies, comparative studies, retrospective, and longitudinal studies. Yin (2009) defines a case study as an empirical study carried out to study a phenomenon in the real-life context and using numerous evidence sources. In addition, focus is placed on presenting a full and accurate explanation and an interpretation of the relationship between the factors involved in each situation in a case study (Rashid et al., 2019).

Table 9.3 Human governance analytics description

Items	*Description*
Talent search and acquisition	
Candidate success profiles	The ideal candidate for the job
Number of qualified candidates per position	The number of candidates that fulfil the criteria for the position
Recruitment analysis	The rate of recruitment processes versus the rate of the selected candidates
Workforce planning (head counting)	Number of the workers needed to accomplish the activity plan of the organization
Employee retention	Rate of the employee retention in the organization
Hiring metrics	Number of the contract's agreement made with the new employees, and the type of contract
Turnover	The ratio between the number of dismissal employees and the number of new entries, to replace them. It is the flow of entries and leaves of employees in an organization
Talent development	
Employee engagement	Employee NPS—Assess the Net Promoter Score of your employee (NPS). Ask your team if they recommend a job at your company. Improve NPS for workers and you can increase engagement and commitment
Succession plans	Percentage of positions that exist to be filled internally or the number of years it takes for the average candidate to be ready for a new role
Employment sustainability	The rate of employability skills provision
ROE (Return on emotions)	Measures emotions and the engagement of the employees to the organization
Induction	Effectiveness of the onboarding program in the organization
Team performance	Performance appraisal of the activity of the teams regarding their goal's achievement with quality

(continued)

Table 9.3 (continued)

Items	*Description*
Employee training	Training effectiveness to measure the degree to which learning improves employee performance
Organisational structures levels	Span of control is a metric that refers to the number of employees under a manager's direct control
Employee mobility	Internal mobility rate represents the number of moves within the several departments of the company being promoted or moving laterally
Employee satisfaction	Percentage of satisfaction regarding the job position and job content, and the relationships between colleagues and managers
Talent performance appraisal	
Employee performance	Performance appraisal of the activity of the employees regarding their goals achievement with quality
Leadership gap	The percentage of negative accountability for the leader actions. They should be accountable for creating a vision,inspiring the workforce, and creating the benchmark for professionalism and excellence
ROI (Return on investment)	A performance measure used to evaluate the efficiency of an investment
Accident levels	Number of accidents in the workplace, and the level of severity
Overtime pay	It is the additional pay rate paid to employees for working more than the normal number of hours
Employee absenteeism	Employee absenteeism is characterized as an employee's frequent absence from work. This form of absence is also categorized as a regular absence that excludes allowed leave or paid time off
Compensation and rewards	Include salary, incentives, and performance bonus
Payroll budget	Includes fixed manpower cost, attrition rate, retention cost, re-hiring cost, expansion cost, training cost, retirement cost, and other related metrics

Source Authors' data analysis

A case study based on Yin (2009) could be suitable for analyzing real events and when the occurrence is of an extraordinary type, as well as posing multiple variables where uncertainty happens very frequently. It is also important when the study involves a contemporary phenomenon, where the boundaries between the phenomenon and its meaning are not well defined.

In this research two case studies will be presented: the first one about analytics in talent search and acquisition and selection and the second regarding talent development and talent performance appraisal.

Case Study 1—Metrics for Senior Civil Servants Recruitment in the Public Administration Context

Introduction

The process of implementing public policies and the way in which Portuguese public senior civil servants are selected and related to political power were analyzed through a questionnaire, specifically developed for this purpose. The questionnaire consisted of a total of 40 questions, organized into four distinct parts, namely:

(i) sociodemographic characterization of the sample (includes issues such as gender, age group, academic qualifications, seniority in public administration, management functions exercised, training carried out, relationship with ministerial offices, performance of political functions or positions of election, political ideology, and party affiliation)
(ii) importance of factors in the selection of leaders (middle and senior) in public administration, considering the internal reality (e.g.)
(iii) perceptions and opinions about political and administrative separation (e.g.), and
(iv) reform perceptions in Portuguese public administration (e.g.).

The questions in Part I were multiple choice, while the questions in the remaining parts allowed answers on a Likert scale, with five answer points. In Part II (where 1 means "nothing important" and 5 means "totally important", including one "I don't know/don't answer" option) and four answer points in Parts III and IV (where 1 means "totally disagree" and 4 means "totally agree", including an "I don't know/don't answer" option).

The data presented in this study refer to the treatment of Part II of the questionnaire—importance of factors in the selection of managers (middle and senior) in public administration, considering the internal reality,—as well as to the analysis of differences in these perceptions considering some of the variable's sociodemographic aspects of Part I. For the purpose of this case study, we will focus on the second part of the cited study.

Procedure

The data presented in this study fall within the scope of a public policy research project carried out at ISCTE–IUL, Instituto Universitário de Lisboa, with the support of INA—Instituto Nacional de Administração, I.P. The study aimed to explore the process of implementing public policies and the way in which Portuguese public officials are selected and related to political power. For this purpose, the collaboration of ISCTE and INA was requested, which made available a database with a total of 8166 emails from Public Administration officers who attended those courses under the EPD (2004–2011). These officers were contacted via email, having been presented with the objectives of the study and ensured ethical care (e.g., anonymity and confidentiality) associated with the collection and treatment of the data collected (explained on the online platform where the questionnaire was completed). A total of 1766 responses were obtained of which 964 were considered valid. The estimated average time to complete the questionnaire was 30 minutes.

The collected data were processed using the statistical software SPSS (Statistical Program for Social Sciences for Windows—version 22). Descriptive statistics analyses were carried out, namely through the use of central tendency measures and dispersion measures, in order to characterize the sample, as well as the results obtained regarding the characterization of the relations between policy and administration, namely the identification of factors that most contribute to the selection of public officials, in the context of the reforms undertaken in recent years in Public Administration. In all analyses, the results of hypothesis tests with a $p \leq 0.05$ were considered statistically significant.

Metrics

In this case study we recover the data by performing the following steps (Ferraz, 2020):

(1) Analyze the anti-image correlation matrix, the sphericity test, and the KMO measurement, to identify whether they are appropriate for this analysis.
(2) Extract the rotation factors using the Varimax method to facilitate their interpretation.
(3) Interpret the factors and analyze the obtained scores.
(4) Validate the model.

By doing these operations, we obtained the factor loading after the rotation which makes it possible to identify the component matrix that explains the selection of top public servants (Table 9.4).

Extraction method: Under principal component analysis, two extracted main components were identified which allow us to better understand the criteria of selection of senior civil servants that can be endorsed to some quantitative analysis of this study (Pillars, Concepts, and Indicators).

In terms of the factors associated with the professional component in the selection of top public servants, which seems to have a greater weight than the political component, the following were identified:

1. Regularly frequent key decision-making circles
2. Political ideology
3. Party affiliation
4. Enjoys proximity to, and confidence of, another person
5. An economic and financial position above the national average
6. Shares the same strategic vision of the government's organization/program
7. Has access to valuable information regarding the leadership position and its functional content.

As professional factors we can highlight the following factors:

1. Knowledge from the area of education/specialization
2. Previous experience in public administration

Table 9.4 Factors which influence the selection of top public servants component matrix (Top public servants)

Component matrix (a)		*Components*	
		1 (Professional)	*2 (Political)*
Talent search and acquisition	Knowledge from area of education/specialization	0.818	
	Previous experience in public administration	0.800	
	Performed similar functions before as a technical specialist in the same area	0.798	
	Behavioral skills of the person	0.794	
	Skills envisaged in the leadership personnel statute demonstrated in front of a competition jury or a leader before the nomination	0.785	
	Political exemption and neutrality	0.709	
	Regularly frequents key decision-making circles		0.765
	Political ideology	−0.473	0.745
	Party affiliation	−0.531	0.711
	Enjoys proximity to, and confidence of, another person		0.697
	An economic and financial position above the national average		0.674
	Shares the same strategic vision of the government's organization/program		0.632
	Has access to valuable information regarding the leadership position and its functional content		0.621

Source Authors' data analysis

3. Performed similar functions before as a technical specialist in the same area
4. Behavioral skills of the person
5. Skills envisaged in the leadership personnel statute demonstrated in front of a competition jury or a leader before the nomination

6. Political exemption and neutrality.

Final Considerations

The results of the case study can contribute to Human Governance providing managers with information to make choices about employee recruitment and engagement and also outputs for their development, as well as to have more understanding of the senior civil service context, functions, tasks, roles, and skills needed to drive public administration to success, especially in the political context of Public Administration and political relations. The data found can promote and enhance the public administration leader's profile in the realm of a new governance paradigm which is intrinsically associated with the inevitable challenges that society will face in the future.

Case Study 2—Metrics for Human Governance Regarding Talent Development and Talent Performance Evaluation in the Context of Public Administration

Introduction

Talent Development and Talent Performance Evaluation as relevant metrics for Human Governance in Public Administration are focused on the internal dimension of the organization, centered on the workers and in the people management policies, especially in areas like competencies development, and performance appraisal.

Procedure

A questionnaire was conceived and applied to a Public Managers sample. Twenty-four people have answered. The participants of the study were working in several organizational areas and job positions (e.g., Financial, Information Technologies, People Management, R&D, and International Projects). The respondents only could select the three most relevant metrics regarding talent performance appraisal and talent training—the most relevant responses are presented in Tables 9.5 and 9.6.

Table 9.5 Human governance training analytics

Talent development	Major adequacy of training to organizational needs	100%
	Specific technical training	100%
	Participation in the diagnostic of training needs	75%
	Behavioral training	75%
	Innovation training	75%

Source Authors' data analysis

Table 9.6 Human governance talent performance appraisal analytics

Talent performance appraisal	Performance levels	87.5%
	Leadership gap	87.5%
	Employee absenteeism	87.5%
	Motivation levels	75%
	Reward systems	75%

Source Authors' data analysis

Metrics

(a) Human governance regarding Talent Development metrics.

The implementation of technical training benefited the talent development system as a whole since it matched the main needs of the organization.

Several training sessions related with innovation and new approaches were put into place to fulfill the new organizational needs that were identified. The training sessions were designed to specifically empower people with the technical and technological skills needed to improve organizational efficiency. The creation of an individual development plan for each person was made through proper diagnostic of the training needs. The aim of the behavioral training was to inspire people to better communicate both internally and with the citizens. Innovation training is associated with developments led by R&D department and is translated into new services for the citizens.

(b) Human governance regarding Talent Performance Appraisal metrics.

As we can see, the participants consider performance, leadership, and employee absenteeism the most relevant, because it conditionates the activity of the organization, especially regarding the absenteeism of the workers that show low levels of motivation, and need to be changed by defining new policies and creating a culture where the employees feel more engaged with the organization, and increasing the affective commitment, linking it to a new style of leadership, where the participation and the teamwork effectively works, making the workers more responsible for their work and performance.

Performance Levels are linked to the performance appraisal system—Integrated System of Management and Performance Assessment in Public Administration (SIADAP). Leadership gap: the organization implemented a major change at the leadership level. Also, the strategic goals, the organizational design, and company mission were defined. Employee absenteeism is a major problem to be solved by the new leadership of the organization. By developing an innovative culture that inspires employee participation and workshops that allowed knowledge sharing, people's motivation levels had a boost. The reward system is a major difficulty to recruit workers with specific and exquisite talent, as the system is not flexible and not competitive.

Case Study Final Considerations

The presented results of this case study can contribute to Human Governance providing managers with information to make decisions about definition of people management practices, framed by the labor legislation. These practices will help to create a more strategic human governance and linked to the major goals of the organization to face the challenges of the external environment, namely, the changes in the political environment, in the economic context, and the advancements in the technology.

In this regard, the talent management practices implemented can potentiate the capacities of the Public Servants in order to develop the new mission and achieve the goals defined by the new leaders of the organization.

Discussion and Conclusions

Human Governance will provide managers with information to make choices about employee engagement and development as well as to have more understanding of job functions, tasks, roles, and skills needed to drive business success (Laursen & Thorlund, 2010). A Human Governance Analytics model can help to track organizational performance on an ongoing basis, which can be compared to strategic priorities and targets (Laursen & Thorlund, 2010).

To track, further evaluate, and act to enhance performance, the findings are used. The subsystem of analytics helps enterprises to develop informed decisions to accomplish strategies with success metrics as well as programs and budgets.

Enabling the company to develop successful plans, to provide a connection to a wide variety of data which is workforce-analogous to encourage adequate preparation, to promote different scenarios, and to allow real-world auditing to accomplish correct decisions of strategic nature.

Companies may change priorities, aims, alter initiatives, and re-allocate funds and resources. In essence, success metrics provide an adequate feedback in the company performance improvement system.

Therefore, human governance means understanding that an organization is committed to the importance of its social meaning by developing the full potential of its human resources in an age in which innovations such as artificial intelligence, big data, nanotechnology, robotics, and cloud computing play an important role. Companies that compete understand the rising importance of accuracy in data analysis in today's economy to encourage competition and help boost efficiency.

This study proposes a model that appeals to organic versatile systems, constantly adaptable to new circumstances, as opposed to hierarchical and centralized structures, in order to face this context. Organizations appear to be creative and more open to improvements in this paradigm, concentrating on the introduction of modern modes of work management and autonomous and participatory decision models, appealing to their collaborators for greater autonomy and accountability. However, in order to achieve organizational growth at this stage, the development of the skills of the staff, in this case the public servants, must require an investment.

Organizations are historically organized by several functional tiers, but they prefer to shift to a model which is horizontal by itself, allowing staff to have a key role in issues related with the process of making decisions (Das, 2021c). Rather than individual jobs, an orientation to the development of work groups, a need for collaboration at work alternatively to a culture characterized by control and decision-making centralization. Furthermore, the components of the work groups have to develop the expertise, the autonomy of the knowledge required to respond to unforeseeable disruptions arising from the environment and technologic processes.

In contrast, the work begins to be coordinated, indicating not only coordination but also, and most importantly, the responsibility assumed by each employee to guarantee the work quality and the achievement of the stipulated goals. The above-mentioned innovations include technological as well as social and relational skills. In this context, in order to resolve the complexity of the digital economy, this key research objective has been accomplished by generating more awareness about the principles of human governance and by presenting a model proposal for its implementation in organizations.

Finally, the small sample of our study is indeed a main limitation as well as the scarcity of studies on human governance that are available. Future research should build a model that allows forecasting the workforce planning and to examine the feasibility of applying AI in talent detection and recruitment to improve public management skills and ultimately, enhance Public Services quality systems and processes.

Future Research Directions

With regard to the management implications of research, it is possible to predict that this model of HG Analytics needs to be part of the global strategy of digital economy organizations Era: encouraging styles of leadership that focus on growth through delegation, job enrichment, greater transparency, and accountability; designing innovative work systems that facilitate the learning process; promoting versatility in work practices, taking into account the diversity of staff, facilities, and materials; concentrating on mental and physical factors such as ethics, protection, and healthy environments; implementing fair practices that inspire the adequate treatment of minorities; developing competencies to build opportunities for employees and managers to improve them; rewarding and recognizing improved results and contributions to the organizations' objectives; improving the commitment of employees to enhance their proactive capacity and inspiring them to creatively innovate (e.g., feedback, thoughts, and idea sharing); implementing processes that facilitate the adequate resolution of problems and that will offer redesigned services to customers; developing innovative processes that promote the creation and implementation of social innovations; creating innovative models of governance to accomplish more productivity and the development of the competencies of each employee; creating improved communication networks to promote the transfer of internal information between all employees, as well as improved ways to connect with customers; and envisioning new opportunities for future organizational advancement.

References

Abeysekera, I. (2013). A template for integrated reporting. *Journal of Intellectual Capital, 14*(2), 227–245.

Arfah, S., & Aziuddin, A. (2009). *Human governance: A paradigm shift in governing corporations*. MPH Publishing.

Bardin, L. (1977). *Content analysis Lisbon: Editions 70.*

Becker, T. E. (1998). Integrity in organizations: Beyond honesty and conscientiousness. *Academy of Management Review, 23*(1), 154–161.

Behera, M., Dash, M., Mohanty, A. K., & Das, S. (2019). Entrepreneurial ecosystem: A geographical upliftment. *Revista Espacios, 40*, 26–36. Retrieved from http://www.revistaespacios.com/a19v40n01/19400126.html

Bersin, J. (2017). *Rewriting the rules for the digital age: Deloitte global human capital trends*. University Press.

Cameron, K. S., Bright, D., & Caza, A. (2004). Exploring the relationships between organizational virtuousness and performance. *American Behavioral Scientist, 47*(6), 766–790.

Campbell, D. T., & Stanley, J. C. (1963). Experimental and quasi-experimental designs for research on teaching. In N. L. Gage (Ed.), *Handbook of research on teaching*. Rand McNally.

Creswell, J. W. (1998). *Qualitative inquiry and research design: Choosing among five traditions*. SAGE Publications.

Das, S. (2020a). Innovations in digital banking service brand equity and millennial consumerism. In *Digital transformation and innovative services for business and learning* (pp. 62–79). IGI Global. https://doi.org/10.4018/978-1-7998-5175-2.ch004

Das, S. (2020b, February). *Media impact of advertising on consumer buying behaviour a comparative study of different media*. Shiksha o Anusandhan University. http://hdl.handle.net/10603/273691

Das, S. (2021a). A systematic study of integrated marketing communication and content management system for millennial consumers. In *Innovations in digital branding and content marketing* (pp. 91–112). IGI Global. https://doi.org/10.4018/978-1-7998-4420-4.ch005

Das, S. (2021b). *Digital entertainment: The next evolution in service sector*. Springer Nature. https://doi.org/10.1007/978-981-15-9724-4. Print ISBN 978-981-15-9723-7. Online ISBN 978-981-15-9724-4

Das, S. (2021c). *Search engine optimization and marketing: A recipe for success in digital marketing* (1st ed.). CRC Press. https://doi.org/10.1201/9780429298509

Davis, J., Schoorman, F. D., & Donaldson, L. (1997). Toward a stewardship theory of management. *Academy of Management Review, 22*(1), 20–47.

Dua, S., Singh, I., & Das, S. (2021). Banking innovative service with digital brand equity for new age consumers: Internet banking and millennial consumerism. In *Innovations in digital branding and content marketing* (pp. 134–159). IGI Global. https://doi.org/10.4018/978-1-7998-4420-4.ch007

Duman, Ü. O., & Das, S. (2021). The dynamic rise of digital brands' market mavens in digital entertainment: A complete know how for curious customers. In *Digital entertainment* (pp. 147–172). Palgrave Macmillan. https://doi.org/10.1007/978-981-15-9724-4_8

Duy, N. T., Mondal, S. R., Van, N. T. T., Dzung, P. T., Minh, D. X. H., & Das, S. (2020). A study on the role of web 4.0 and 5.0 in the sustainable tourism ecosystem of Ho Chi Minh City, Vietnam. *Sustainability, 12*(17), 7140. https://doi.org/10.3390/su12177140

Falk, R. (1995). *On humane governance: Toward a new global politics*. Pennsylvania State University Press.

Ferraz, D. (2020). (A)Political administration? The public manager's portrait and selection factors. *Brazilian Journal of Public Administration, 54*(5), 1166–1187. Retrieved from http://bibliotecadigital.fgv.br/ojs/index.php/rap/article/view/82207

Flick, U. (2009). Qualitative Methoden in der Evaluationsforschung. *Zeitschrift für qualitative Forschung, 10*(1), 9–18.

Foss, N. J. (2007). The emerging knowledge governance approach: Challenges and characteristics. *Organization, 14*(1), 29–52.

Gould-Williams, J. (2003). The importance of HR practices and workplace trust in achieving superior performance: A study of public-sector organizations. *The International Journal of Human Resource Management, 14*(1), 28–54.

Graham, J., Plumptre, T. W., & Amos, B. (2003). *Principles for good governance in the 21st century*. Institute on Governance.

Gupta, D. K., Jena, D., Samantaray, A. K., & Das, S. (2019). HRD climate in selected public sector banks in India. *Revista ESPACIOS, 40*(11), 14–20.

Hanapiyah, Z. M., Daud, S., & Abdullah, W. M. T. W. (2016). Human governance and level of corruption risk. *Procedia Economics and Finance, 35*, 127–135.

Hanapiyahak, Z. M., Dauda, S., & Abdullaha, W. M. T. W. (2016). Human governance and level of corruption Ris7. *Procedia Economics and Finance, 35*, 127–135.

Hooda, A., & Singla, M. L. (2020). Core competencies A key to future oriented and sustainable e-governance implementation: A mixed method research. *Transforming Government: People, Process and Policy.*

ILO. (2017). *World employment and social outlook: Trends 2017*. http://www.ilo.org/global/research/global-reports/weso/2017/WCMS_541211/lang–en/index.htm

Kalliath, T. J., & Brough, P. (2008). Work-life balance: A review of the naming of the construct. *Journal of Management and Organization, 14*(3), 323–327.

Kelliher, C., Richardson, J., & Boiarintseva, G. (2019). All of work? All of life? Reconceptualising work-life balance for the 21st century. *Human Resource Management Journal, 29*(2), 97–112.

Laursen, G. H. N., & Thorlund, J. (2010). *Business analytics for managers: Take business intelligence beyond reporting*. Wiley.

Leonard-Barton, D. (1990). The intraorganizational environment: Point-to-point versus diffusion. *Technology Transfer: A Communication Perspective*, 43–62.

Licklider, J. (1990). *Man–computer symbiosis* [ebook]. Systems Research Center of Digital Equipment Corporation. http://memex.org/licklider.pdf

Marler, J. H., & Boudreau, J. W. (2017). An evidence-based review of HR Analytics. *The International Journal of Human Resource Management, 28*(1), 3–26.

Mohanty, P. C., Dash, M., Dash, M., & Das, S. (2019). A study on factors influencing training effectiveness. *Revista Espacios, 40*, 7–15. Retrieved from http://www.revistaespacios.com/a19v40n02/19400207.html

Mondal, S. R. (2020a). A systematic study for digital innovation in management education: An integrated approach towards problem-based learning in Vietnam. In *Digital innovations for customer engagement, management, and organizational improvement* (pp. 104–120). IGI Global. https://doi.org/10.4018/978-1-7998-5171-4.ch006

Mondal, S. R. (2020b, February). *Factors influencing store image loyalty and satisfaction from customer perspective an empirical study in retail sector*. Shiksha o Anusandhan University. http://hdl.handle.net/10603/273688

Mondal, S. R. (2021). A systematic study of new age consumer engagement and exploration for digital entertainment for over-the-top platforms in various digital media. In *Innovations in digital branding and content marketing* (pp. 113–133). IGI Global. https://doi.org/10.4018/978-1-7998-4420-4.ch006

Mondal, S. R., & Das, S. (2021). Examining diabetic subjects on their correlation with TTH and CAD: A statistical approach on exploratory results. In

Machine learning and the internet of medical things in healthcare (pp. 153–177). Academic Press. https://doi.org/10.1016/B978-0-12-821229-5.00007-0

Mondal, S., & Sahoo, K. K. (2020). A study of green building prospects on sustainable management decision making. In *Green building management and smart automation* (pp. 220–234). IGI Global. https://doi.org/10.4018/978-1-5225-9754-4.ch011

Nadanyiova, M., & Das, S. (2020). Millennials as a target segment of socially responsible communication within the business strategy. *Littera Scripta, 13*(1), 119–134. https://doi.org/10.36708/Littera_Scripta2020/1/8

OECD. (2019). *Education at a Glance 2019 OECD Indicators* (p. 4). OECD.

Ones, D. S., Viswesvaran, C., & Schmidt, F. L. (1993). Comprehensive meta-analysis of integrity test validities: Findings and implications for personnel selection and theories of job performance. *Journal of Applied Psychology, 78*(4), 679.

Rashid, Y., Rashid, A., Warraich, M. A., Sabir, S. S., & Waseem, A. (2019). Case study method: A step-by-step guide for business researchers. *International Journal of Qualitative Methods, 18*(1609406919862424).

Ravi, S., & Mondal, S. R. (2021). Digital entertainment based do it yourself content & advertisement as a factor of driving force for trust & customer patronage. In *Digital entertainment* (pp. 127–146). Palgrave Macmillan. https://doi.org/10.1007/978-981-15-9724-4_7

Roe, M. J. (2003). *Political determinants of corporate governance: Political context, corporate impact*. Oxford University Press on Demand.

Sarawati, S. (2018). Human governance: The art of emotional intelligence of leader through the model of spirituality. *International Journal of Engineering and Technology, 7*(2.29), 383–388.

Schabracq, M. J. (2003). Everyday well-being and stress in work and organisations. In M. J. Schabracq, J. A. M. Winnubst, & C. L. Cooper (Eds.), *The handbook of work and health psychology*. Wiley.

Sharma, E., & Das, S. (2020). Measuring impact of Indian ports on environment and effectiveness of remedial measures towards environmental pollution. *International Journal of Environment and Waste Management, 25*(3), 356–380. https://doi.org/10.1504/IJEWM.2019.10021787

Sharma, E., & Das, S. (2021). Integrated model for women empowerment in rural India. *Journal of International Development, 33*(3), 594–611. https://doi.org/10.1002/jid.3539

Sharma, E., Nigam, N., & Das, S. (2020). Measuring gap in expected and perceived quality of ICT enabled customer services: A systematic study of top ten retailers of India. *International Journal of Applied Systemic Studies, 9*(2), 159–184. https://doi.org/10.1504/ijass.2020.113260

Singh, L. B., Mondal, S. R., & Das, S. (2020). Human resource practices & their observed significance for Indian SMEs. *Revista ESPACIOS, 41*(7). Retrieved from http://www.revistaespacios.com/a20v41n07/20410715.html

Singh, S., Mondal, S., Singh, L. B., Sahoo, K. K., & Das, S. (2020). An empirical evidence study of consumer perception and socioeconomic profiles for digital stores in Vietnam. *Sustainability, 12*(5), 1716. https://doi.org/10.3390/su12051716

Siri, R., & Das, S. (2021). A study on processing of information storage & use of new age consumers in digital wellness sector through story telling & creating interest. In *Digital entertainment* (pp. 45–63). Palgrave Macmillan. https://doi.org/10.1007/978-981-15-9724-4_3

Siri, R., Mondal, S. R., & Das S. (2020). Hydropower: A renewable energy resource for sustainability in terms of climate change and environmental protection. In *The handbook of environmental chemistry*. Springer. https://doi.org/10.1007/698_2020_635

Van, N. T. T., Vrana, V., Duy, N. T., Minh, D. X. H., Dzung, P. T., Mondal, S. R., & Das, S. (2020). The role of human–machine interactive devices for post-COVID-19 innovative sustainable tourism in Ho Chi Minh City Vietnam. *Sustainability, 12*(22), 9523. https://doi.org/10.3390/su12229523

Van Weyenbergh, G. (2019, June). Distributed participatory governance. In *Proceedings of the 20th Annual International Conference on Digital Government Research* (pp. 515–516).

Yegen, C., & Mondal, S. R. (2021). Sharenting: A new paradigm of digital entertainment of new age parenting and social media. In *Digital entertainment* (pp. 213–231). Palgrave Macmillan. https://doi.org/10.1007/978-981-15-9724-4_11

Yin, R. K. (2009). *Case study research: Design and methods* (Vol. 5). Sage.

CHAPTER 10

Analysing Users' Engagement with eSports Team: Does Covid-19 Matter?

Francesca Di Virgilio, Mohammad Soliman, Muhammad Anwar ul Haq, and Sara Fantini

Introduction

Social media platforms have been a widespread uptake and adoption in the business environment by offering to many organizations the opportunity to build new market space in terms of competitiveness and innovation (Mount & Martinez, 2014), find new customers (Baird & Parasnis, 2011), understand customers' needs (Sashi, 2012),

F. Di Virgilio (✉) · S. Fantini
Department of Economics - University of Molise, Campobasso, Italy
e-mail: fradivi@unimol.it

M. Soliman
University of Technology and Applied Sciences, Salalah, Oman
e-mail: msoliman.sal@cas.edu.om

Present Address:
Faculty of Tourism & Hotels, Fayoum University, Faiyum, Egypt

S. R. Mondal et al. (eds.), *HR Analytics and Digital HR Practices*,
https://doi.org/10.1007/978-981-16-7099-2_10

rethink new business models (Bleicher & Stanley, 2018), and provide benefits in organizational communication (Tajudeen et al., 2018).

Previous studies, in many disciplines including health, marketing, innovative business, human resources, and knowledge management continue to discover new applications for social media platforms (Chang et al., 2015; Culnan et al., 2010; Di Virgilio, 2018; Hansen & Levin, 2016; López-Bolás et al., 2019; Robertson & Kee, 2017). In this context, a ground-breaking innovative business develops: eSports, as a product of globalization that is spreading among hundreds of millions of viewers from different countries (Cunningham et al., 2018; Filo et al., 2015; Heere, 2018). In the literature, eSports is described as an electronic version of sports where professional gaming and cyber-athletics played and organized among professional players, in teams or individually that compete with each other in a specific game and create attraction for viewers, who watch them live or streaming, everywhere and anytime, through social media platforms (Funk et al., 2018; Hamari & Sjöblom, 2017; Reitman et al., 2020). In these years, eSports activities are increasing competitiveness by reaching new and more entrepreneurs and consumers, promoting and developing massive revenues (Scholz, 2019), despite this, to make business decision, the analysis of the users' engagement regards an event or a team, provides an unusually productive information to invest in this digital business (Jenny et al., 2018). There is a growing body of literature on eSports that recognizes users' engagement (Chmait et al., 2020; Hilvert-Bruce et al., 2018), in terms of performance (Matsui et al., 2020; Behnke et al., 2019), of interactive experiences with regard to viewer–streamer interaction (Wohn & Freeman, 2020), and of the gamer as an influencer (Sjöblom et al., 2017).

Surprisingly, a search of the recent literature on eSports revealed the lack of studies of the effects of COVID-19 period on users' engagement trends. COVID-19 (Coronavirus) is a global pandemic and has led to a strong global health issue with effects on the global economy and in

---

M. Anwar ul Haq
Department of Management Sciences Pakistan, University of Gujrat, Gujrat, Punjab, Pakistan
e-mail: anwar.haq@uog.edu.pk

business shutting down in all sectors (Ratten, 2020a; Das, 2021a). From a sport industry perspective (Mondal, 2021; Ratten, 2020b), there has been a dramatic interruption of the activities during the lockdown, this crisis has been unprecedented event worldwide, heavily influencing physical and psychological well-being of the communities (Dua et al., 2021; Duy et al., 2020; Van et al., 2020).

In this scenario, to fill the gap in the literature, the aim of this chapter is to investigate how pandemic period has affected users' engagement trends compared to the previous period, with a particular focus on how it has influenced users' sentiments and moods expressed by comments on Instagram profile of the Italian eSports team: namely Dropz. In order to achieve these goals, a combination mixed of quantitative and qualitative approaches was used in the data analysis by a powerful tool: NVivo 11 (Bazeley & Jackson, 2013).

The findings of this study highlight significant contributions to interdisciplinary both scholars and practitioners interested in studying the users' engagement of eSports teams. Mainly, it is the first study that analyzes the impact of the COVID-19 on users' engagement trends of an eSports team, highlighting the potentiality for future investments and business development on all social media platforms also in the time of the global crisis. Furthermore, a methodological approach was applied in a more dynamic and innovative manner, proposing metrics to assess users' sentiment and to extract six mood states, helping to understand how the comments within the engagement, generated by users, as an important source of information to monitor the teams' brand image (Culotta & Cutler, 2016) and to understand consumers' need (Sashi, 2012) by their moods (Gardner, 1985; Thelwall & Buckley, 2013).

Background: Main Focus of the Chapter

ESports Overview

eSports are born from the traditional professional sports (Heere, 2018; Cunnigham et al., 2018; Siri et al., 2020; L.B. Singh et al., 2020), but it involves new means and requires not so traditional skills (Funk et al., 2018; Hallmann & Giel, 2018); for this reason, several researchers did not define it as a simple electronic version of sports (Hamari & Sjöblom, 2017; Taylor, 2012), but as a form of sports that links the virtual contest through social media platforms where gamers and teams, respectively, compete with each other in games divided into categories, within events such as leagues, ladders, and tournaments and the viewers watch them live or streaming in a digital way (Hallmann & Giel, 2018; L. B. Singh et al., 2020; Sharma & Das, 2020).

eSports have led to a proliferation of studies across disciplines offering a number of insights and showing its relevance from various perspectives (Cunningham et al., 2018; Filo et al., 2015; Hallmann & Giel, 2018; Reitman et al., 2020). In the context of social media studies, the researchers focus their studies on how eSports community is spread and how viewers support their teams or players within the interactions with gameplay on social media platforms (Das, 2020; Mondal, 2020; Sjöblom et al., 2017). The social interaction is more easily reachable between viewers and players or teams by their followers and streamers followed on their channels of different social platforms (Cunningham et al., 2018; Nadanyiova & Das, 2020). Existing research in informatics has been published on the broadcast popularity and on the level of institutional infrastructure of eSports activities (Funk et al., 2018; Holt, 2016) recognizing the critical role played by technological progress (Mondal & Sahoo, 2020; Turtiainen et al., 2020), to favor accessibility to an increasing number of followers on different social platforms simultaneously (Behera et al., 2019; Cunningham et al., 2018; Gupta et al., 2019; Mohanty et al., 2019). Moreover, new web technologies make the game better organized and improve physical skills and knowledge of the professional players by using them regularly (Hallmann & Giel, 2018; Taylor, 2012). Considering that players or teams in sports industry are sponsored by numerous business organizations (Hamari & Sjöblom, 2017), in order to gain sponsorship is essential for them to become more professional, to increase their revenues, and attract new followers (Jenny et al., 2018).

In cognition science, experimental researches in eSports is less common but growing as showed by Gray et al. (2018). Previously published studies have analyzed complex human behavior through the study of players' performance (Bednárek et al., 2018), to better understand the games or team composition (Mora-Cantallops & Sicilia, 2019), and to identify higher skill levels in competitive events (Behnke et al., 2019; Matsui et al., 2020). In this field, the motivations and the consumption by players have led to a renewed interest, in order to understand the possible benefits, in terms of leisure, positive well-being, to escape from real-life, self-improvement, motivations, and socialization (Hilvert-Bruce et al., 2018; Jang & Byon, 2020; Weiss & Schiele, 2013; Wohn & Freeman, 2020). The researchers have measured many of the factors leading to consumption, the most commonly adopted perspective is the gratification theory framework (Hilvert-Bruce et al., 2018; Whiting & Williams, 2013). The main research area to understand users experience was on the online games (Whiting & Williams, 2013; Wu et al., 2010) and on the social media platforms such as Facebook, Twitter, and Twitch (Chen, 2011; Sjöblom et al., 2017) through two most widely measurement scales: the motivation for eSports consumption (Khan, 2017) and fan motivation (Wann, 1995).

In this scenario and according to Scholz (2019), eSports seem to be a business with limitless potential growth; however, the study of the change in the level of engagement and the motivations leading to consumptions remains a major challenge to develop this sector.

Users' Engagement with eSports

Social media engagement is a major area of interest within the field of social media platforms, to understand the strategic role of sharing into online experiences by consumers' interactions (Dolan et al., 2016; Khan, 2017; Sashi, 2012). The core consumers of the eSports are mainly characterized by young people who spend more time every day alone or with their group of friends to produce contents on multiple platforms simultaneously which they can comment on the performances and cheer for their favorite teams or players (Freeman & Wohn, 2019). Users' interaction is one of the main drivers to study the level of engagement regarding a team or event, due to the fact that every gamer influences to produce contents and in parallel they use social networks such as Twitch.tv and YouTube gaming, to follow online video streaming, achieving their image by Facebook and Instagram and to strengthen their fan base by Twitter announcements (Establés et al., 2019; Hilvert-Bruce et al., 2018). Some researchers have pointed out the motivations that drive users to be more engaged in online games for extended period of time every day, in relationship to the team composition, the characteristics of the game, or the game ranking systems (Brubaker & Wilson, 2018; Hilvert-Bruce et al., 2018; Mora-Cantallops & Sicilia, 2019; Sjöblom et al., 2017). Furthermore, many businesses are approaching the context of eSports sector to sponsor teams, events, or to open a new market and are realizing the benefits in their marketing strategies to advertise their products and services, to know in-depth the rise of users' engagement in terms of comments, likes, and shares (Brubaker & Wilson, 2018). Therefore, many companies involve users in the corporate sharing process as co-marketers, inviting their friends to play and emphasizing them to share contents as photos or videos or to use specific hashtags, because their contents becoming viral may reach the highest number of potential consumers which could turn into economic value (Jenny et al., 2018).

In this scenario, it is interesting to analyze how COVID-19 may impact the trend of users' engagement of an eSports' team, leading us to the first research question:

RQ1. How the pandemic has impacted on users' engagement trends in terms of followers, likes, and comments?

Users' Sentiment Expressions

An increasing number of empirical analyses of sentiments and moods on social media platforms have shown their predictive role as economic indicators (e.g., Bollen et al., 2010). Studies of eSports show the importance of engagement in eSports can arise emotions and sentiments (Hallmann & Giel, 2018), connectedness to their behavioral patterns on such platforms (Matsui et al., 2020; Freeman & Wohn, 2019) as Facebook or live-stream platforms (Ellison et al., 2007; Hilvert-Bruce et al., 2018), highlighting the domain of positive youth development (Johnston et al., 2013), where users feel safe both psychologically and physically and every competitive and entertaining activity may bring associated with various positive or negative sentiments such as fun, leisure, or aggression and loneliness (Hallmann & Giel, 2018; Weiss & Schiele, 2013) creating easily a stronger connection with their favorite players or teams (Danish et al., 2004; Holt, 2007).

There is still uncertainty in the literature about why people play online eSports, and which of them provides positive or negative personal experiences (Yin et al., 2020) and influences their moods. The users' mood following their team or event can lead to attitude toward the consumptions on eSports as general consumer behavior theory suggests (Gardner, 1985; Isen, 1989). It is revealed from Hilvert-Bruce et al. (2018, p. 60), the main motivations from psychological perspective to engage people watch live streaming are: social interaction, social anxiety, entertainment, sense of community, meeting new people, information seeking, social support, and external support.

Nevertheless, more recently, literature has emerged that offers contradictory findings of enjoyment into different perspectives: the enjoyment as positive sentiment by using the chat function as suspense of the video game outcome (Wulf et al., 2018), as opposed, the enjoyment of aggression behavior as a rather common for players to exhibit this negative sentiment during gaming experience or to cheer their favorite team or player (Wann et al., 1999; Wann & Martin, 2008).

Users' sentiments and moods are expressing through comments by text information, emoticons, and emoji, the most common on the social media platforms such as Facebook and Instagram. In particular, emoticons and emoji were an important means of online modern communication technology (Chairunnisa & Benedictus, 2017; Kannan & Shreya, 2017). Emoticon is a symbol or a short character usually resembling facial expression, portraying a particular activity or emotional form such as smileys (Derks et al., 2008; Dresner & Herring, 2010). Instead, emoji is a symbol that facilitates better communications by messages with wider concepts and ideas such as people, celebrations, weathers, animals, and nature, vehicles and buildings, food and drink, activity, travel and places, objects, symbols, and flags.

According to Novak et al. (2015), nearly half of the texts on Instagram contains emoticon—emoji and express users' opinions, sentiments, evaluations, attitudes, and emotions with the meaning positive, neutral, or negative.

Therefore, it is plausible to assume that there may be negative influence on users' sentiment expressed by comments, during a period of lockdown due to the COVID-19 pandemic compared with the previous period, leading to the following question:

RQ2. How the pandemic has impacted on the users' sentiments expressed by comments?

Methodology

The Case

The context of the current chapter involves an Italian's eSports team, namely, Dropz. As asserted by the co-founders of the team during a direct interview, Dropz was born in November 2018 and competes in League of Legends, Fortnite, and Apex. In a few months, the team won the third prize at the B series of ESL Vodafone Championship of League of Legends, two months later it placed fifth in the ranking of the A series of the same competition, which is one of the most important for League of Legends in Italy, together with the PG Nationals, to which Dropz succeeded in participating in June 2019. Constituted as a sporting association, Dropz is a professional eSports team and it has a specific organizational structure. On the top of the pyramid there are the three co-founders, who are also the president, the sponsorship responsible, and the bursar. They manage a content manager, who deals with the creation of content on social media, and three team managers. Everyone administers coaches, assistant coaches, and gamers of each eSports in which Dropz competes, so there are gamers for League of Legends, those for Fortnite and those for Apex (www.dropzesports.com). In addition, on their Facebook profile (Dropz), we can find more information about their vision, i.e., enriching the management of the traditional sports industry with that one of the innovative eSports team, by involving as many people as possible in a competitive team. Moreover, in the same section of their Facebook page, there's an interesting description of the meaning of the logo (a drop of water) which is closely connected to their hashtag (#can't stop the wave!).

The team is active on different social media platforms such as Facebook, Instagram, Twitter, YouTube Gaming, Twitch, and Discord. Currently the team is focusing upon the Instagram profile in order to better manage its image, showing its players' abilities through videos, announce events, and attract new followers. Indeed, Instagram is also the platform where the team reached the highest number of followers among its social media pages, as we can see on Dropz's Instagram profile (@teamdropz), the social media analytics we used, Ninjalitics, and as emerged from the direct interview to the co-founders of the team.

Data Collection and Analysis Procedures

The operational part of the case study about the eSports team Dropz consisted of collecting data to address our research questions regards the level of engagement (RQ1) in terms of number of followers, likes, and comments by post (Brubaker & Wilson, 2018) and the users' sentiment (RQ2) expressed by comments with their contents that the team Dropz's Instagram profile attracted on the posts they published in the period from August 2019 to March 2020, before and during COVID-19. The procedure of data collection can be divided into two phases.

Phase 1: Data Collection of Trends (RQ1)

First of all, information was collected about the number of followers of the profile and how the number changed during COVID-19 period and the number of followers' reactions to the posts published. We used a specific social media analytics website (www.Ninjalitcs.com) which is specialized in searching for all the information related to the activity of all the Instagram profiles. Through that tool, we managed to discover how the number of followers changed day by day in the period from August 2019 to March 2020 and the total number of likes and comments to each post in the same period, as well.

We reported all information in an Excel file, which has been split up into three parts: (1) In the first part, we reported the number of followers, likes, and comments by post; (2) In the second part, we calculated the arithmetic average of the number of followers, likes, and comments recorded each month; and (3) in the third part, we calculated the marginal amount of followers and the arithmetic average of the number of likes and comments recorded each month.

Phase 2: Analyzing Sentiments Express Through Comments (RQ2)

For peeping into the users' sentiment by analyzing the comments made as a reaction to each post released by the team, we followed a three-step process proposed by Abdous and He (2011) and applied by He et al. (2017) also. The steps are outlined below:

(a) Identification of the text (data extraction): The online comments on the Instagram posts of Dropz eSports team were retrieved. The comments were arranged into an Excel Spreadsheet. Each comment was individually reviewed by an expert of our team before making it part of the Excel sheet for further analysis. This pre-processing was necessary because of (a) finding any repetitive comments and (b) for translation; many of the comments were made in Italian, a language expert, versed in both English and Italian, translated the same into English. For validation of the translation, another expert translated the comments back into Italian, minor adjustments were made for further analysis. We followed the forward–backward translation method to avoid bias as recommended by Brislin (1970); (c) for conversion of emoticon and emoji: many of the followers expressed their emotion and sentiment, using emoticon and emoji, a frequent and easy medium of expression on social media sites, the same was translated according to Novak et al. (2015) into their textual counterparts. After the pre-processing, there were 1396 comments for analysis.
(b) Data processing: In this step that comments were arranged data-wise and month-wise. For each month there was a separate spreadsheet with each comment entered into unique cell differentiated by the date commented. All the spreadsheets were then imported into NVivo 11 (QSR, 2016), a powerful tool for qualitative analysis. NVivo is used to analyze the qualitative data. It can help to analyze various forms of data, i.e., text, videos, and audio. Using NVivo, various queries can be performed such as word frequency query and word search query. Data can be easily coded into categories and themes can be identified. NVivo can also help analyze sentiments (Bazeley & Jackson, 2013).
(c) Recognize actionable information: After importing the data into NVivo, various queries such as text search and word frequency were run to establish an initial feel out of the data. Moods were then identified using Node coding in NVivo. We also conducted sentiment analysis for identifying positive and negative sentiments expressed by the fans for their team (Abdous & He, 2011).

Findings

Initial Analysis of Trends

Figure 10.1 reveals the growth of followers from August 2019 to March 2020. The dotted line shows the cumulative growth of followers, the solid line shows the marginal growth of followers each month. By 1 August 2019, there were only 3045 followers of the team Dropz, which had grown over to 5062 by the end of November, thus an increase of 2019 followers over four months. In December 2019, there was only a marginal addition of 56 members. This was immediately before COVID-19 started to emerge. Among the following months, March 2020 saw the highest rise with 640 followers. We can infer from the above that while COVID-19 started to grip the lives, the people had no choice but to stay home and engage in online activities, such as subscribing to eSports.

Figure 10.2 demonstrates the number of comments between August 2019 and March 2020. In August 2019, only 17 comments were posted. The trend kept upwards in September and October 2019. In December 2019, 51 comments were posted. March 2020 recorded the peak, 416 comments. It can be inferred that with the advent of COVID-19, the followers engaged more with the team.

Figure 10.3 shows the trend of users' likes. There were only 93 likes in August 2019. The trend fell in November 2019 and December 2019 with 76 and 86 likes, respectively. In January 2020, there was a rise again

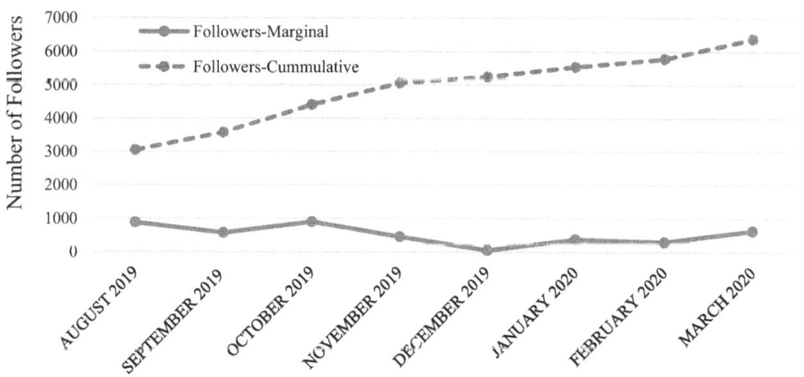

Fig. 10.1 Followers' growth on Instagram (*Source* Authors' own analysis by NVivo 11)

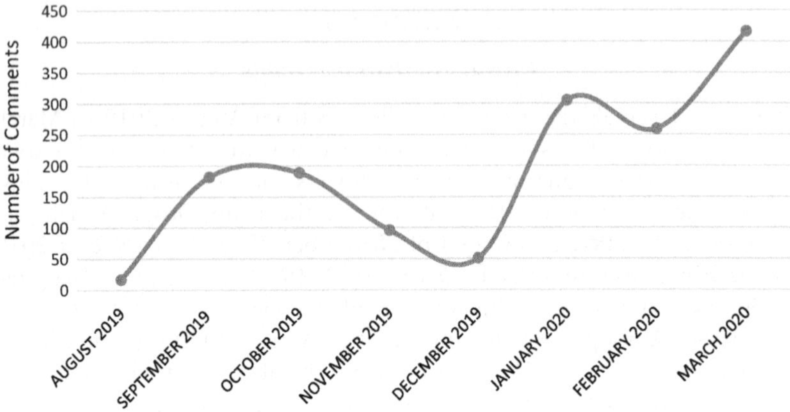

Fig. 10.2 Number of comments (*Source* Authors' own analysis by NVivo 11)

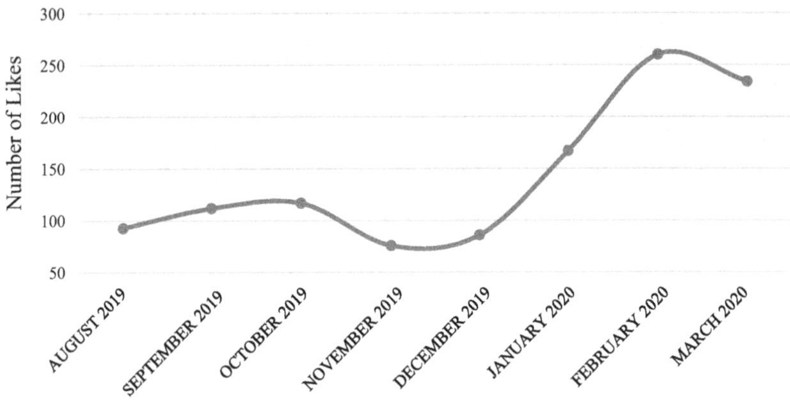

Fig. 10.3 The trend of Instagram likes by followers (*Source* Authors' own analysis by NVivo 11)

in the number of likes. The number of likes, post-COVID-19, was clearly higher in the months of February and March 2020.

Content Analysis

Word Frequency

There were a total of 1394 comments made on Instagram posts. For extracting the usable information and to draw inferences, we also excluded characters (i.e., ! @, #, $, and &). Furthermore, vowels or the text having no inferential values were also dropped. Using the word frequency query in Nvivo 11, in the first step, we extracted the frequency with which the expressions were used in the data set. Table 10.1 shows the top 20 expressions used by the followers. The expression "heart" was used as much as 1172 times at different instances. On the lower side, the expression "drop" was used 94 times. It is also notable that similar expressions were stemmed together, such as, "heart, hearts", "wave, waves, waving".

Table 10.1 Top 20 expressions

S. No	*Word*	*Length*	*Count*	*Weighted percentage (%)*	*Similar words*
1	Hearts	6	1172	8.18	heart, hearts
2	Fire	4	938	6.55	Fire
3	Face	4	801	5.59	face, faces
4	blue	4	574	4.01	Blue
5	wave	4	438	3.06	wave, waves, waving
6	smiling	7	353	2.47	smiling
7	water	5	301	2.10	Water
8	biceps	6	230	1.61	biceps
9	flexed	6	230	1.61	flexed
10	eyes	4	222	1.55	eye, eyes
11	hands	5	194	1.35	hand, hands
12	droplet	7	176	1.23	droplet, droplets
13	Joy	3	168	1.17	Joy
14	tears	5	168	1.17	Tears
15	black	5	124	0.87	Black
16	suit	4	122	0.85	suit, suits
17	muscle	6	114	0.80	muscle
18	shaped	6	108	0.75	shaped
19	apex	4	105	0.73	Apex
20	drop	4	94	0.66	drop, dropping, drops

Source Authors' own analysis

Fig. 10.4 Dominantly used expressions (*Source* Authors' own analysis by NVivo 11)

The following word cloud generated from NVivo11 further elucidates the above frequently occurring expressions (Fig. 10.4).

Identification of Moods

Based on the frequency of the expression, we tracked the occurrence of the expressions in the text in each instance. Each comment was scrutinized again for identifying the type and the level of engagement of followers with the team. Six moods emerged which are categorized the manner in which those following the Instagram account engaged with the team through posting various comments. Details follow:

Involvement/Celebration: After assessing the comments, it was revealed that the majority of the fans engaged with the team on highly positive terms. They celebrated the success of the team by expressing in the form of text or by posting smileys such as heart, fire, bomb, etc. There were 452 instances in which the fans celebrated the activities of the team.

Appreciation/Support: Another set of fans engaged with the team by expressing their appreciation and support for the team. The intensity of expression in this category was lesser than those in the celebration category. The followers used terms such as good luck, congratulations, etc. There were 487 comments in which followers appreciated/supported the team activities.

Suggestion: Another theme that emerged out of the comments was the followers giving various suggestions to the team. There was a total of 87 comments in which different suggestions were given to the team.

Dislike: All the followers did not happen to like the team. In certain cases, the followers also expressed their dislike for the activities of the team. However, the dislike was not very much prevailing in the comments. There were 39 comments in which followers did not like the post by the team.

Questions/Replies: In a few comments, 95, the followers engaged with the team by asking various questions. However, such was a very meager ratio in the overall number of engagements. The followers usually asked about the activities or the future plans of team. Some even inquired about the possibilities to join the team.

Irrelevant/Neutral: Lastly, some comments could not particularly be categorized into one of the above themes. They were irrelevant to the theme of the post or did not express any opinion. A major chunk of comments into this category was mentions/tags. A total of 227 comments fall in this category.

An example for each theme is presented in Table 10.2.

Analyzing the Trend of Engagement

In the following chart, we explain how the followers engaged with the team over the period August 2019–March 2020. In August 2019, among the overall 14 comments, seven were made celebrating the team, six were made as appreciation, and one comment was suggestive. None of the followers disliked team activity. In September 2019, the engagement of followers was much higher than August 2019. In total, 198 times the

Table 10.2 Examples related to themes

Name	*Description*	*Examples*
Involvement/celebration	Refers to the use of celebrating expressions by followers	Well done guys! Hold the flag high + emoticon heart
Appreciation/support	Refers to the use of appreciative expression by followers	Congratulations, you deserve it! Great and Good luck! tag + emoticon praying hands
Suggestion	Refers to the use of suggestive expressions by followers	More years together! Stay humble! + emoticon face
Question/reply	Refers to the use of expressions asking questions	Seriously we can play in the third person? Tag + which rank do you aim to? + emoticon face
Dislike	Refers to the use of expressions showing dislike	tag + You're illegal Ridiculous! + emoticon face
Irrelevant/neutral	Refers to comments not falling in any of the above categories	Tag + Goat GG + tag

Source Authors' own analysis of data

followers made comments out of which 76 were for celebration, 86 were supportive, 11 were suggestive, three were disliking, one asking question, and 21 were irrelevant. Almost a similar trend persisted in October 2019. A total of 190 comments were made. Among the total, 91 were celebrative, 54 supportive, four suggestive, six disliking, 35 were neutral, and none asked a question. In November 2019, we observed a major decline in how the followers engaged with the team with only 89 comments. There were only 44 celebrative comments, 25 were supportive, 10 were suggestive, and one comment each for the themes of dislike and asking questions. There were eight irrelevant comments.

In December 2019, as the COVID-19 started to surge, we observe a further decline. Only 43 comments were posted. There were 11 celebrative comments, ten supportive, seven suggestive, two expressing dislike, 11 asking a question, and two were irrelevant comments. In January 2020, the follower engagement again started to rise with 299 comments made by the fans. Among the total, 132 were celebrative, 53 were supportive, six were suggestive, only two disliking, 33 asking a question, and as much as 73 were irrelevant. In February 2020, there was a sharp decline with only 211 comments posted by the fans. There were 47 celebrative comments, 94 were supportive, 18 were suggestive, six disliking, 23 each for asking a question or were neutral. In March 2020, the fan's engagement with the team recorded a peak with 343 comments overall. There were 44 celebrative comments, 159 supportive, 30 suggestive, 19 disliking, 26 asking a question, and 65 were irrelevant comments.

We further conclude from the chart that team support is constantly on the rise after December 2019 with peak in March 2020. Similarly, though negligible, comments showing dislike were also on the rise after December 2019 and witnessing a rise till March 2020. March 2020 was the peak time of COVID-19 cases. The follower seemed to have the highest level of engagement with the eSports during March 2020. Since the outdoor activities had been locked down, people spent their time in indoor activities such as engaging in eSports (Fig. 10.5).

In December 2019, we can observe there is a lesser level of engagement by the follower. This might be attributed to: (1) lesser investment in the promotion of posts, (2) lesser number of events in the gaming world, (3) change of players in the team who took away their followers, (4) the number of posts published was lesser, and (5) the team was more engaged in promotion activities on other platforms.

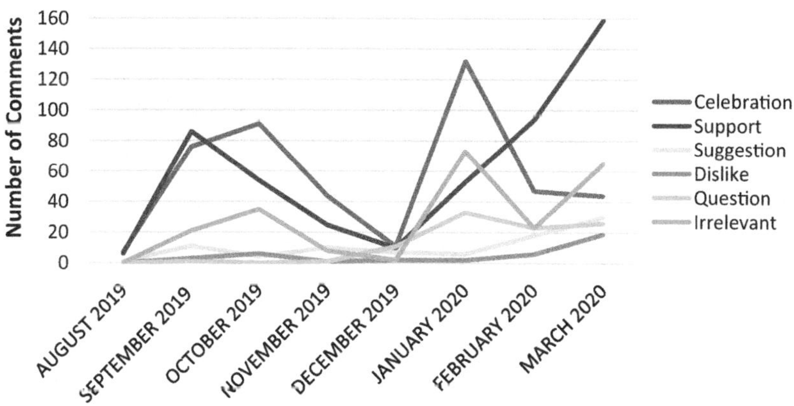

Fig. 10.5 Thematic trend analysis (*Source* Authors' own analysis by NVivo 11)

Sentiment Analysis

In the next phase, we conducted sentiment analysis. Sentiment analysis is used to identify the sentiments prevalent in the text and seeking to address how and if pandemic period impacted positive or negative on users' sentiment. The analysis turns out the results in positive, negative, and neutral sentiments. For this purpose, a sentiment analysis query was run in NVivo 11. The chart (see Fig. 10.6) shows a variable trend of engagements over the period August 2019–March 2020. In September and October, the neutral sentiments were on the rise as compared to August, while again fell down in November and December. There is a peak in January 2020 with more than 250 neutral sentiments. After falling to 170 in February 2020, March 2020 sees a growth surpassing 300. The notable trend is that positive and negative sentiments both have remained below a tally of 50 over the period of August 2019 to March 2020.

In order to further understand the trend of positive sentiments, along with the overall positive, two other categories, very positive, and moderately positive were plotted. There has been a rise in the positive sentiments in September 2019 as compared to adjacent months. After dipping down in November, December 2019 and January 2020 see a rise with February 2020 hitting the peak. In March 2020, there is a fall yet again. Very

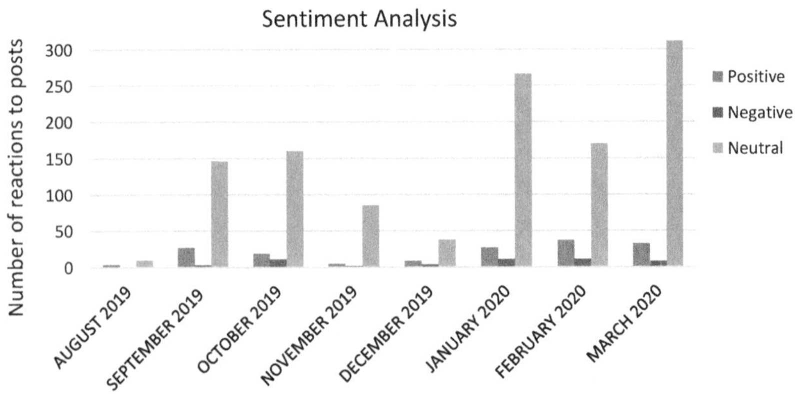

Fig. 10.6 Sentiment analysis-overall (*Source* Authors' own analysis by NVivo 11)

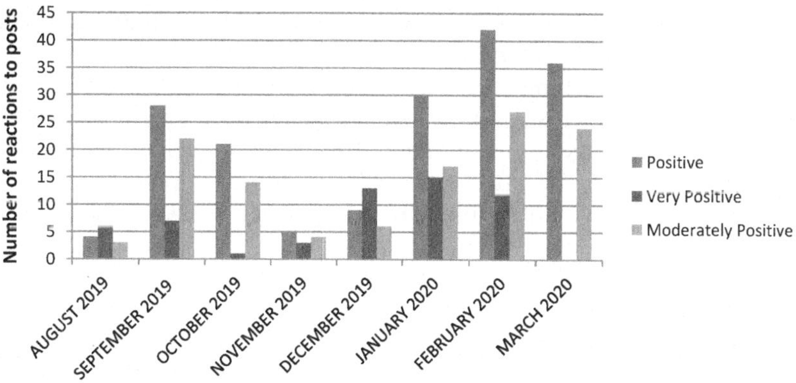

Fig. 10.7 Sentiment analysis-positive (*Source* Authors' own analysis by NVivo 11)

positive and moderately positive sentiments also showed a similar trend (Fig. 10.7).

Conclusions

Discussion

This chapter is one of the first of its kind to investigate the users' engagement level on Instagram of the Italian eSports team, during crisis situation due to the COVID-19, and to determine if it has had an influence positive or negative on users' sentiments, since the individuals have been confined to their home and this has led a reliance more online rather than physical communication. To achieve this, we systematically examined the number of followers, the likes, and the posts and their content published in the period from August 2019 to March 2020.

More importantly, we introduced content analysis to unravel the underlying sentiment on the comments of the posts, we tracked the occurrence of the expression in the text in each comment.

The results show that, in times of global health crisis, highest rise of followers in the months during lockdown due to the COVID-19 was significantly associated with the main outcome related to the numbers of comments and likes. Interestingly, we find that team support is constantly on the rise after December 2019 with a peak in March 2020 alongside the peak time of COVID-19 in Italy.

Meanwhile, matching between months of the crisis and moods expressed by comments, we find that the expressions regarding involvement, support suggestion are more than dislikes, replies, or neutral, directly determines the effect of social support that followers give to their team in line with literature (Hilvert-Bruce et al., 2018; Sjöblom & Hamari, 2017).

This empirical study also reveals that posts with emoticons and emoji attached relating to the comments in the months of the pandemic still express the most users' engagement; this could attribute to a lack of external support in real life as studied in previous research (Hilvert-Bruce et al., 2018; Sjöblom & Hamari, 2017), in which the users are more likely to engage following their team on Instagram profile also during the crisis. Regarding sentiment analysis, when posts are related to the pandemic period, stronger positive emotions lead to team, enhancing user relationship and creating a stronger association between followers and their team. The social interaction has been shown to be of great importance in the past studies (Chen, 2011; Hamari & Sjöblom, 2017), as much of the motivations of eSports consumption takes place online, the connection between consumers and teams is more easily reachable by their followers and streamers followed on Instagram such as in the different social platforms (Cunningham et al., 2018). The findings of this research offer the following useful insights for theory and practice.

Theoretical Contributions

The findings of this study should be of interest to interdisciplinary scholars to understand methodological approaches as well as types of data used to explore, observe users' engagement and users' sentiment on Instagram profile of an Italian eSport team.

Research aimed at answering is one of the few theoretically informed attempts of applying an innovative methodological approach to assess the effect of COVID-19 on users' engagement and sentiments compared to the previous period. The quantitative analysis aimed at exploring the level of engagement in terms of followers, likes, and comments (Brubaker & Wilson, 2018) can be valuable for future scholars with an interest to monitor the teams' brand image (Culotta & Cutler, 2016) also in time of crisis.

In particular, compared to most of the existing studies that are not explicit about the criteria but also remarks for lacking rigor or critical thinking about user engagement trend on Instagram for an eSport team, this study proposes a bespoke approach for doing this.

The qualitative analysis in the research phase 2 makes an important contribution to research on eSport team exploring, by a powerful tool: NVivo 11 (Bazeley & Jackson, 2013), the comments for each post released by the users can hold and their relationship with sentiments and moods, expressed within textual information, emoticons-emojis, which is the concept mostly overlooked in current research, especially during a period of lockdown due to COVID-19. The rise of followers and comments on Instagram profile shows no signs of slowing down during the period of global business shutting down in sport industry (Ratten, 2020a). These results are in line with previous studies which stated that the consumption of social media products in our society increases constantly (Culotta & Cutler, 2016).

Lastly, time of crisis due to the global pandemic seems to be an important motivator to follow their team, as it has a positive impact on not just the number of followers and comments into positive sentiments and moods, in fact the results of world frequency of the expression shows that the social interaction is facilitated on Instagram and fill a very real role for positive sentiment not only through play but also through following a team. This can clearly be seen from the associations between positive sentiments and an increased number of the various comments that express positive moods such as involvement/celebration, appreciation/support, and suggestion.

As been stated in previous research the users feel safe both psychologically with various positive or negative sentiments on eSports environment (Hallmann & Giel, 2018; Weiss & Schiele, 2013) and creating easily a stronger connection with their favorite teams (Danish et al., 2004; Holt, 2007).

Furthermore, the qualitative analysis on the second phase contributes to an increase of scientific knowledge in the eSport studies on users' sentiment and mood perspective applying a content analysis with NVivo, to analyze textual information emoticon-emoji available within the comments on the Instagram profile of the team. This approach provides a framework of the engagement-updating process by analyzing trend engagement and sentiment express through comments thus calling for further investigations that can help to enrich the research on eSport teams or players to monitor their brand image (Culotta & Cutler, 2016; Das, 2021b) and to understand users' need by their comments on social media platforms such as Instagram.

Contribution to Practice

Our study has several important practical implications because organizations are investing in eSports promoting both their products and services, they would be interested in exploring what kind of results these efforts can achieve. Drawing on the findings of phase 1 and the findings of the analysis of the comments on Instagram profile of phase 2, eSports companies can design more tailored interventions for strengthening the management of their teams and image on Instagram, as these are directly connected to a successful level of engagement.

Thus for addressing the emerging need for explaining comments of users, we studied the conversion of emotions and emoji expressed in each post. We processed six themes that express moods that emerged in various comments. All of these activities helped to explain users' behavior on Instagram to support and to follow their team which various moods and sentiments extract through a systematically and scientific approach based on two phases.

The surprising result was that in the months during lockdown due to COVID-19, the followers seemed to have highest level of engagement in terms of likes, comments, and followers and may bring toward aspects of mood as a driver that shapes various consumption-related responses (Gardner, 1985; Isen, 1989).

Perhaps the strongest results of the present study highlight the fact that social experiences related to both the rise of engagement and the means of sentiments and moods express by comments are an immensely important aspect to examine users' behavior in order to make business decision about future investments and business development.

Finally, seeking findings as users' engagement grows, eSport represents a digital industry with substantial growth potential on Instagram (Acuti et al., 2018), by new actors and activities in a timely manner.

This study on eSports gives to scholars and practitioners a dynamic model to study the engagement process and user behavior on eSport team before and during COVID-19 pandemic as the researches surrounding has not kept pace with this perspective.

Limitation and Future Research

Like any study, the current chapter has some limitations to be considered for future research directions. Firstly, this chapter aims to analyze the content of the Instagram site of eSports team. Thus, the generalization of the results for eSports teams using other social media sites such as Facebook and Twitter may be limited because of the specific characteristics of Instagram. Consequently, further research could analyze the data of other social media platforms (e.g., Facebook, Twitter, etc.) of the selected team. Additionally, the analysis of social media content of other eSport teams in Italy could be a venue for future studies (S. Singh et al., 2020). Secondly, the current chapter focused on eSports team in Italy. Thus, future research should be conducted in other nations in Europe. A comparative study between Italy and another European country is also recommended to outline the similarities and differences regarding the analysis of social media platforms on eSports. Thirdly, this chapter employed Nvivo software to conduct content analysis and sentiment analyses for Instagram data. Further studies are recommended to use other software programs (e.g., ATLAS.ti, MAXQDA, etc.). Fourthly, the data were collected during the period from August 2019 to March 2020. Future research could, therefore, analyze the data for a long period to provide solid arguments by comparing the results of social media content analysis on eSports. Lastly, the current study conducted a qualitative approach to analyze the data of Instagram site related to eSports team. Future studies could follow a quantitative method by conducting online surveys to examine the level of users' engagement toward eSports teams in different countries. Further studies are also recommended to employ text mining to conduct a competitive analysis for the user-generated data on social media platforms on eSports.

References

Abdous, M., & He, W. (2011). Using text mining to uncover students' technology-related problems in live video streaming. *British Journal of Educational Technology, 42*(1), 40–49.

Acuti, D., Mazzoli, V., Donvito, R., & Chan, P. Y. L. (2018). An Instagram content analysis for city branding in London and Florence. *Journal of Global Fashion Marketing, 9*(3), 185–204.

Baird, H. C., & Parasnis, G. (2011). From social media to social customer relationship management. *Strategy & Leadership, 39*(5), 30–37.

Bazeley, P., & Jackson, K. (Eds.). (2013). *Qualitative data analysis with Nvivo.* Sage.

Bednárek, D., Kruliš, M., Yaghob, J., & Zavoral, F. (2018). Player performance evaluation in team-based first-person shooter eSport. *Communications in Computer and Information Science, 814*, 154–175.

Behera, M., Dash, M., Mohanty, A. K., & Das, S. (2019). Entrepreneurial ecosystem: A geographical upliftment. *Revista Espacios, 40*, 26–36. Retrieved from http://www.revistaespacios.com/a19v40n01/19400126.html

Behnke, M., Kosakowski, M., & Kaczmarek, L. D. (2019). Social challenge and threat predict performance and cardiovascular responses during competitive video gaming. *Psychology of Sport & Exercise, 46*, 101584.

Bleicher, J., & Stanley, H. (2018). Digitization as a catalyst for business model innovation a three-step approach to facilitating economic success. *Journal of Business Management, 4*(2), 62–71.

Bollen, J., Mao, H., & Zeng, X.-J. (2010). Twitter mood predicts the stock market. *Journal of Computational Science, 2*(1), 1–8.

Brislin, R. W. (1970). Back-translation for cross-cultural research. *Journal of Cross-Cultural Psychology, 1*(3), 185–216.

Brubaker, P. J., & Wilson, C. (2018). Let's give them something to talk about: Global brands' use of visual content to drive engagement and build relationships. *Public Relations Review, 44*(3), 342–352.

Chairunnisa, S., & Benedictus, A. S. (2017). Analysis of emoji and emoticon usage in interpersonal communication of Blackberry Messenger and WhatsApp application user. *International Journal Social Sciences Management, 4*(2), 120–126.

Chang, Y., Yu, H., & Lu, H. (2015). Persuasive messages, popularity cohesion, and message diffusion in social media marketing. *Journal of Business Research, 68*(4), 777–782.

Chen, G. M. (2011). Tweet this: A uses and gratifications perspective on how active Twitter use gratifies a need to connect with others. *Computers in Human Behavior, 27*(2), 755–762.

Chmait, N., Westerbeek, H., Eimea, R., Robertson, S., Sellitto, C., & Reid, M. (2020). Tennis influencers: The player effect on social media engagement and demand for tournament attendance. *Telematics and Informatics, 50*, 101381.

Culnan, M., McHugh, P., & Zubillaga, J. (2010). How large U.S. companies can use Twitter and other social media to gain business value. *MIS Quarterly Executive, 9*(4), 243–259.

Culotta, A., & Cutler, J. (2016). Mining brand perceptions from Twitter social networks. *Marketing Science, 35*(3), 343–362.

Cunningham, G. B., Fairley, S., Ferkins, L., Kerwin, S., Lock, D., Shaw, S., & Wicker, P. (2018). eSport: Construct specifications and implications for sport management. *Sport Management Review, 21*, 1–6.

Danish, S., Forneris, T., Hodge, K., & Heke, I. (2004). Enhancing youth development through sport. *World Leisure Journal, 46*(3), 38–49.

Das, S. (2020). Innovations in digital banking service brand equity and millennial consumerism. In *Digital transformation and innovative services for business and learning* (pp. 62–79). IGI Global. https://doi.org/10.4018/978-1-7998-5175-2.ch004

Das, S. (2021a). A systematic study of integrated marketing communication and content management system for millennial consumers. In *Innovations in digital branding and content marketing* (pp. 91–112). IGI Global. https://doi.org/10.4018/978-1-7998-4420-4.ch005

Das, S. (2021b). *Search engine optimization and marketing: A recipe for success in digital marketing* (1st ed.). CRC Press. https://doi.org/10.1201/9780429298509

Derks, D., Bos, A. E., & Von Grumbkow, J. (2008). Emoticons in computer-mediated communication: Social motives and social context. *CyberPsychology & Behavior, 11*(1), 99–101.

Di Virgilio, F. (2018). *Social media for knowledge management applications in modern organizations*. IGI Global.

Dolan, R., Conduit, J., Fahy, J., & Goodman, S. (2016). Social media engagement behaviour: A uses and gratifications perspective. *Journal of Strategic Marketing, 24*(3–4), 261–277.

Dresner, E., & Herring, S. C. (2010). Functions of the nonverbal in CMC: Emoticons and illocutionary force. *Communication Theory, 20*, 249–268.

Dua, S., Singh, I., & Das, S. (2021). Banking innovative service with digital brand equity for new age consumers: Internet banking and millennial consumerism. In *Innovations in digital branding and content marketing* (pp. 134–159). IGI Global. https://doi.org/10.4018/978-1-7998-4420-4.ch007

Duy, N. T., Mondal, S. R., Van, N. T. T., Dzung, P. T., Minh, D. X. H., & Das, S. (2020). A study on the role of web 4.0 and 5.0 in the sustainable tourism ecosystem of Ho Chi Minh City, Vietnam. *Sustainability, 12*(17), 7140. https://doi.org/10.3390/su12177140

Ellison, N. B., Steinfield, C., & Lampe, C. (2007). The benefits of Facebook "friends": Social capital and college students' use of online social network sites. *Journal of Computer-Mediated Communication, 12*, 1143–1168.

Establés, M. J., Guerrero-Pico, M., & Contreras-Espinosa, R. S. (2019). Gamers, writers and social media influencers: Professionalisation processes among teenagers. *Revista Latina De Comunicación Social, 74*, 214–236.

Filo, K., Lock, D., & Karg, A. (2015). Sport and social media research: A review. *Sport Management Review, 18*(2), 166–181.

Freeman, G., & Wohn, D. Y. (2019). Understanding eSports team formation and coordination. *Computer Supported Cooperative Work (CSCW), 28*(1), 95–126.

Funk, D. C., Pizzo, A. D., & Baker, B. J. (2018). eSport management: Embracing eSport education and research opportunities. *Sport Management Review, 21*, 7–13.

Gardner, M. P. (1985). Mood states and consumer behavior: A critical review. *Journal of Consumer Research, 12*(3), 281–300.

Gray, P. B., Vuong, J., Zava, D. T., & McHale, T. S. (2018). Testing men's hormone responses to playing league of legends: No changes in testosterone, cortisol, DHEA or androstenedione but decreases in aldosterone. *Computers in Human Behavior, 83*, 230–323.

Gupta, D. K., Jena, D., Samantaray, A. K., & Das, S. (2019). HRD climate in selected public sector banks in India. *Revista ESPACIOS, 40*(11), 14–20.

Hallmann, K., & Giel, T. (2018). eSports—Competitive sports or recreational activity? *Sport Management Review, 21*, 14–20.

Hamari, J., & Sjöblom, M. (2017). What is eSports and why do people watch it? *Internet Research, 27*(2), 211–232.

Hansen, J. M., & Levin, M. L. (2016). The effect of apathetic motivation on employees' intentions to use social media for businesses. *Journal of Business Research, 69*, 6058–6066.

He, W., Tian, X., Tao, R., Zhang, W., Yan, G., & Akula, V. (2017). Application of social media analytics: A case of analyzing online hotel reviews. *Online Information Review, 41*(7), 921–935.

Heere, B. (2018). Embracing the sportification of society: Defining e-sports through a polymorphic view on sport. *Sport Management Review, 21*, 21–24.

Hilvert-Bruce, Z., Neill, J. T., Sjöblom, M., & Hamari, J. (2018). Social motivations of live-streaming viewer engagement on Twitch. *Computers in Human Behavior, 84*, 58–67.

Holt, J. (2016). Virtual domains for sports and games. *Sport, Ethics and Philosophy, 10*, 5–13.

Holt, N. L. (2007). *Positive youth development through sport*. Routledge.

Isen, A. M. (1989). Some ways in which affect influences cognitive processes: Implications for advertising and consumer behavior. In A. M. Tybout & P. Cafferata (Eds.), *Advertising and consumer psychology* (pp. 91–117). Lexington Books.

Jang, W., & Byon, K. K. (2020). Antecedents of esports gameplay intention: Genre as a moderator. *Computers in Human Behavior, 109*, 106336.

Jenny, S. E., Keiper, M. C., Taylor, B. J., Williams, D. P., Gawrysiak, J., Manning, R. D., & Tutka, P. M. (2018). eSports venues: A new sport business opportunity. *Journal of Applied Sport Management, 10*(1), 34–49.

Johnston, J., Harwood, C., & Minniti, A. M. (2013). Positive youth development in swimming: Clarification and consensus of key psychosocial assets. *Journal of Applied Sport Psychology, 25*(4), 392–411.

Kannan, S., & Shreya, N. (2017). Understanding emoticons: Perception and usage of emoticons in WhatsApp. *Artha-Journal of Social Sciences, 16*(3), 49–68.

Khan, M. L. (2017). Social media engagement: What motivates user participation and consumption on YouTube? *Computers in Human Behavior, 66*, 236–247.

López-Bolás, A., Valderrama-Santomé, M., & Di Virgilio, F. (2019). Claves del éxito para la viralización de contenidos de salud. El caso de las redes sociales del Hospital Povisa. *El profesional de la información, 28*(5), e280502.

Matsui, A., Sapienza, A., & Ferrara, E. (2020). Does streaming esports affect players' behavior and performance? *Games and Culture, 15*(1), 9–31.

Mohanty, P. C., Dash, M., Dash, M., & Das, S. (2019). A study on factors influencing training effectiveness. *Revista Espacios, 40*, 7–15. Retrieved from http://www.revistaespacios.com/a19v40n02/19400207.html

Mondal, S. R. (2020). A systematic study for digital innovation in management education: An integrated approach towards problem-based learning in Vietnam. In *Digital innovations for customer engagement, management, and organizational improvement* (pp. 104–120). IGI Global. https://doi.org/10.4018/978-1-7998-5171-4.ch006

Mondal, S. R. (2021). A systematic study of new age consumer engagement and exploration for digital entertainment for over-the-top platforms in various digital media. In *Innovations in digital branding and content marketing* (pp. 113–133). IGI Global. https://doi.org/10.4018/978-1-7998-4420-4.ch006

Mondal, S. R., & Sahoo, K. K. (2020). A study of green building prospects on sustainable management decision making. In *Green building management and smart automation* (pp. 220–234). IGI Global. https://doi.org/10.4018/978-1-5225-9754-4.ch011

Mora-Cantallops, M., & Sicilia, M. Á. (2019). Team efficiency and network structure: The case of professional league of legends. *Social Networks, 58*, 105–115.

Mount, M., & Martinez, M. G. (2014). Social media: A tool for open innovation. *California Management Review, 56*(4), 124–143.

Nadanyiova, M., & Das, S. (2020). Millennials as a target segment of socially responsible communication within the business strategy. *Littera Scripta, 13*(1), 119–134. https://doi.org/10.36708/Littera_Scripta2020/1/8

Novak, K. P., Smailović, J., Sluban, B., & Mozetič, I. (2015). Sentiment of emojis. *PLoS One, 10*(12), e0144296.

QSR. (2016). *NVivo11.* QSR International Pty Ltd.

Ratten, V. (2020a). Coronavirus and international business: An entrepreneurial ecosystem perspective. *International Business Review, 62*(5), 629–634.

Ratten, V. (2020b). Coronavirus disease (COVID-19) and sport entrepreneurship. *International Journal of Entreprenueurial Behavior & Research, 26*, 1355–2554.

Reitman, J. G., Anderson-Coto, M. J., Wu, M., Lee, J. S., & Steinkuehler, C. (2020). Esports research: A literature review. *Games and Culture, 15*(1), 32–50.

Robertson, B. W., & Kee, K. F. (2017). Social media at work: The roles of job satisfaction, employment status, and Facebook use with co-workers. *Computers in Human Behavior, 70*, 191–196.

Sashi, C. M. (2012). Customer engagement, buyer–seller relationships, and social media. *Management Decision, 50*(2), 253–272.

Scholz, T. (2019). *eSports is business: Management in the world of competitive gaming*. Palgrave Macmillan.

Sharma, E., & Das, S. (2020). Measuring impact of Indian ports on environment and effectiveness of remedial measures towards environmental pollution. *International Journal of Environment and Waste Management, 25*(3), 356–380. https://doi.org/10.1504/IJEWM.2019.10021787

Singh, L. B., Mondal, S. R., & Das, S. (2020). Human resource practices & their observed significance for Indian SMEs. *Revista ESPACIOS, 41*(7). Retrieved from http://www.revistaespacios.com/a20v41n07/20410715.html

Singh, S., Mondal, S., Singh, L. B., Sahoo, K. K., & Das, S. (2020). An empirical evidence study of consumer perception and socioeconomic profiles for digital stores in Vietnam. *Sustainability, 12*(5), 1716. https://doi.org/10.3390/su12051716

Siri, R., Mondal, S. R., & Das, S. (2020). Hydropower: A renewable energy resource for sustainability in terms of climate change and environmental protection. In *The handbook of environmental chemistry*. Springer. https://doi.org/10.1007/698_2020_635

Sjöblom, M., & Hamari, J. (2017). Why do people watch others play video games? An empirical study on the motivations of Twitch users. *Computers in Human Behavior, 75*, 985–996.

Sjöblom, M., Torhonen, M., Hamari, J., & Macey, J. (2017). Content structure is king: An empirical study on gratifications, game genres and content type on Twitch. *Computers in Human Behavior, 73*, 161–171.

Tajudeen, F. P., Jaafar, N. I., & Ainin, J. S. (2018). Understanding the impact of social media usage among organizations. *Information & Management, 55*(3), 308–321.

Taylor, T. L. (2012). *Raising the stakes, e-sports and the professionalization of computer gaming*. MIT Press.

Thelwall, M., & Buckley, K. (2013). Topic-based sentiment analysis for the social web: The role of mood and issue-related words. *Journal of the American Society for Information Science and Technology, 64*(8), 1608–1617.

Turtiainen, R., Friman, U., & Ruotsalainen, M. (2020). Not only for a celebration of competitive overwatch but also for national pride: Sportificating the Overwatch World Cup 2016. *Games and Culture, 15*(4), 351–371.

Van, N. T. T., Vrana, V., Duy, N. T., Minh, D. X. H., Dzung, P. T., Mondal, S. R., & Das, S. (2020). The role of human–machine interactive devices for post-COVID-19 innovative sustainable tourism in Ho Chi Minh City, Vietnam. *Sustainability, 12*(22), 9523. https://doi.org/10.3390/su12229523

Wann, D. L. (1995). Preliminary validation of the sport fan motivation scale. *Journal of Sport & Social Issues, 19*(4), 377–396.

Wann, D. L., & Martin, J. (2008). The positive relationship between sport team identification and social psychological well-being: Identification with favourite teams versus local teams. *Journal of Contemporary Athletics, 3*, 81–91.

Wann, D. L., Carlson, J. D., & Schrader, M. P. (1999). The impact of team identification on the hostile and instrumental verbal aggression of sport spectators. *Journal of Social Behavior and Personality, 14*, 279–286.

Weiss, T., & Schiele, S. (2013). Virtual worlds in competitive contexts: Analysing eSports consumer needs. *Electronic Markets, 23*, 307–316.

Whiting, A., & Williams, D. (2013). Why people use social media: A uses and gratifications approach. *Qualitative Market Research: An International Journal, 16*(4), 362–369.

Wohn, D. Y., & Freeman, G. (2020). Live streaming, playing, and money spending behaviors in eSports. *Games and Culture, 15*(1), 73–88.

Wu, J.-H., Wang, S.-C., & Tsai, H.-H. (2010). Falling in love with online games: The uses and gratifications perspective. *Computers in Human Behavior, 26*, 1862–1871.

Wulf, T., Schneider, F. M., & Beckert, S. (2018). Watching players: An exploration of media enjoyment on Twitch. *Games and Culture, 15*(3), 328–346.

Yin, K., Zi, Y., Zhuang, W., Gao, Y., Tong, Y., Song, L., & Liu, Y. (2020). Linking esports to health risks and benefits: Current knowledge and future research needs. *Journal of Sport and Health Science, 9*(6), 485–488.

Index

A

Academician, 102, 200–204, 206
Analytics, 4, 8, 9, 12, 137, 138, 141, 145, 147, 148, 188, 218, 219, 222, 223, 228, 235, 236, 250, 251

B

Bed and Breakfast (B&B), 26–29, 31–35, 38–41
Big Data (BD), 2–7, 9–18, 186, 223, 235
Big Data Analytics Capability (BDAC), 4, 7, 8, 10

C

Case study/Case studies, 73, 75, 81, 82, 89, 90, 133, 225, 228–230, 232, 234, 251
Change management, 80
Colleges & universities & learning, 202, 204, 205
Content analysis, 225, 261, 263, 265
COVID-19, 1, 11, 18, 27, 34, 41, 51, 56, 58, 59, 64, 65, 73, 74, 78, 80, 81, 83, 84, 86, 87, 89, 90, 101, 119, 128–132, 134, 136–140, 143–146, 149, 151, 153–159, 172, 173, 175, 177, 178, 180, 187–189, 191–193, 199, 201–211, 244, 248, 249, 251, 253, 258, 259, 261–265
COVID-19 health emergency, 58, 59, 61, 65, 110

D

Digital communication, 190
Digitalisation, 55, 66
Distance work, 115, 129, 132
Dual strategy, 4, 9

E

Education service, 200, 205, 206
eSports, 244–248, 250–253, 259, 261–265

S. R. Mondal et al. (eds.), *HR Analytics and Digital HR Practices*,
https://doi.org/10.1007/978-981-16-7099-2

Evaluation, 1, 2, 15, 33, 40, 57, 61, 103, 104, 110, 114–118

F
Flexible working, 78, 88, 104, 105, 145

H
Home work, 132, 154
HRD capabilities, 2
HR Department (HRD), 2–7, 9, 11–14, 16, 18
HR management (HRM), 2, 5, 6, 8, 12, 15, 75, 80, 81, 102, 105, 110, 111, 114, 117, 147, 148, 172, 223
HRM systems, 103, 104, 110
Human governance, 218–223, 232–236
Human resource analytics, 172, 218

I
Impact of COVID-19, 89, 152, 211, 245
Information and Communications Technology (ICT), 15, 56, 65, 76–80, 129, 130
Instagram, 39, 40, 42, 245, 247, 249–252, 255, 256, 261–265
Italy, 28, 34, 41, 58, 105, 134, 137, 140, 146, 149, 154, 250, 262, 265

J
Job Redesign, 73

M
Mobility and development, 103, 110, 113

N
New ways of working, 13, 64, 74, 175

O
Organisational flexibility, 52–54, 62, 65
Organizational change, 7, 192
Organizations, 4–9, 11, 13–18, 27, 29–32, 39–43, 73–82, 84–86, 88, 89, 101–110, 112–116, 118, 119, 128–135, 137, 138, 141–145, 147, 148, 158, 171–176, 183, 191, 192, 201, 202, 209, 217–224, 230, 233–236, 243, 246, 264

P
Pandemic, 1, 2, 6, 11, 13, 15, 16, 18, 27, 41, 56, 61, 65, 73–75, 77, 81, 85, 90, 110, 119, 127–131, 134, 137–140, 143, 145, 149, 151–153, 155–158, 171–173, 175–178, 180, 183, 190–192, 199, 202, 203, 207–210, 217, 244, 245, 248, 249, 260, 262, 263, 265
People Analytics (PA), 3, 6, 11, 158
Performance, 1, 2, 8, 11, 13, 14, 26, 27, 30–34, 38–43, 54–58, 60, 82, 85–87, 102, 107, 108, 110, 113–119, 138, 147, 172, 176, 190, 192, 201, 202, 219–222, 224, 228, 232, 234, 235, 244, 246
Public Administration (PA), 51–53, 55, 57–60, 62, 64–66, 75, 77, 81, 82, 84, 88, 89, 218, 225, 228–230, 232
Public organisations, 52, 59, 61, 64–66, 218

R

Remote work/Remote working, 13, 54, 75, 78–81, 84, 85, 89, 102, 104–111, 114–119, 128–148, 150–155, 157–160, 192, 208
Rewards, 116, 234

S

Sentiment analysis, 157, 252, 260, 262
Service delivery, 172, 177, 178, 191, 222
Smart work/Smart working (SW), 52–66, 78–80, 84, 85, 88, 101–118, 176
Smart worker, 52, 54, 61, 64, 80, 102, 103, 106–116, 118, 119
Social media usage (SMU), 27, 30–32, 34, 35, 37–43

T

Teaching, 200–209
Technology changes, 222
Telework, 78, 80, 104, 105, 110–114, 129, 132, 152
Top management orientation, 27, 41

U

Users' engagement, 244, 245, 248, 261, 262, 264, 265

W

Workforce management, 201, 202, 205
Workforce (teachers) management, 201
Work-life balance (WLB), 65, 85, 108, 221
Work organization, 104, 110, 119

The manufacturer's authorised representative in the EU is Springer Nature Customer Service Centre GmbH, Europaplatz 3, 69115 Heidelberg, Germany. If you have any concerns regarding our products, please contact ProductSafety@springernature.com

Printed and bound by CPI Group (UK) Ltd, Croydon, CR0 4YY
30/09/2026
02225499-0012